PULP
the art of Rob Davis

AIRSHIP 27 PRODUCTIONS

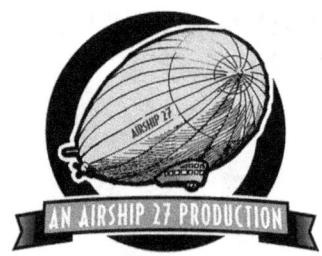

Pulp: The Art of Rob Davis
© 2015 Rob Davis

I dedicate this book to my ever patient wife and soul-mate, Theresa, and to our children Rachel and Ryan. Thanks for putting up with me and my obsession.
—Rob Davis

Published by Airship 27 Productions
www.airship27.com
www.airship27hangar.com

Cover and interior illustrations © 2015 Rob Davis
Cover coloring by John Wilson

Editor: Ron Fortier
Production and design by Rob Davis.

ISBN-13: 978-0692466230 (Airship 27)
ISBN-10: 0692466231

Printed in the United States of America

10 9 8 7 6 5 4 3 2 1

PULP: The Art of Rob Davis

TABLE OF CONTENTS

Opening a book is a story in its own right.

First there's the way you came across the volume, in an old cardbox box in a seedy goodwill store you never found again, or it was a final gift from a beloved uncle, or maybe one day when you were feeling blue you saw your favourite author had a new title out and you rushed through the rain to grab the last copy.

Then there's the cover, setting the tone, and maybe the blurb on the back, shouting out like a sideshow barker or establishing the scene like a Shakespeare prologue. There's the smell of the printing, the rustle of the paper, the weight and grain and texture of the leaves.

Before ever we read a word, a book has already made an imprint on us.

And from the earliest times, from days when stories were told on papyrus with seagull-feather quills and deep-sea squid ink, through years when medieval monks spent lifetimes preparing a single tome to rough raw Depression times where adventure yarns came on yellow pulp paper, alongside the words and as much a part of the reading experience as them, were the pictures.

Every art book introduction tries to avoid repeating the old maxim that a picture is worth a thousand words. But today let's go there. Pictures *can* accomplish very succinctly what prose would require long descriptive paragraphs to convey. Even then, the two mediums would pass on slightly different messages in different ways. Pictures and words might have an exchange rate, but that doesn't make them interchangeable or the same thing.

Take a peek ahead at page 113 of the barker and showgirl doing their "Tah-Dah" introduction. Look at the body language, the expressions, the position of the characters in the frame and their relationship to the background. The text can tell all of that to the reader, but the picture shoots that narrative beat right into our hindbrain where we feel it raw.

Or consider Robin Hood and his Merry Men as they stand on page 119, each offering a character study, collectively demonstrating a group dynamic. We know something of the cast, and how this story's versions of those iconic figures are going to turn out, before we read a single word.

So narrative art and narrative prose do slightly different things, serving slightly different purposes. Saws and screwdrivers are both important tools. Narrative art and prose storytelling are both appropriate mechanisms to get the job done when a yarn must be spun.

Rob Davis is a *narrative* artist. He can't help it. Even his portraits tell tales. Look at the vignettes on page 88, where each face betrays a backstory. Shudder at the Sheriff of Nottingham on page 126 (my personal favourite of all the art in this volume) as he sits surrounded by bold black shadows while a man is dragged to his doom. Pity the lady's grief and solitude on page 97, as she sits hunched up, deliberately small in stark moody surroundings. Rob invites us to supply our own stories as we interpret the images he offers up.

It is unsurprising that Rob is best known for his work in pulp fiction and comic books. Both mediums use images to forward the storytelling, to evoke visceral reactions, to capture a mood or a moment, or to forward the action. Those are the skills on display in this volume. That is why Rob is a successor to those golden age pulp artists like Walter Baumhofer, Virgil Finlay, Norman Saunders, Rudolph Belarski and the rest, and an inheritor of the Victorian periodical artists like Sidney Paget and Hablot Knight Browne who came before them.

Like them, Rob's work is shaped towards the medium in which it is presented. Many of those artists first contributed their work to cheap magazine publications, the Penny Dreadfuls and Pulp Monthlies of their eras. The contemporary equivalent of those outlets is the small-press pulp publishing industry, and its modern chosen format is the 6x9" paperback edition. These books are offered in print and electronic versions, and many of them retain or revive the long-held tradition of offering interior as well as cover art.

And Rob knows a secret…

He knows how to compliment a narrative. He knows how to show cause and effect in a single image (see page 40), how to convey personality (page 163), how to capture a moment (page 11), how to suggest a mood (page 145). As an author of many of the stories that Rob has illustrated, I'm always grateful when an artist offers that extra punch to keep the reader reeling and reacting to the tale. That different cognitive and emotional input from a great piece of art rounds out the reader/viewer experience and amplifies the impact.

There are no lengths to which Rob will not go in service of a good story. This volume includes a map and a castle diagram I demanded for *Robin Hood: Forbidden Legend*. Rob supplied. There are complicated scenes requiring a detailed and intelligent understanding of the tale being illustrated. There are bold, stark, simple images using Rob's trademark swathes of pure black and white and there are complex, technically precise pictures executed with a draughtsman's patience.

All of which brings us to *this* book, a book where the pictures *are* the story. The experience you'll get from this volume is of ideas leaping from the page into your mind. Each leaf offers another moment. Appreciate the technical skill or just let the moods and situations wash over you, as you please. Each picture will lead you somewhere. Every picture will take you through the work and world of one of the early 21st century's outstanding narrative artists.

When you've finished admiring Rob's work, store this volume carefully. All those Dickensian and Sherlockian illustrators' images and many of the golden age pulp artists' outputs are now public domain. A century from now people will be hunting down Rob's out-of-copyright catalogue to plunder for their 3-D laser holonovels. Until then this tome is your only chance of being in on Rob's secret.

Opening this book is story. Each picture will tell you another. Rob Davis is the spotlighted storyteller this time.

Proceed to chapter one.

I.A. Watson
On the same page
3rd June, 2015

CHAPTER 1
THE BIZARRE HEROES

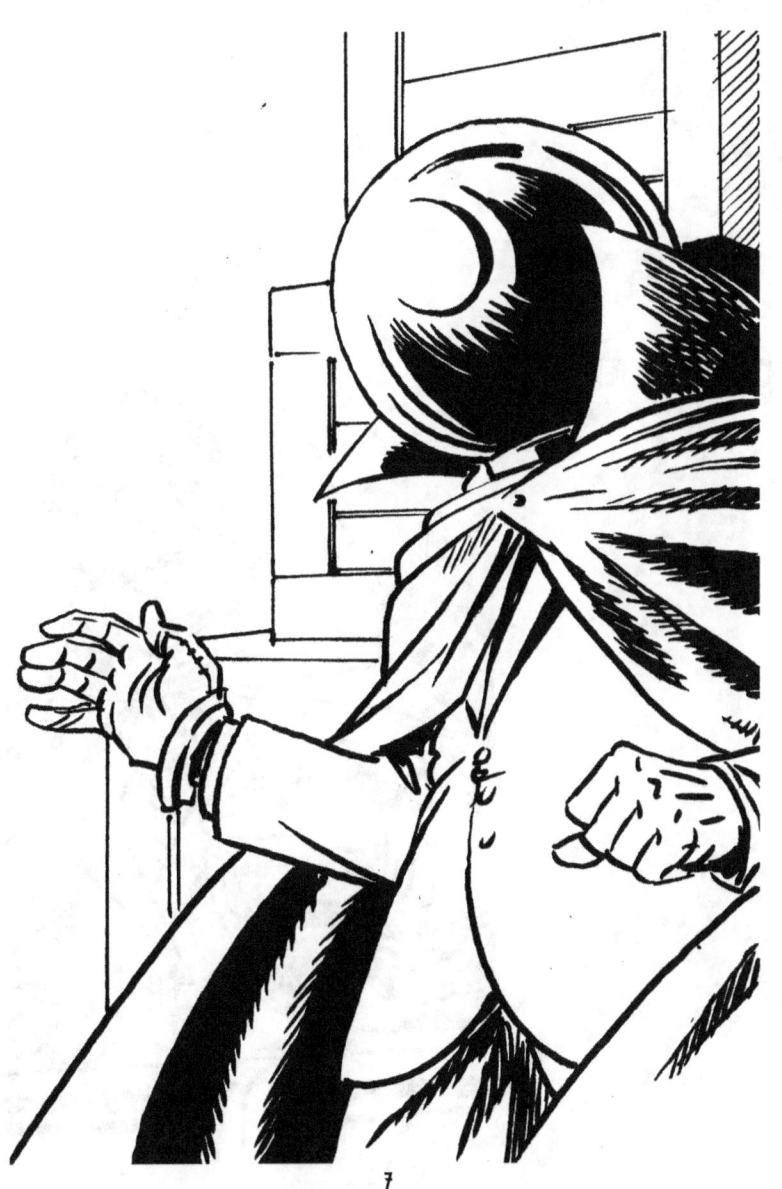

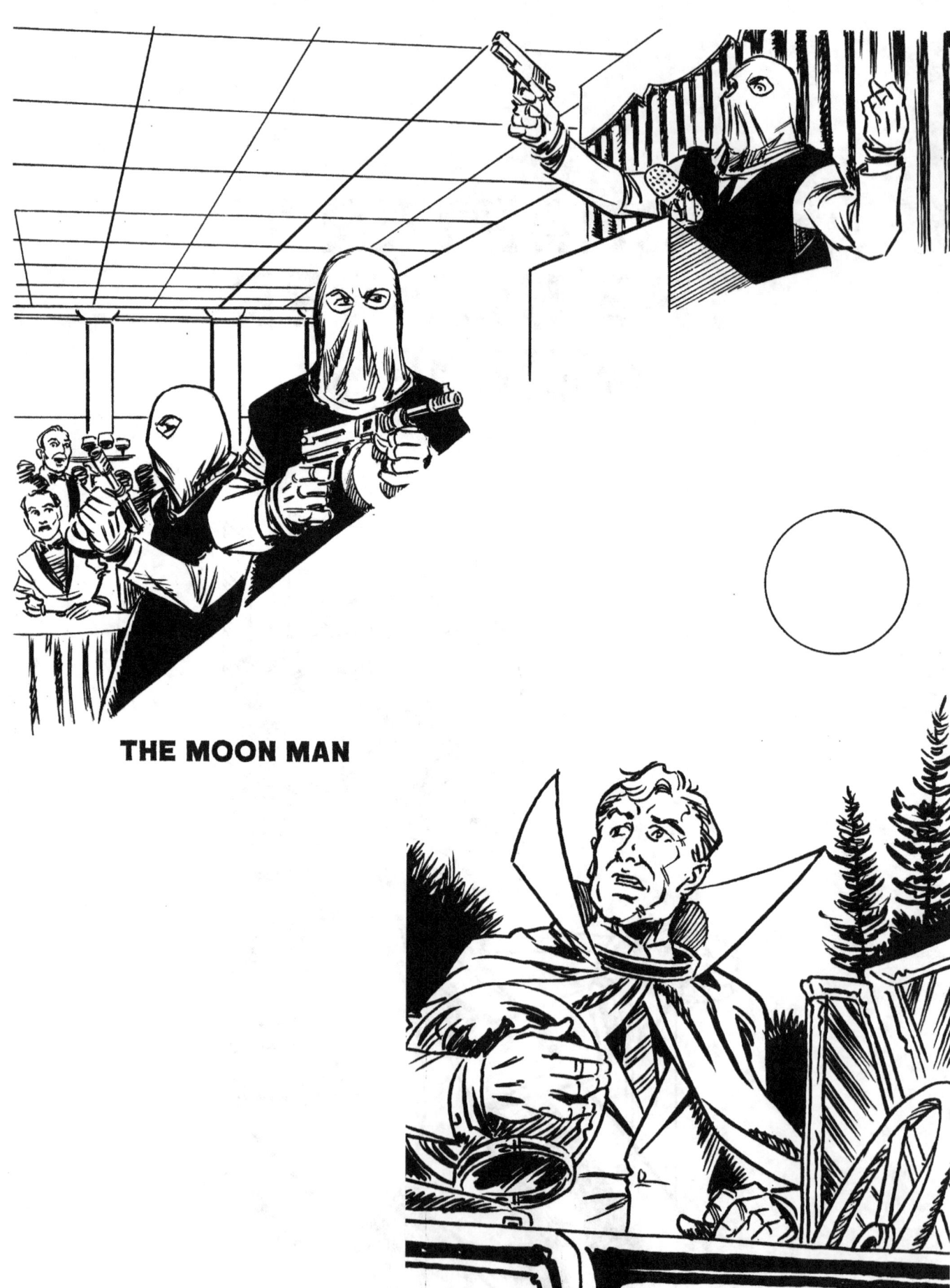

THE MOON MAN

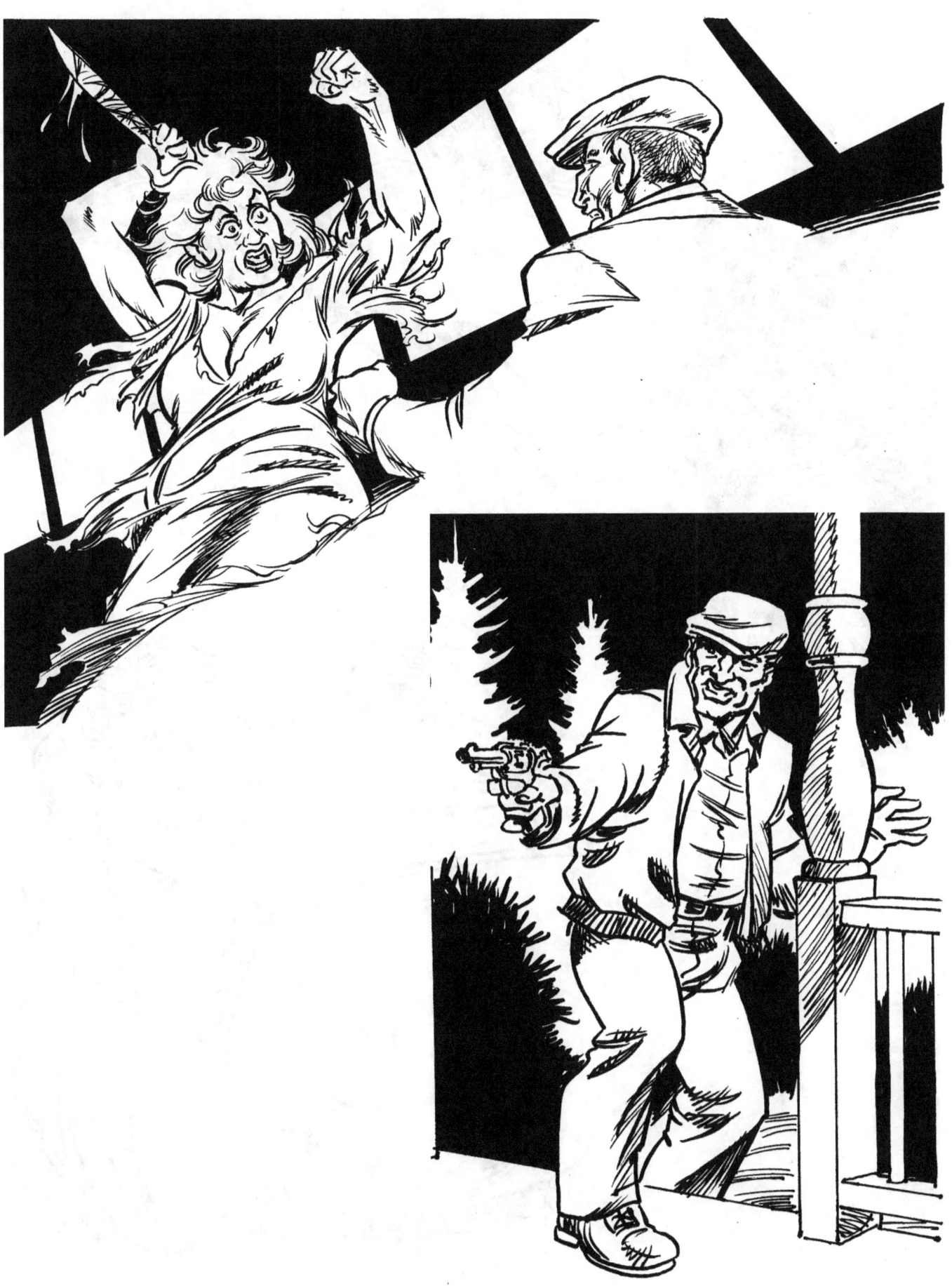

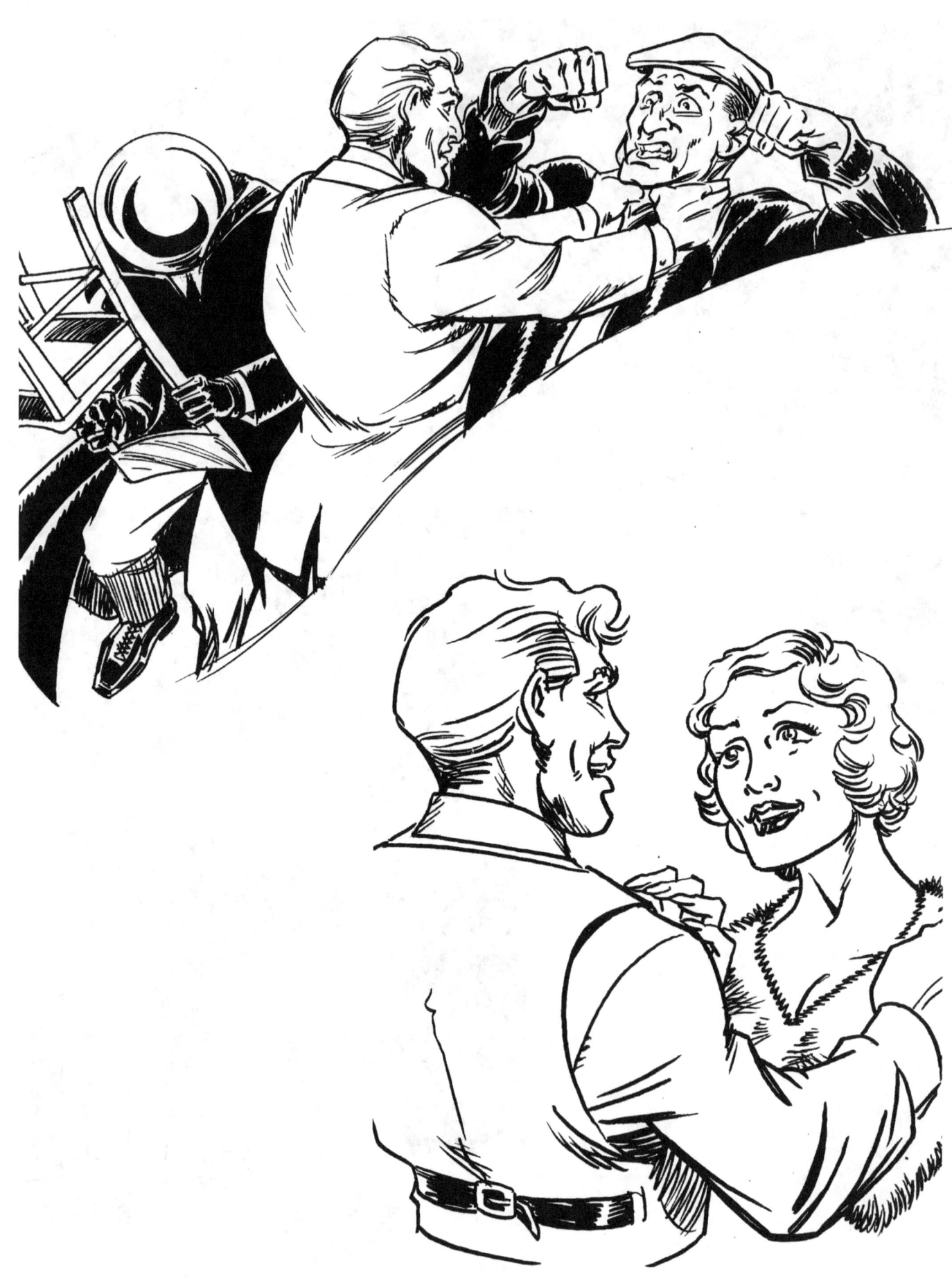

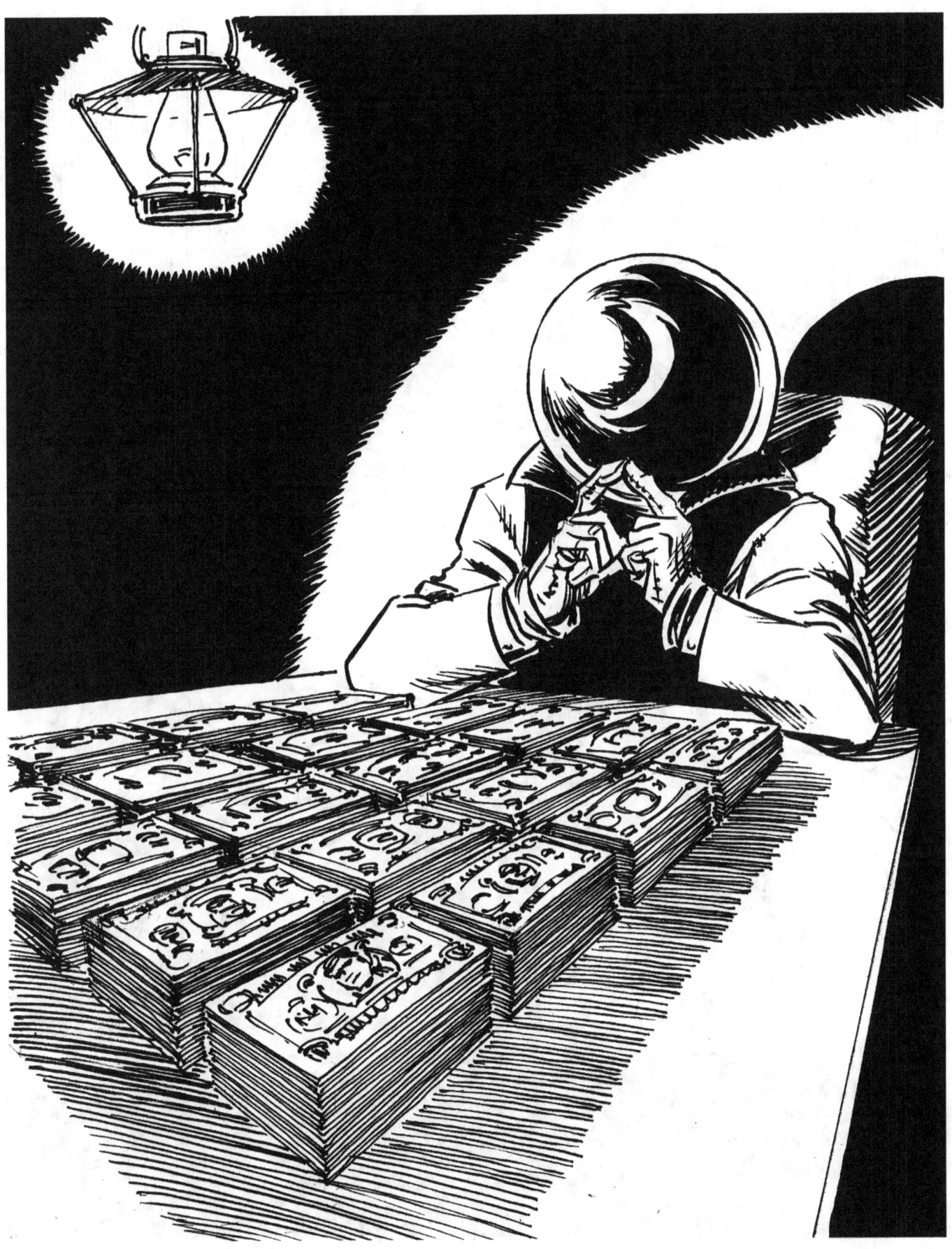

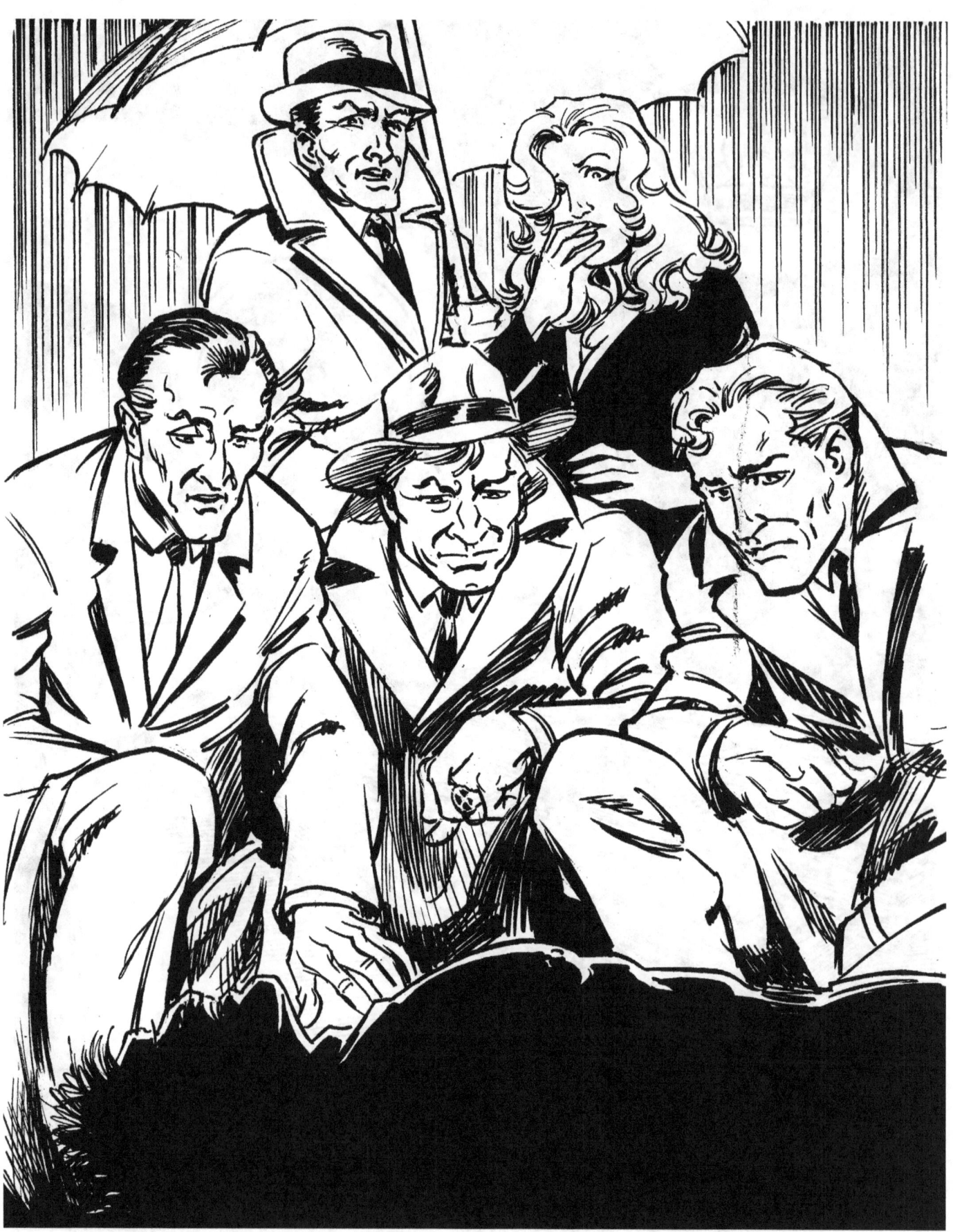

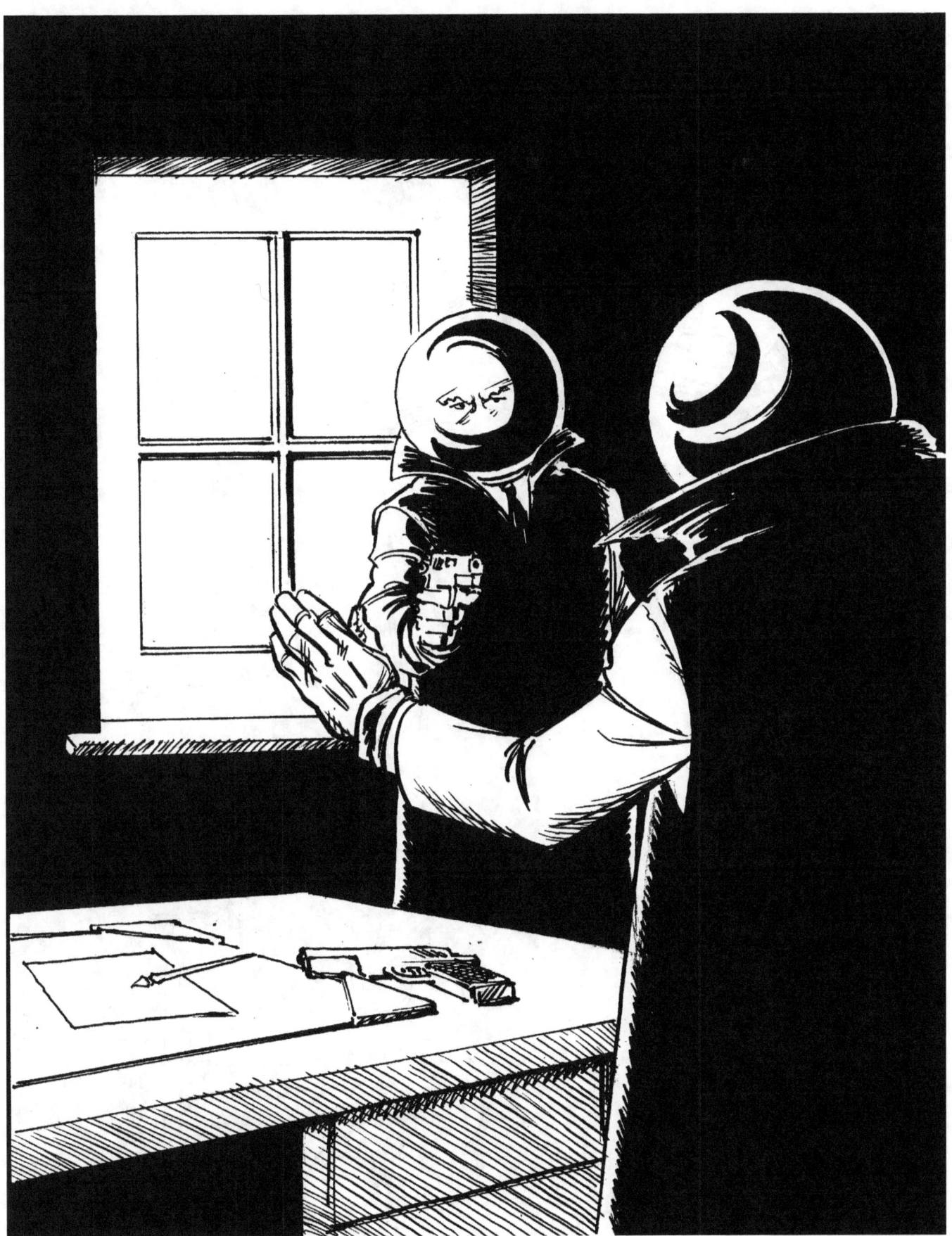

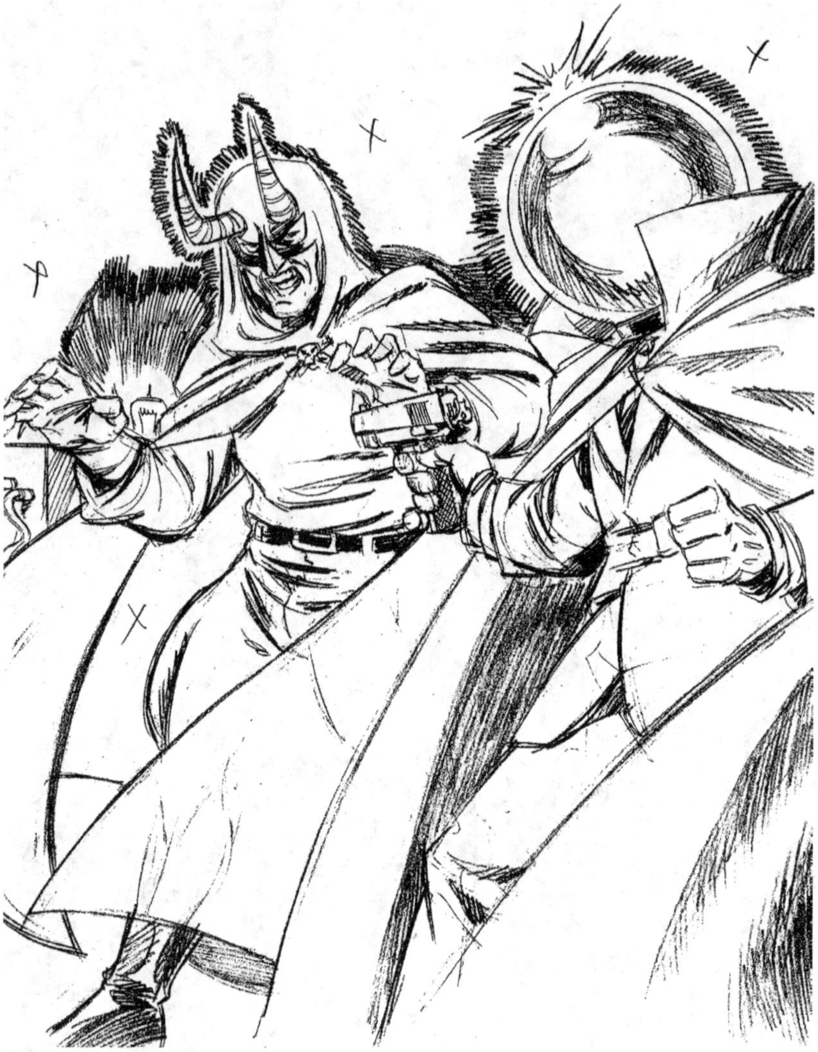

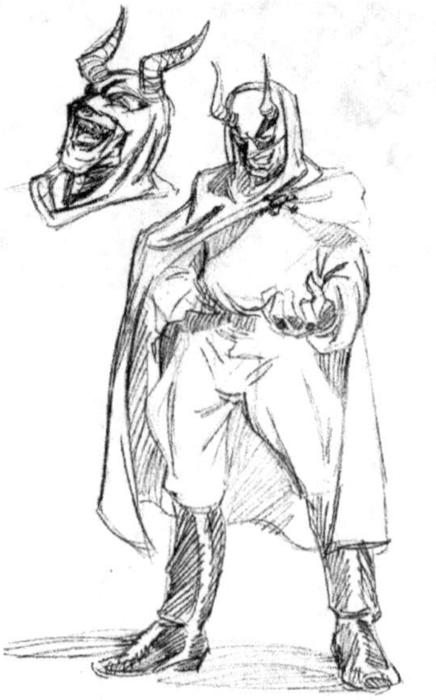

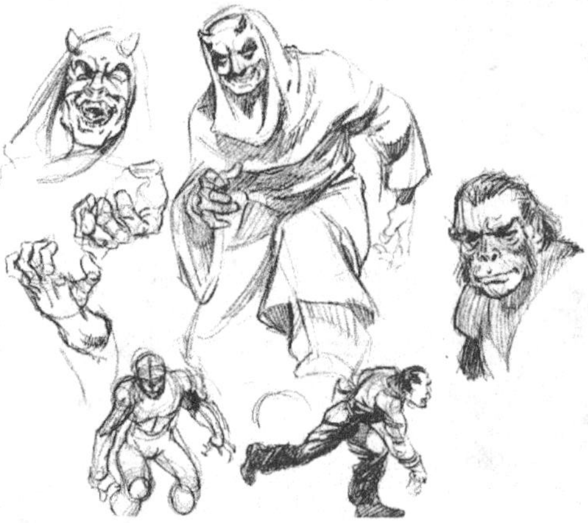

DR. SATAN

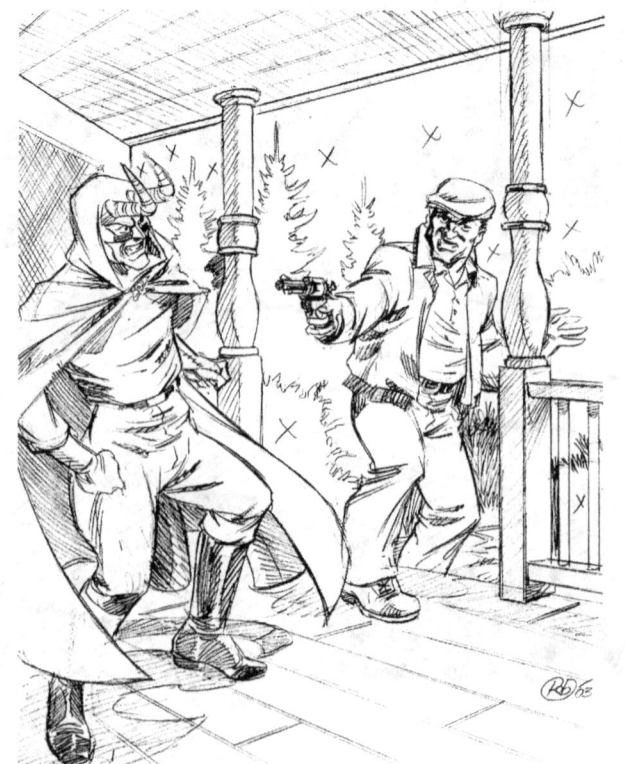

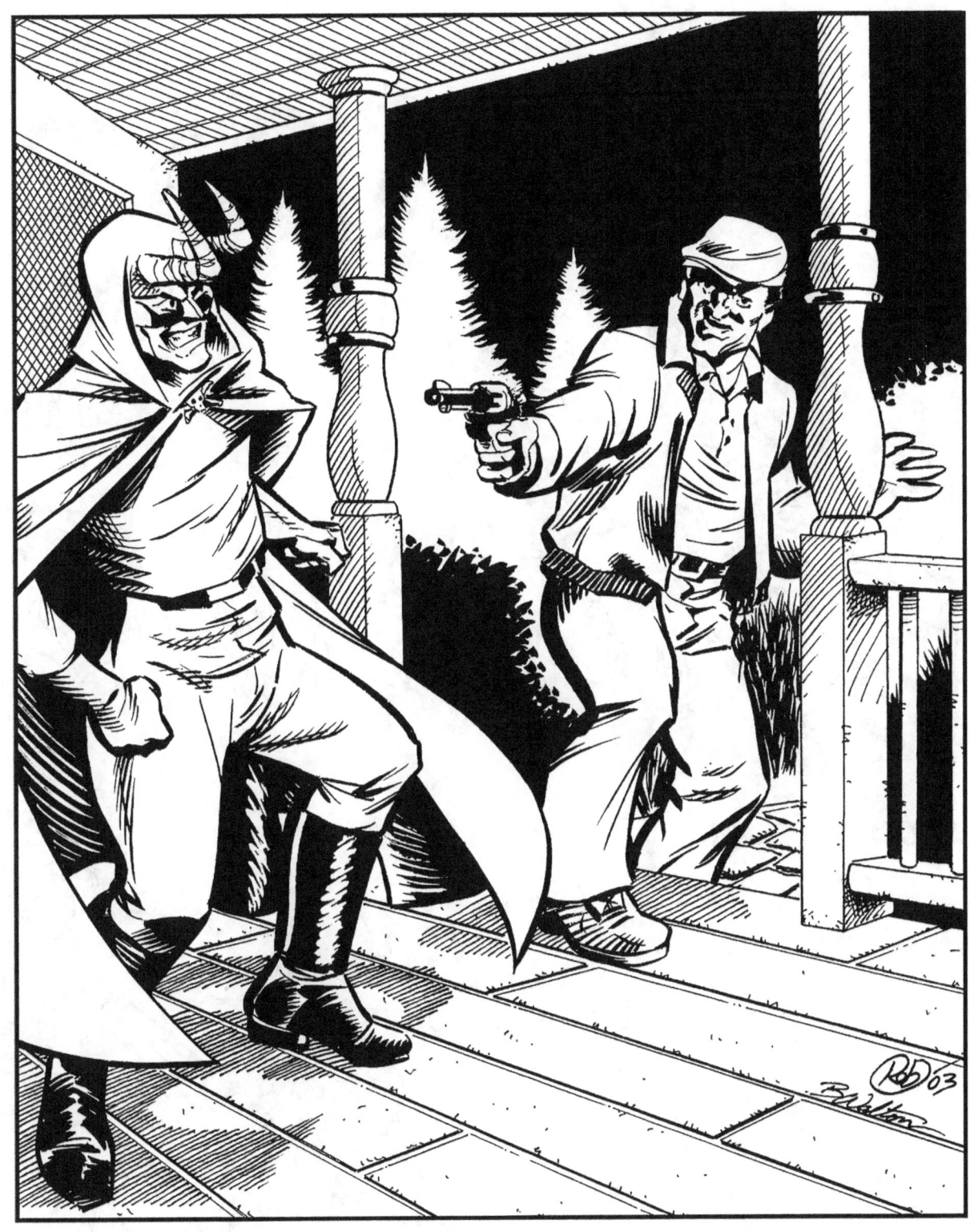

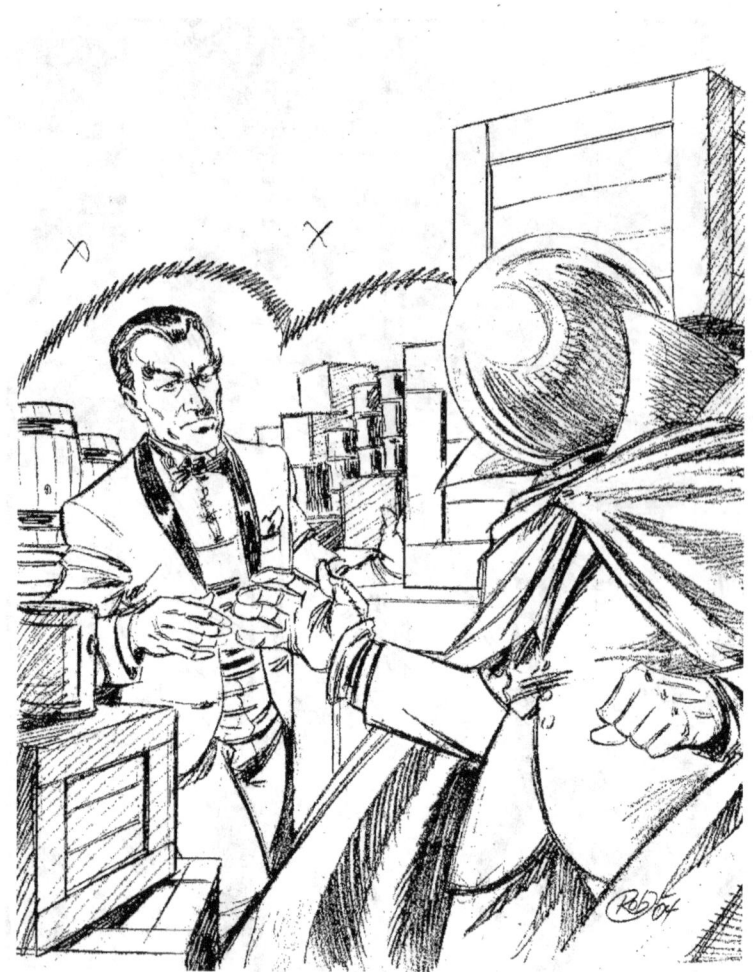

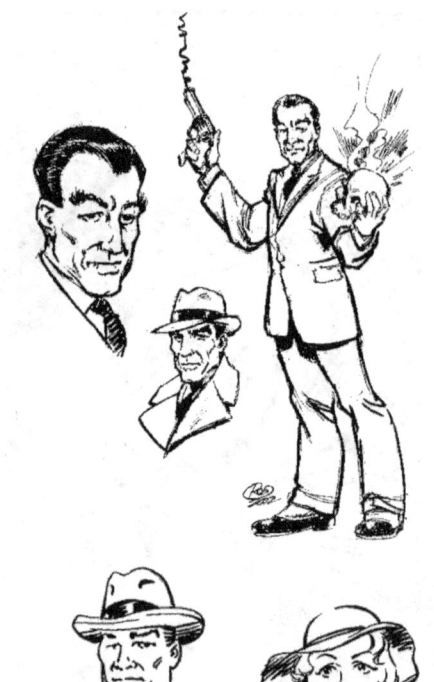

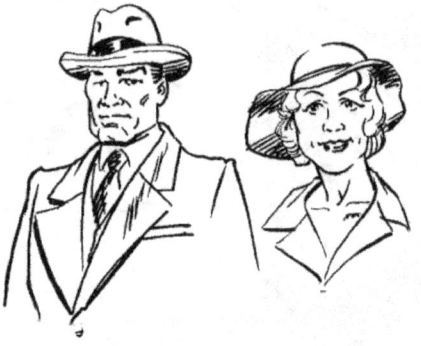

ASCOTT KEANE

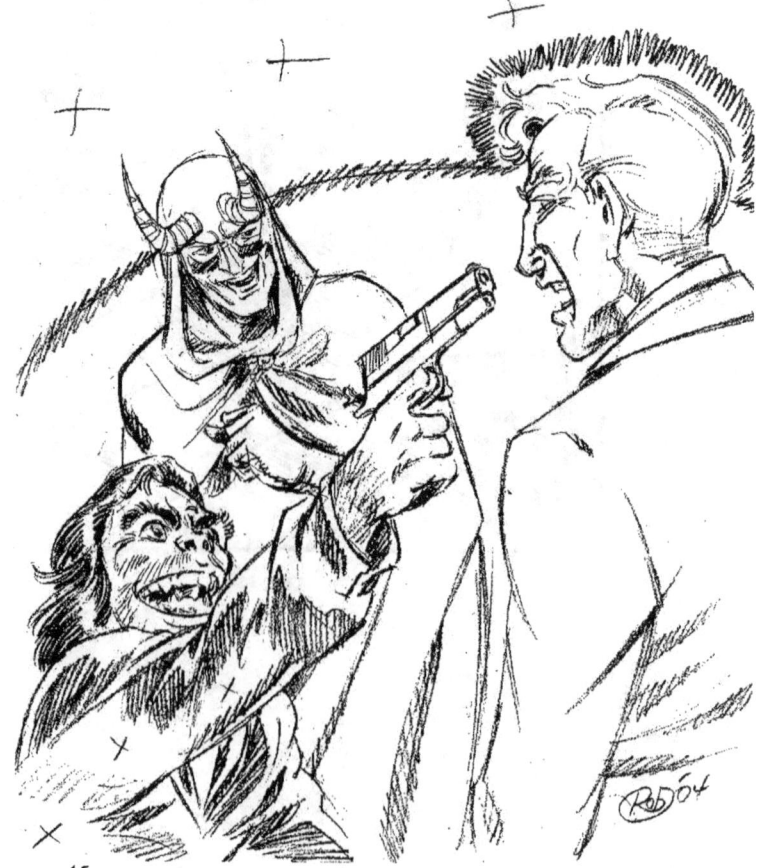

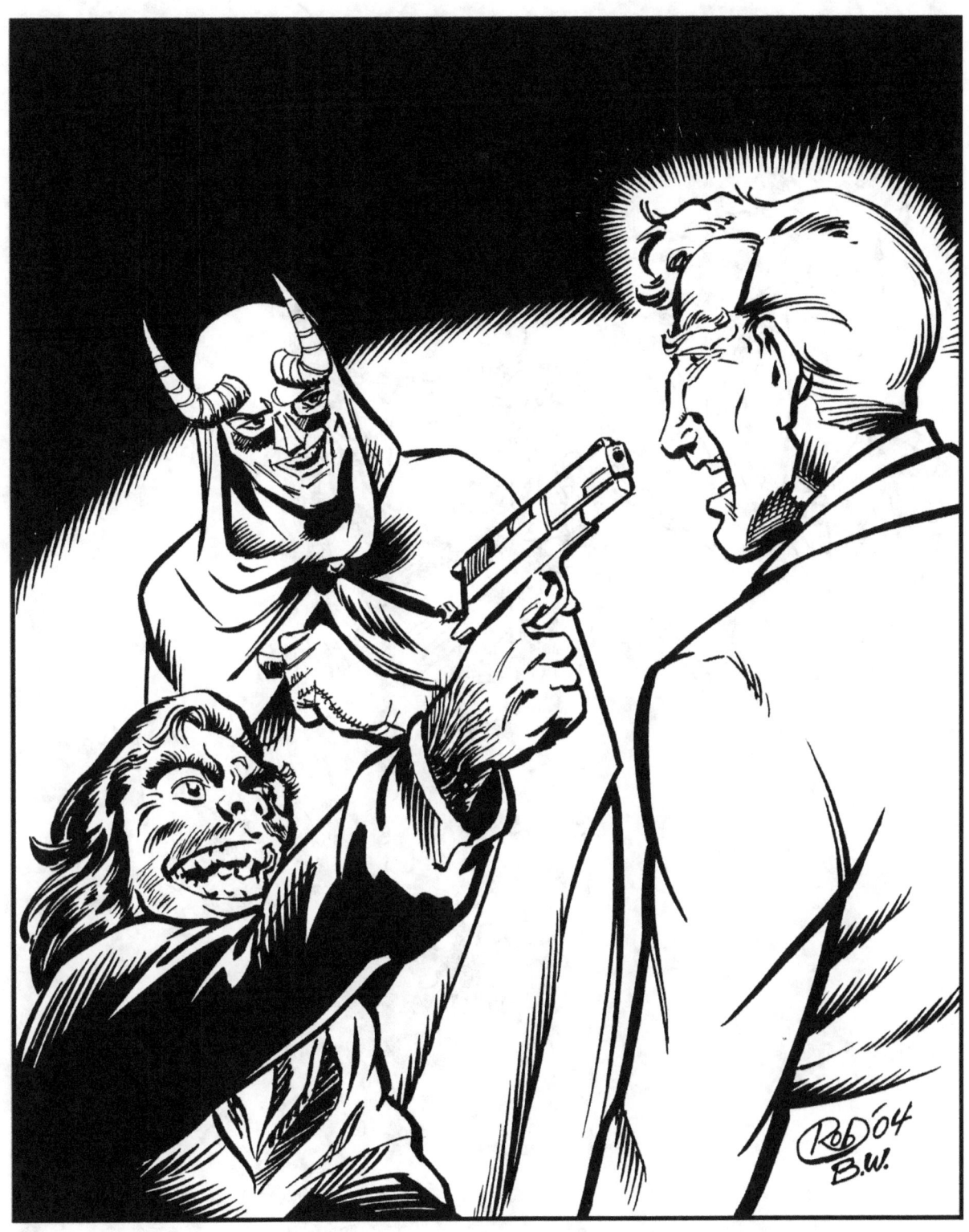

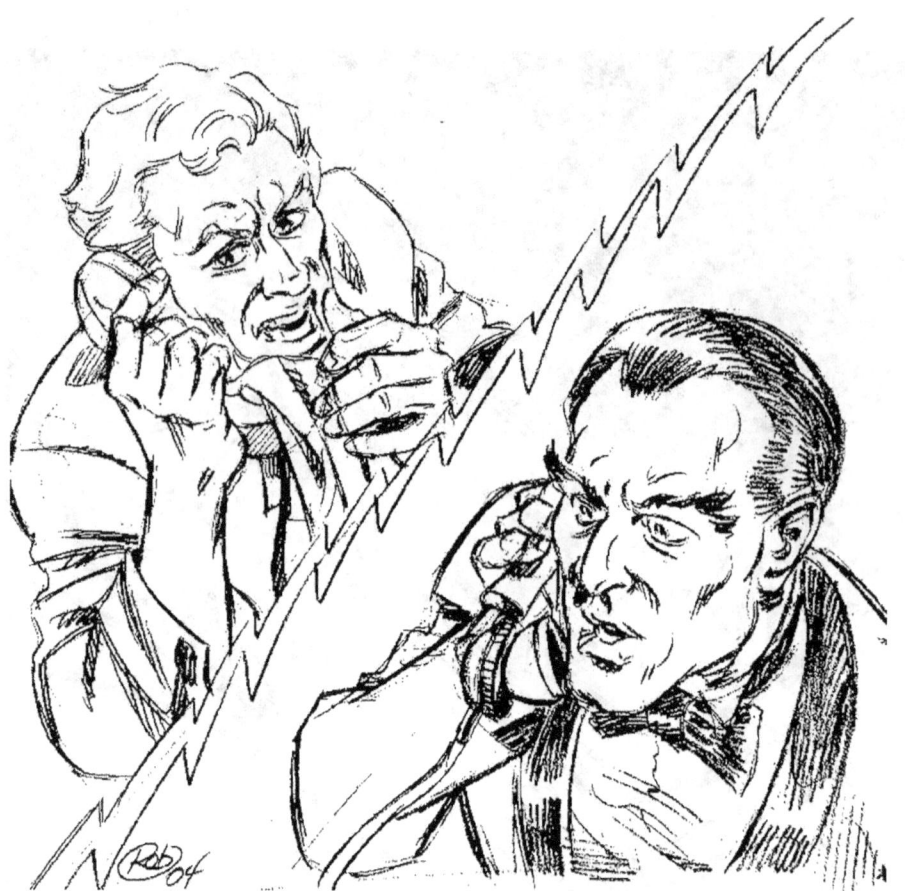

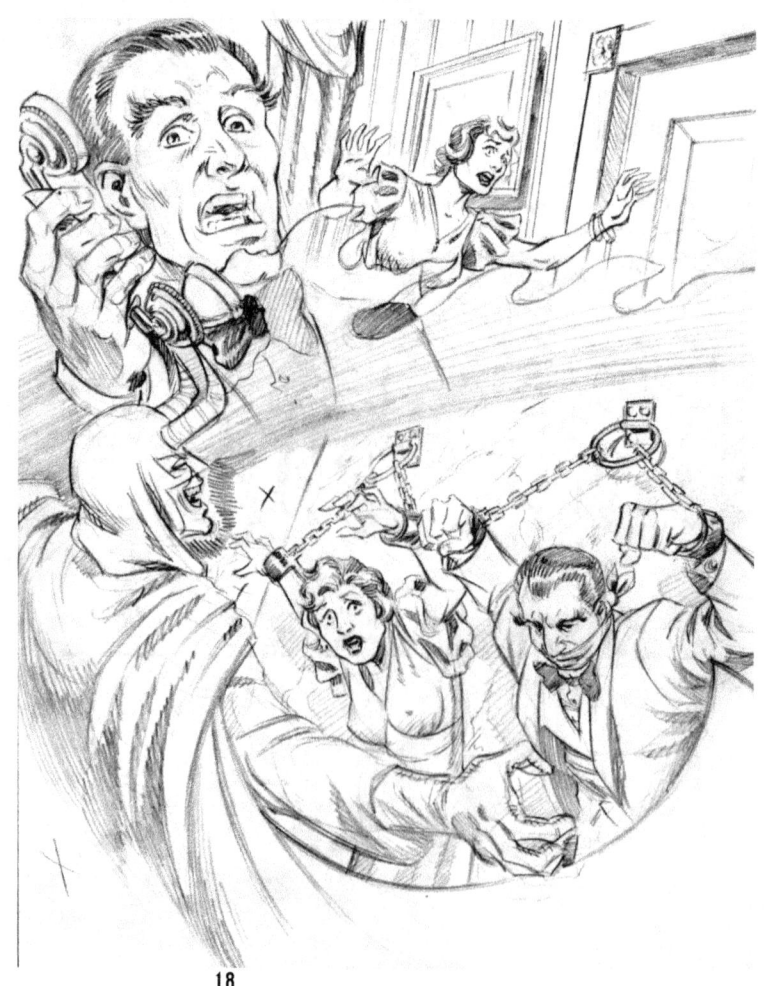

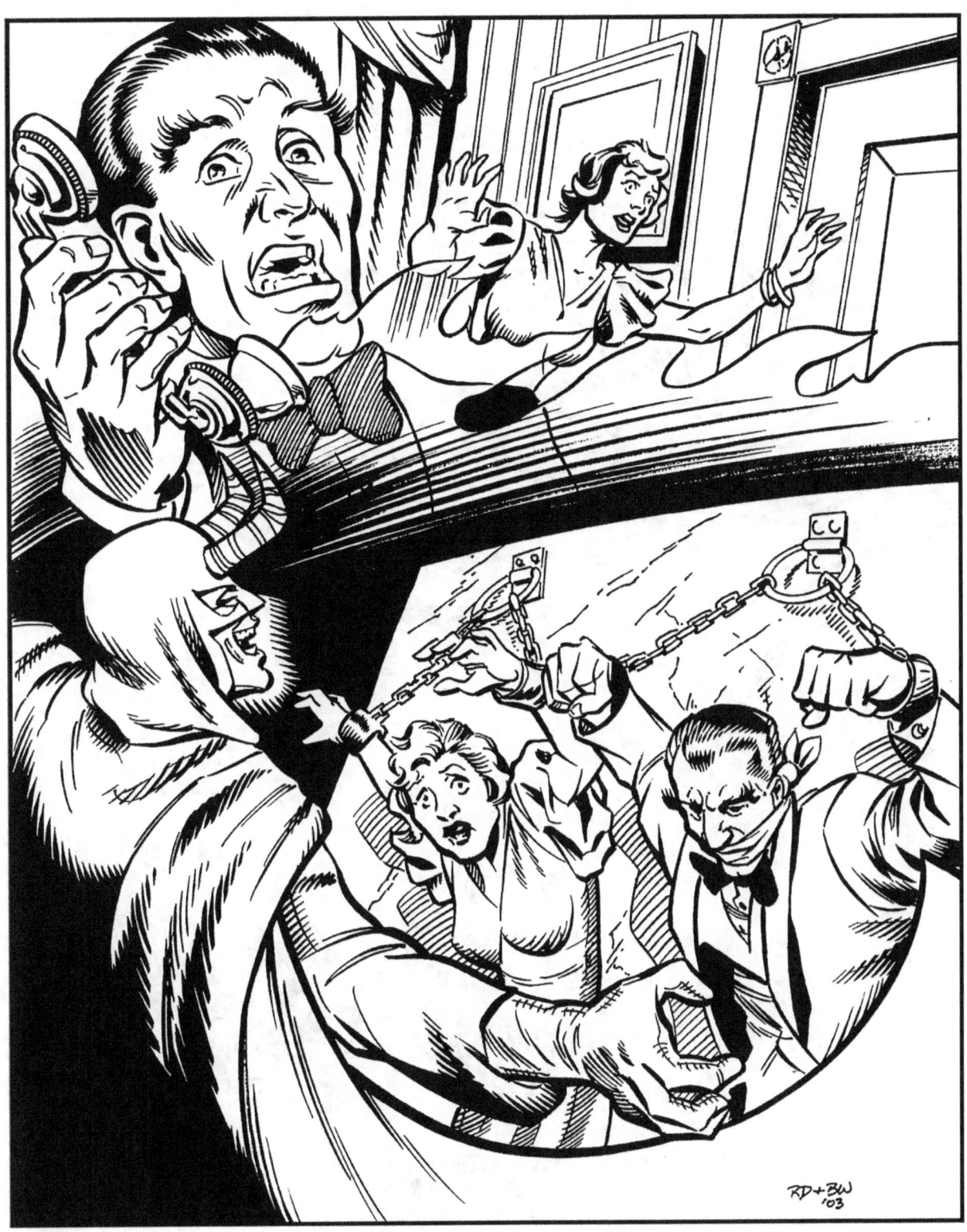

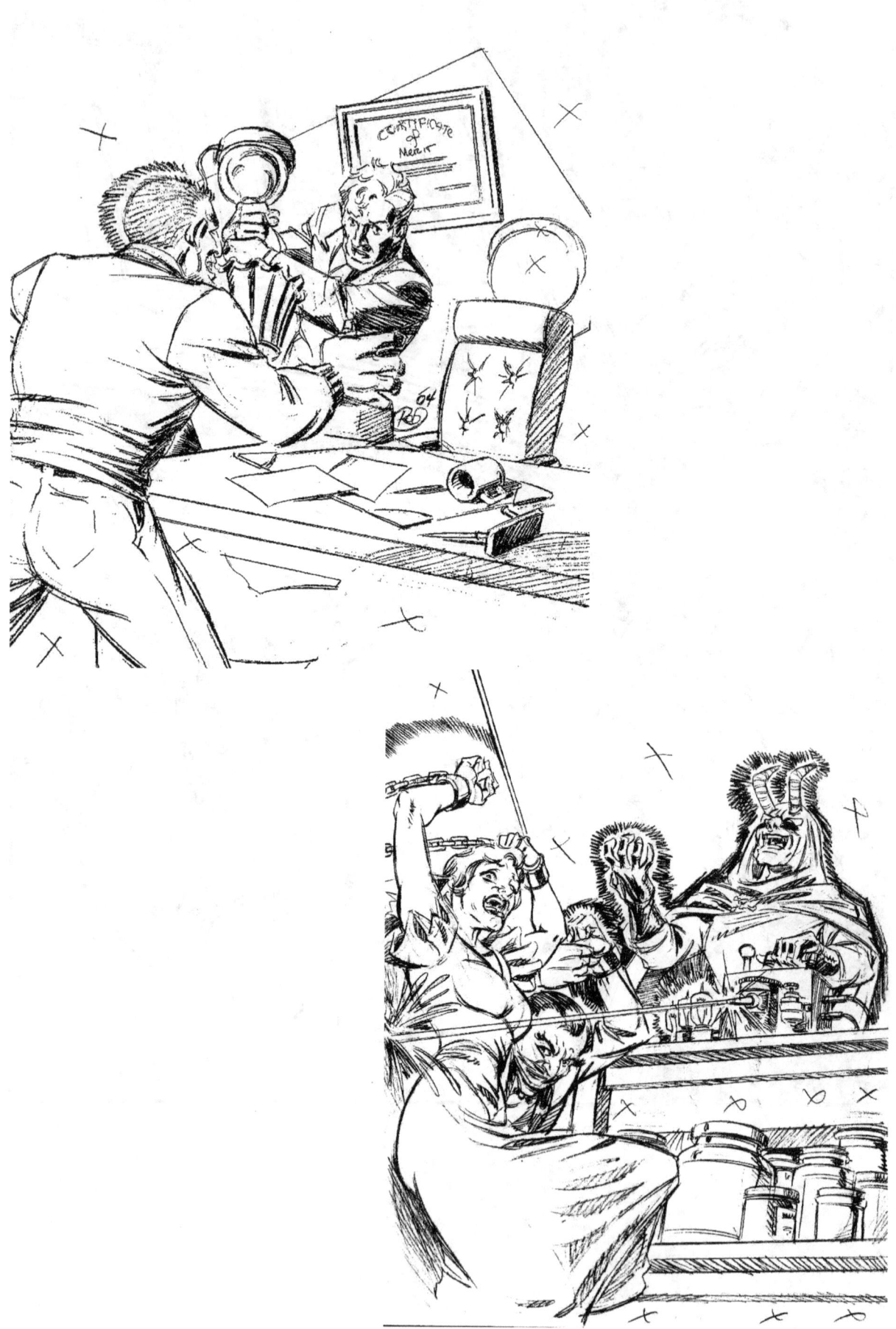

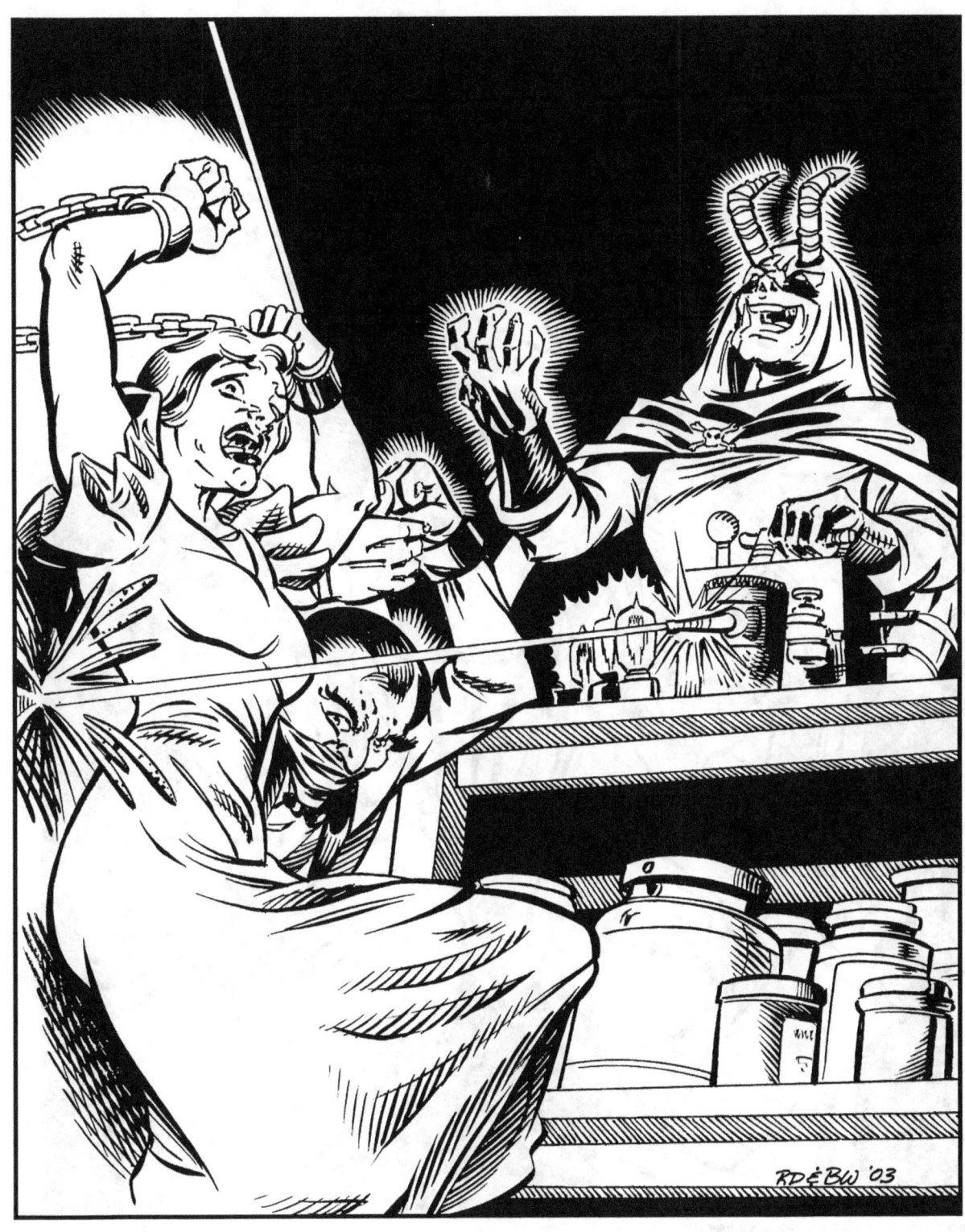

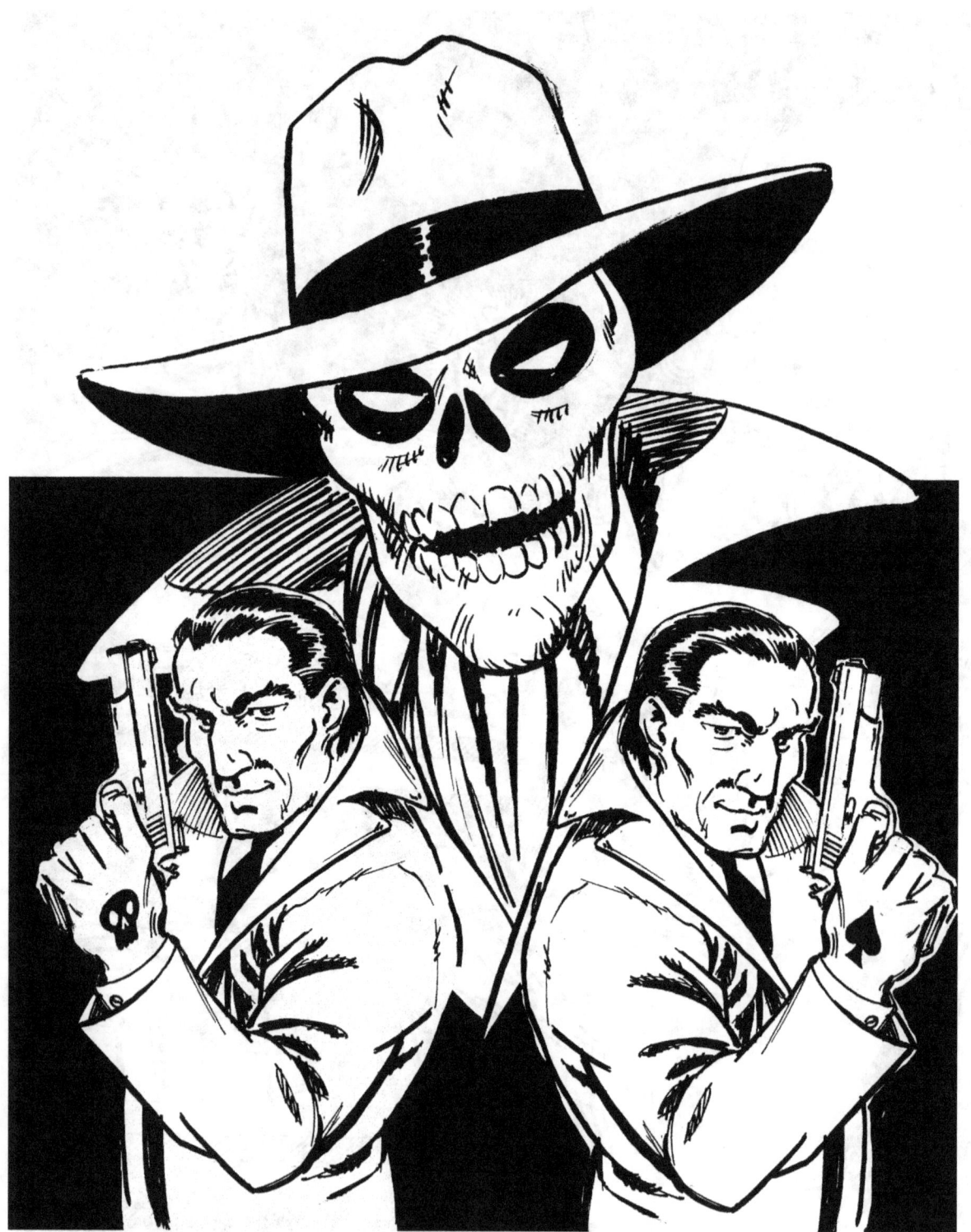

BROTHER BONES

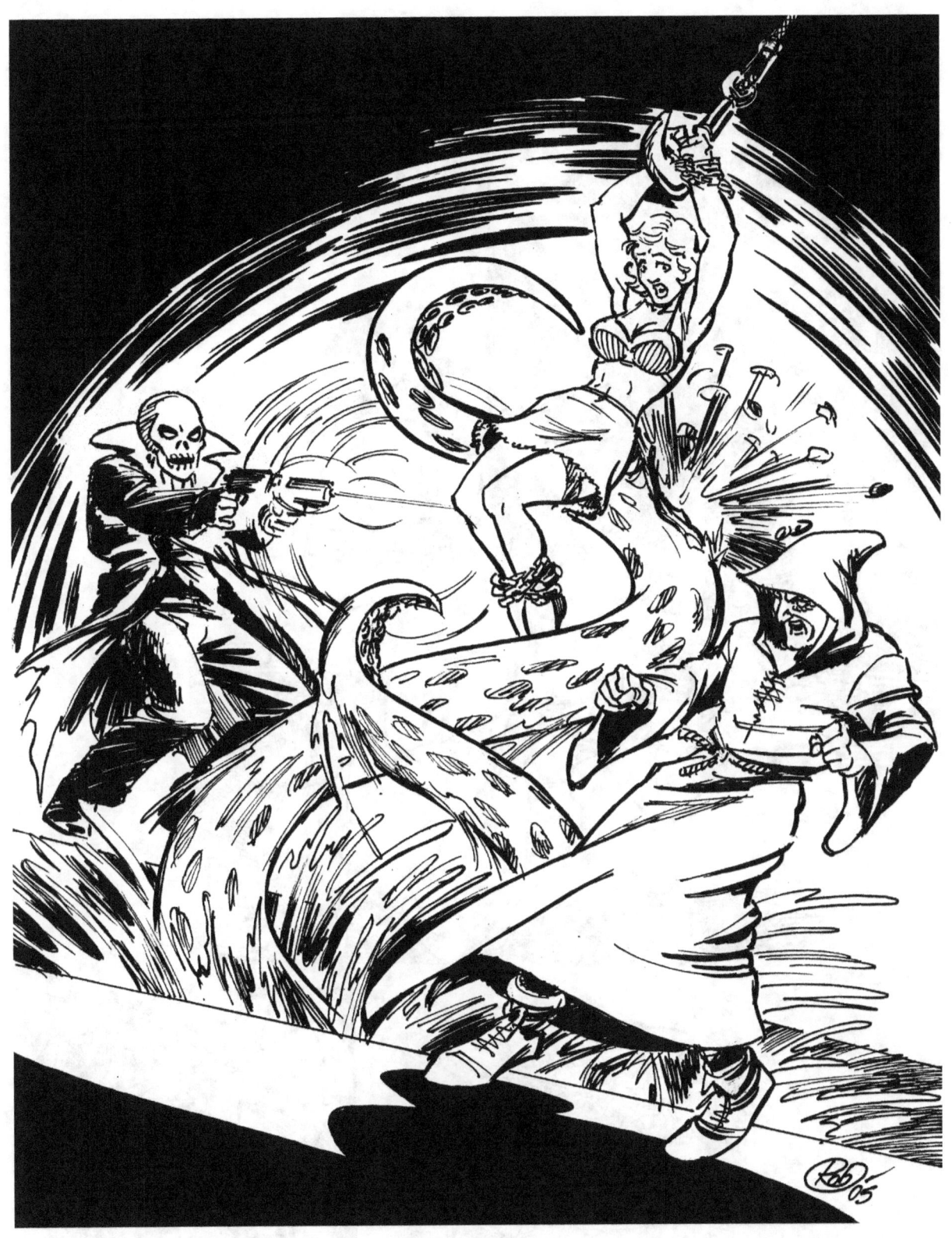

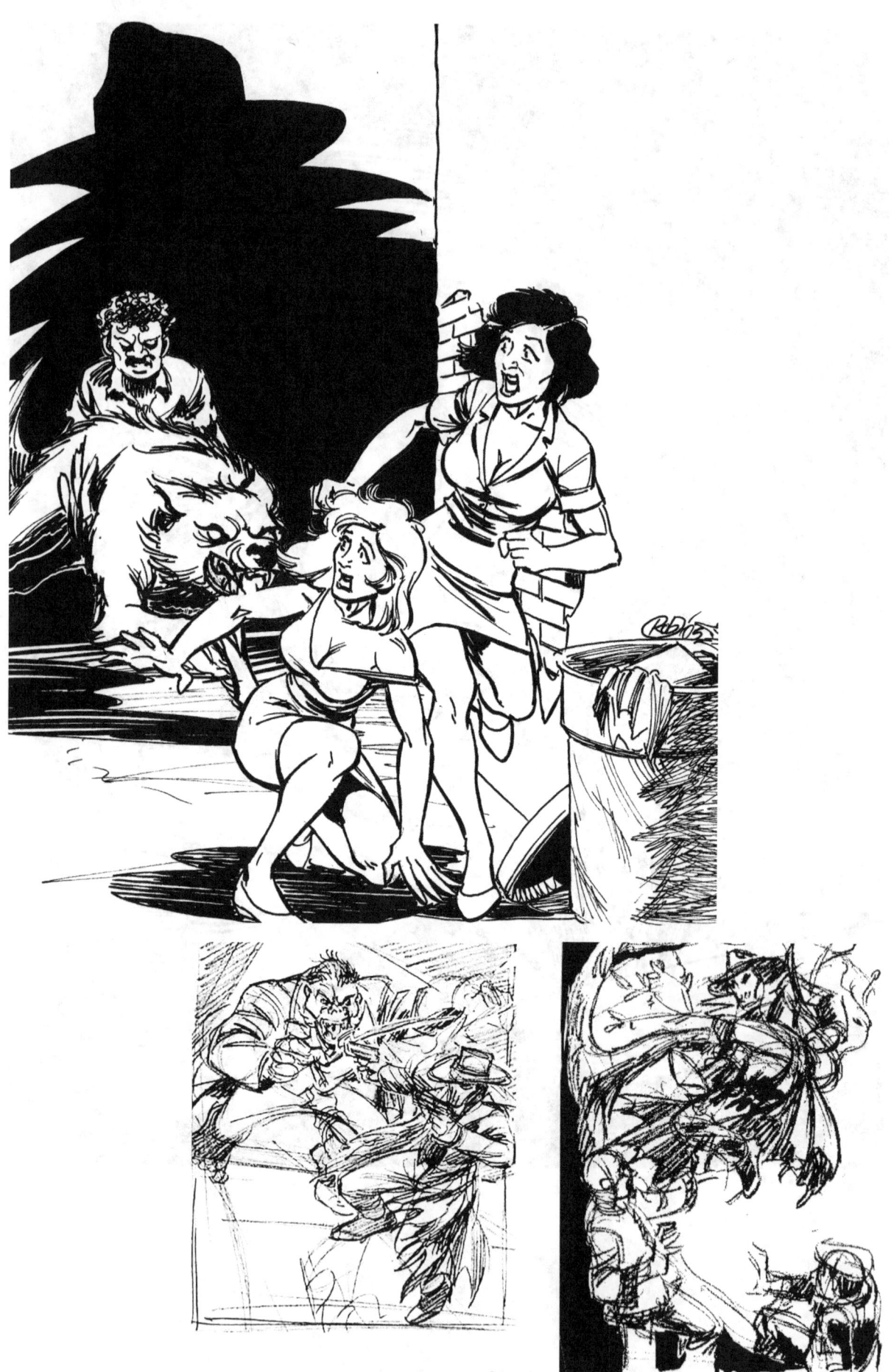

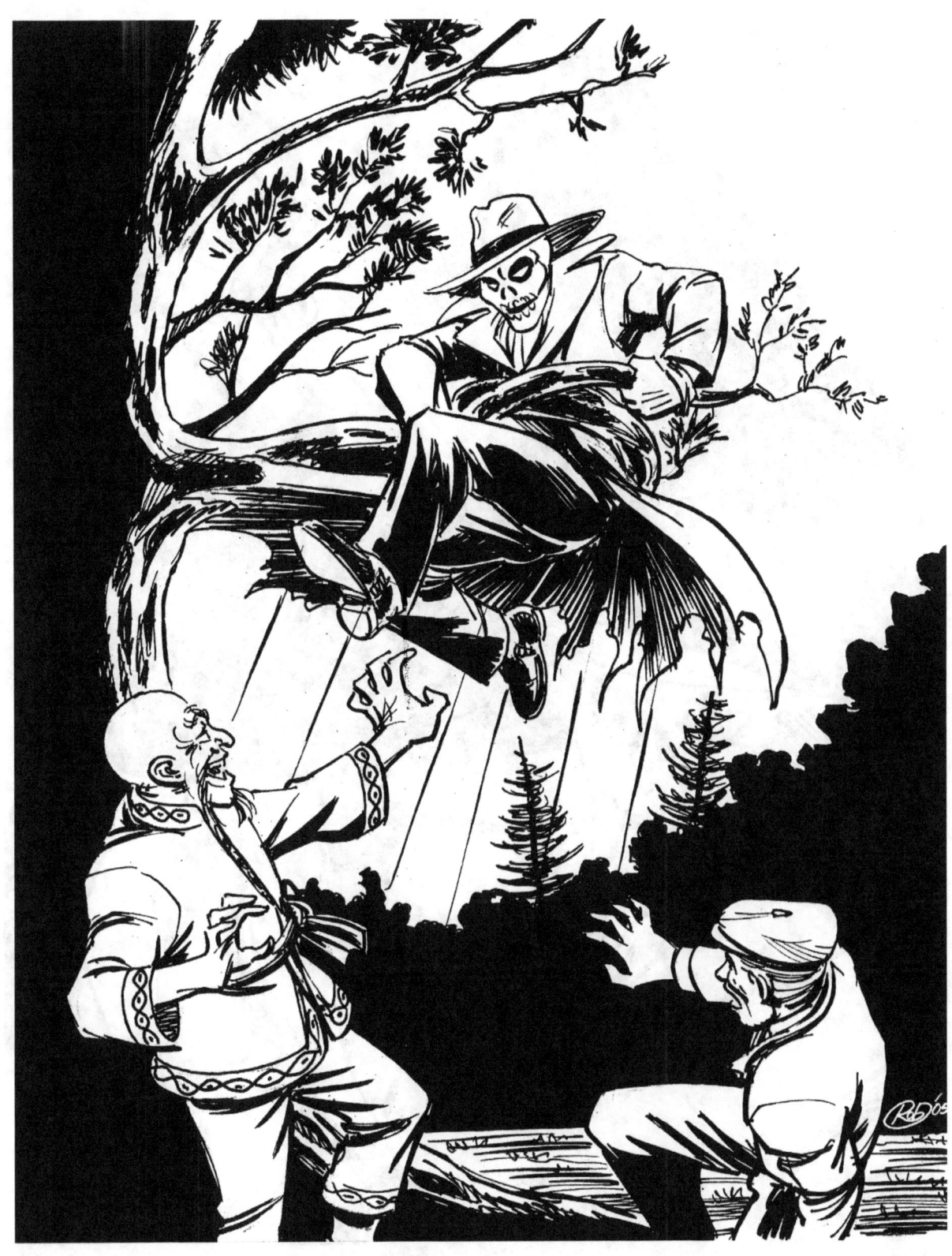

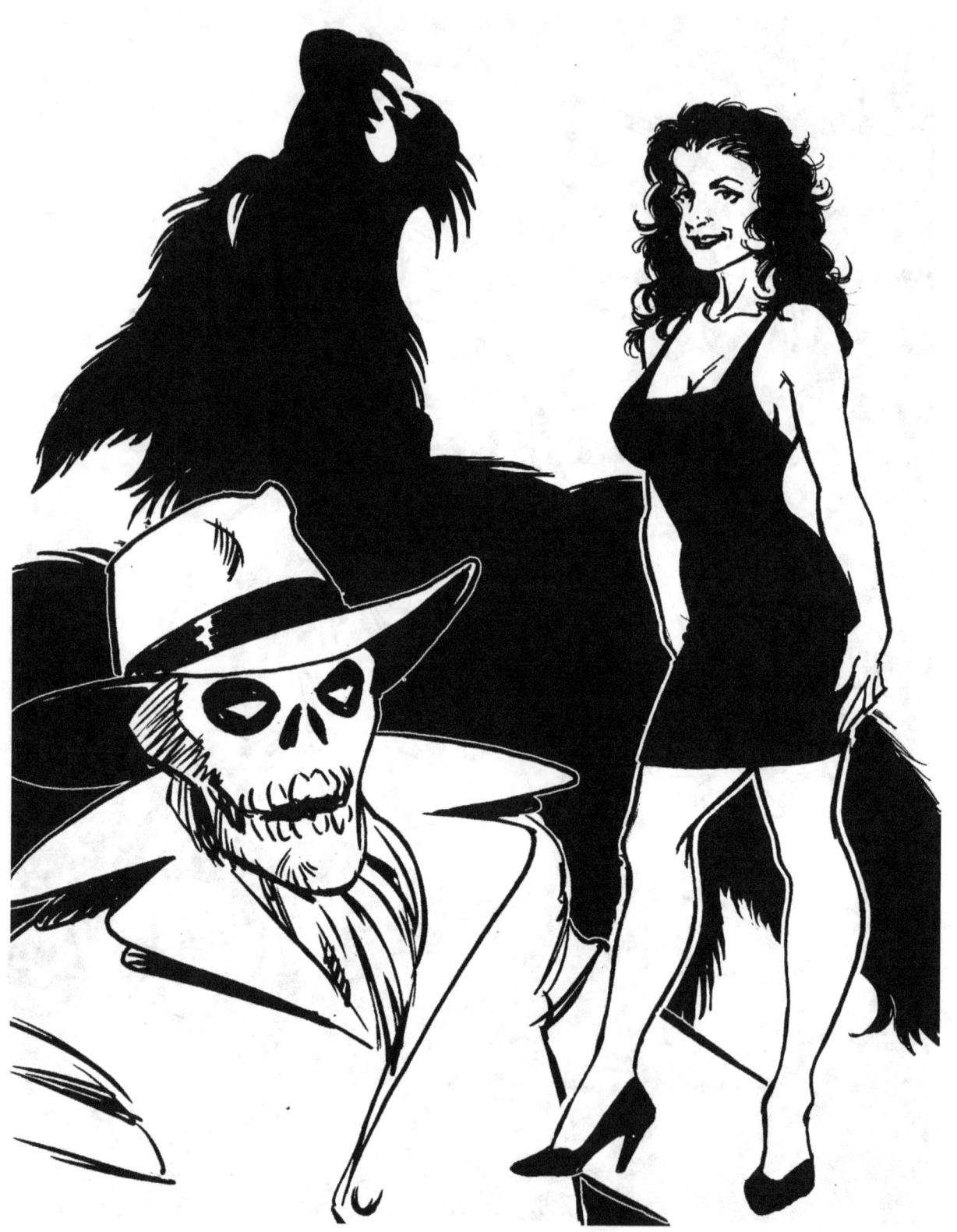

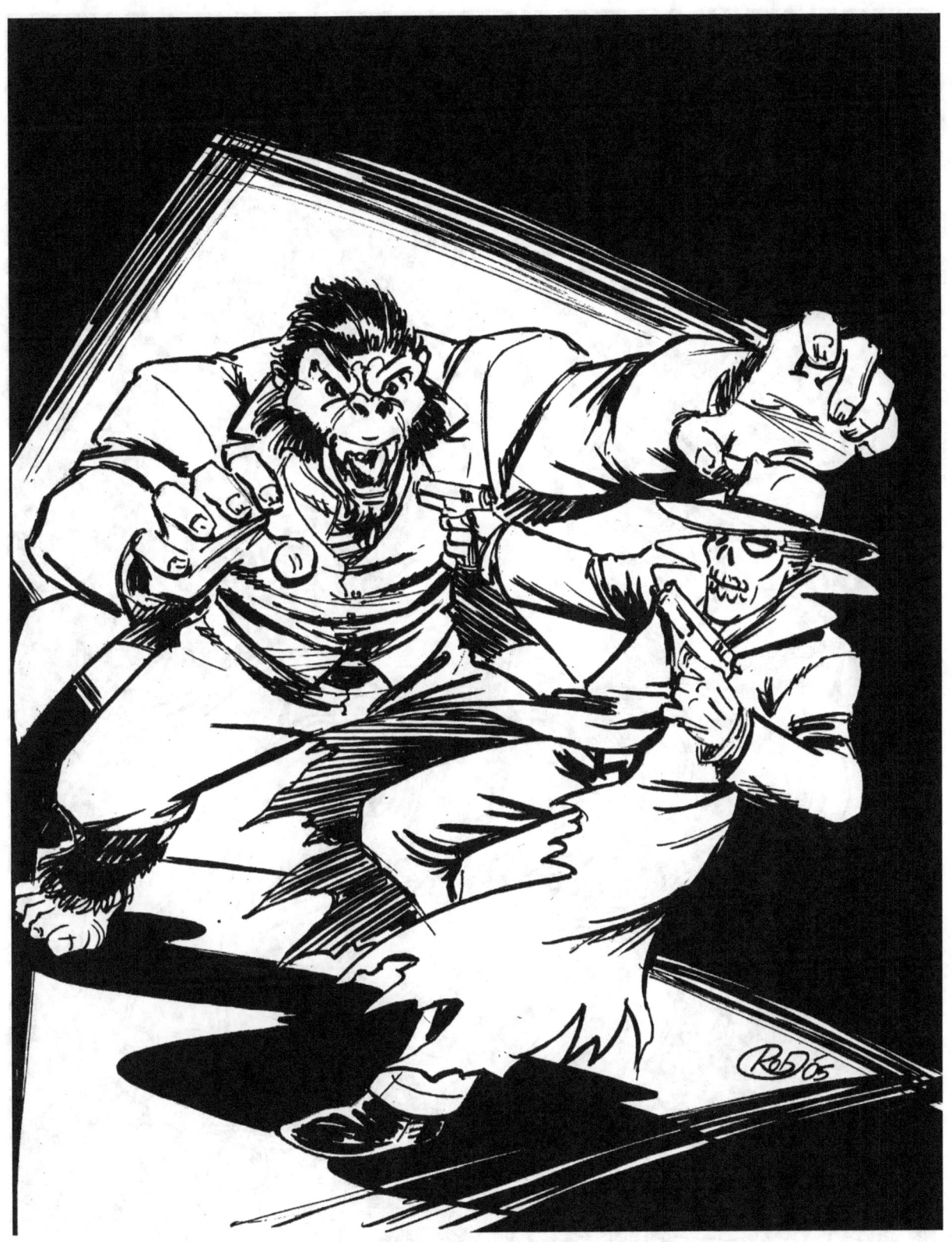

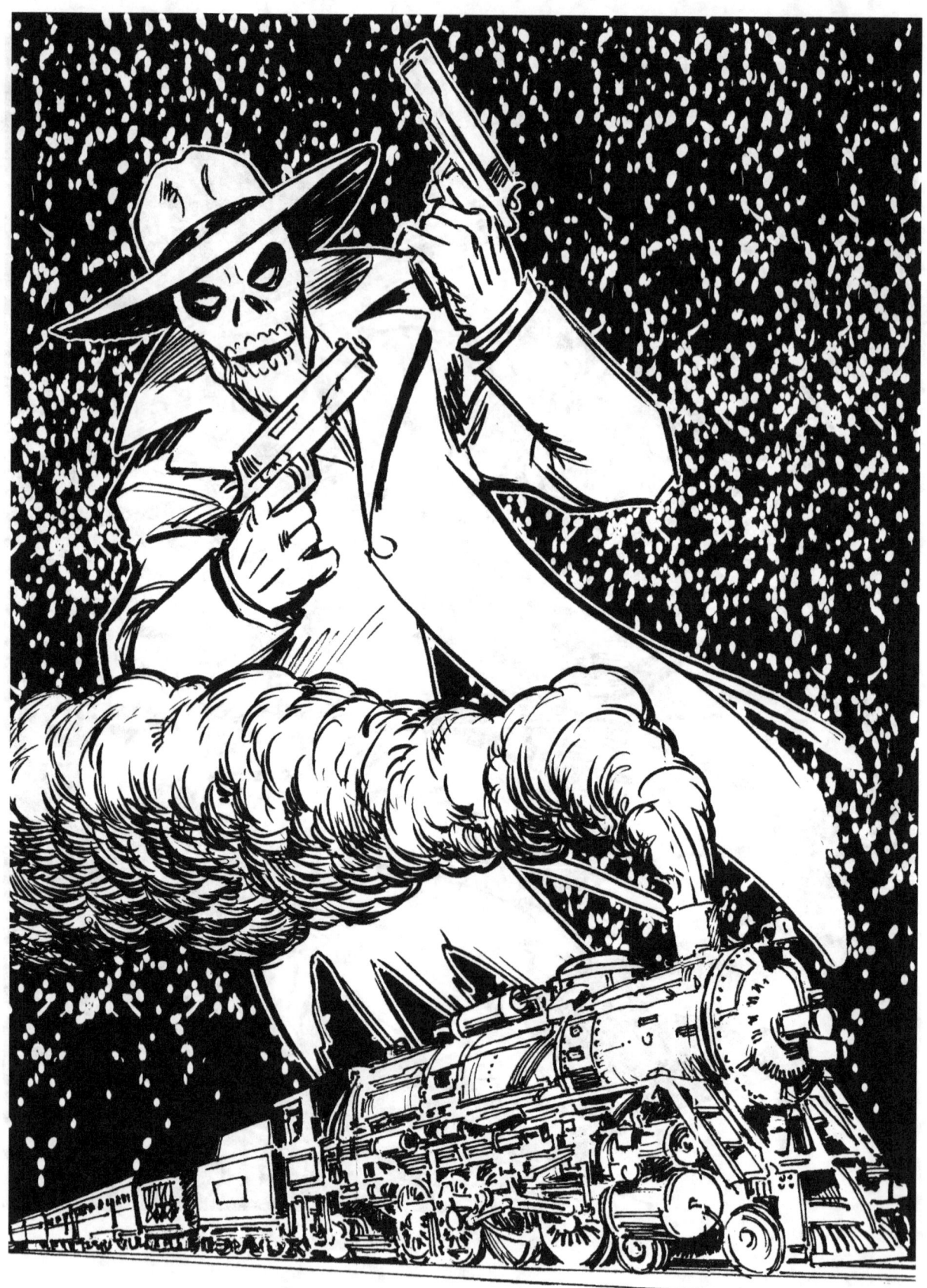

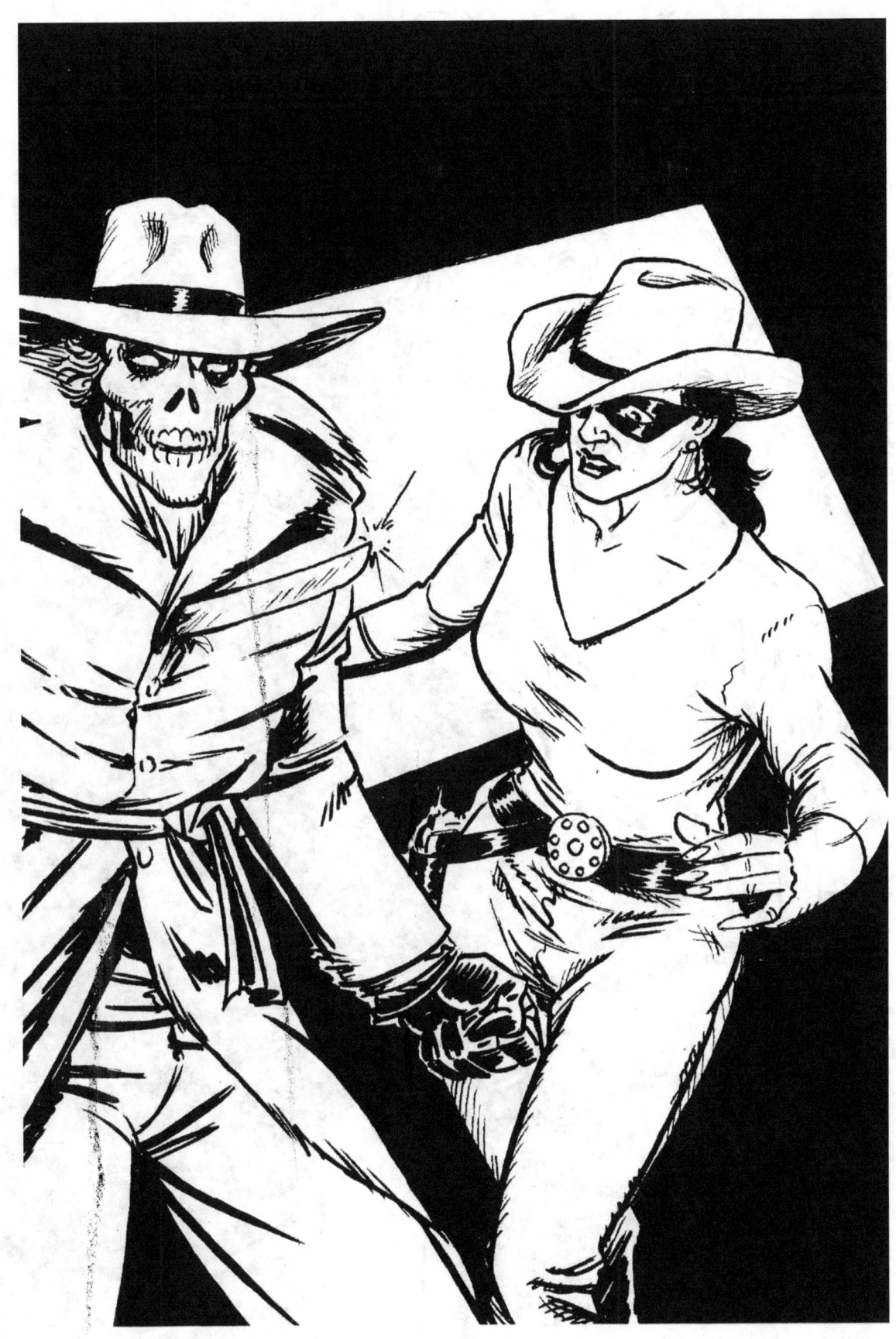

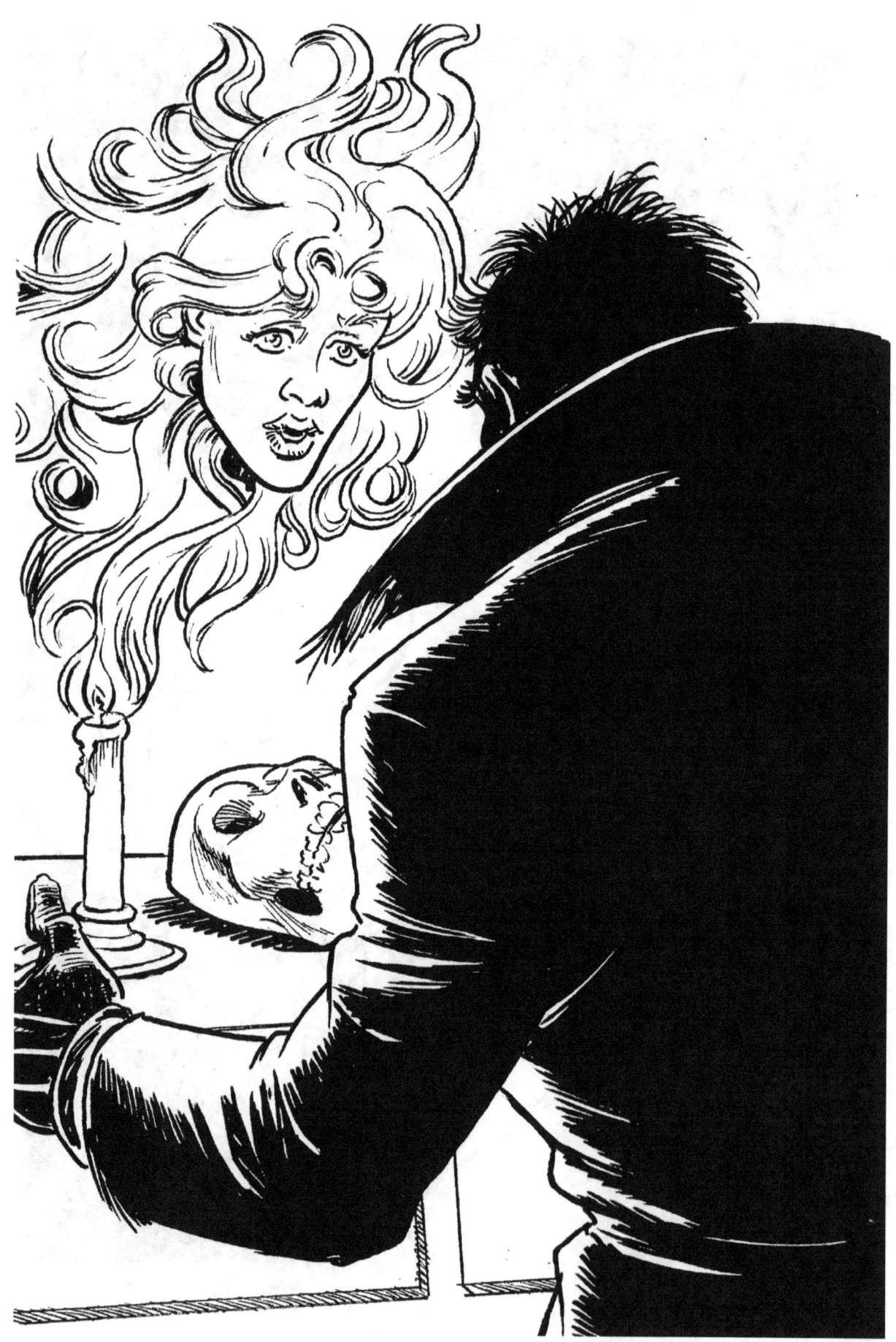

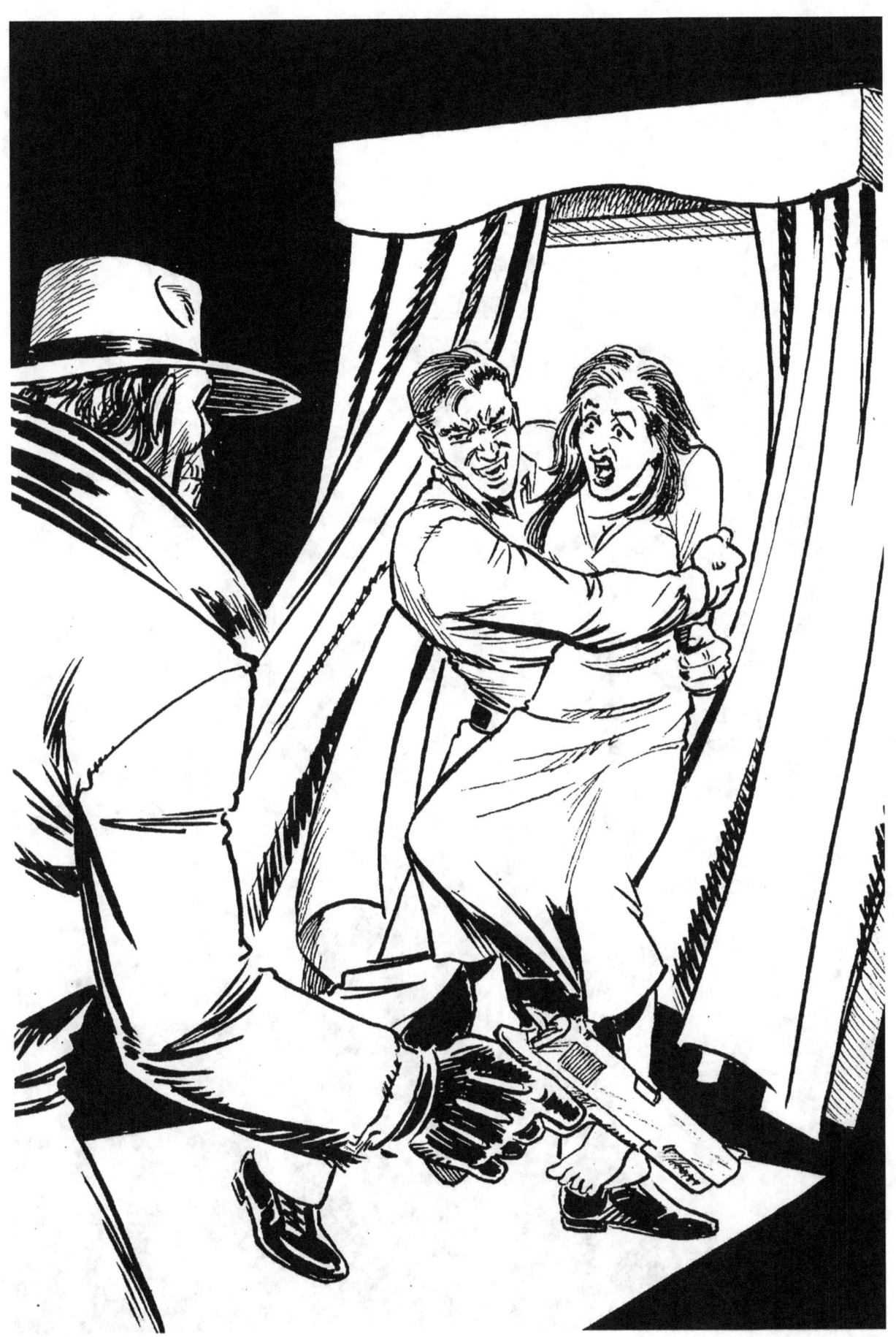

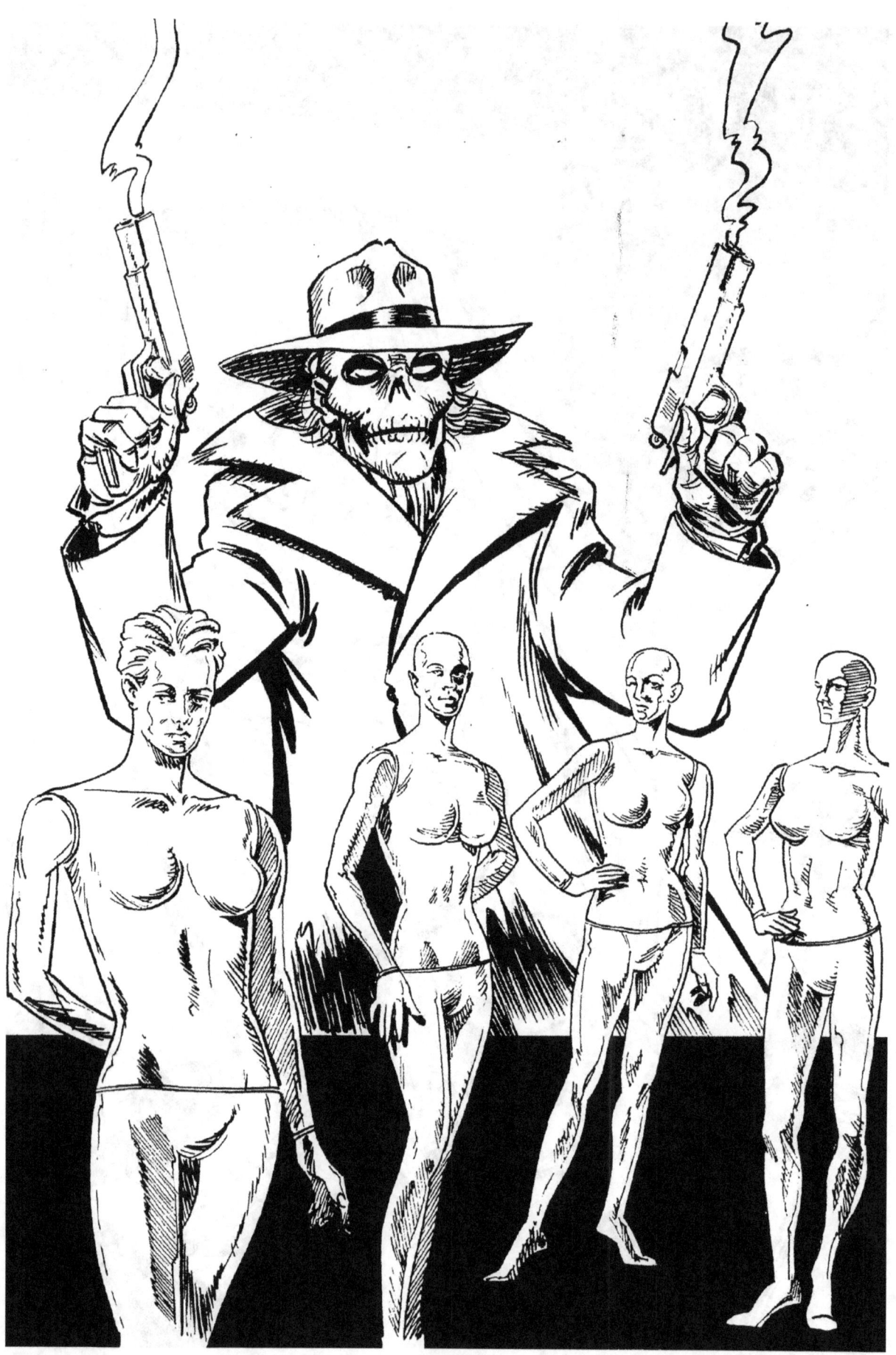

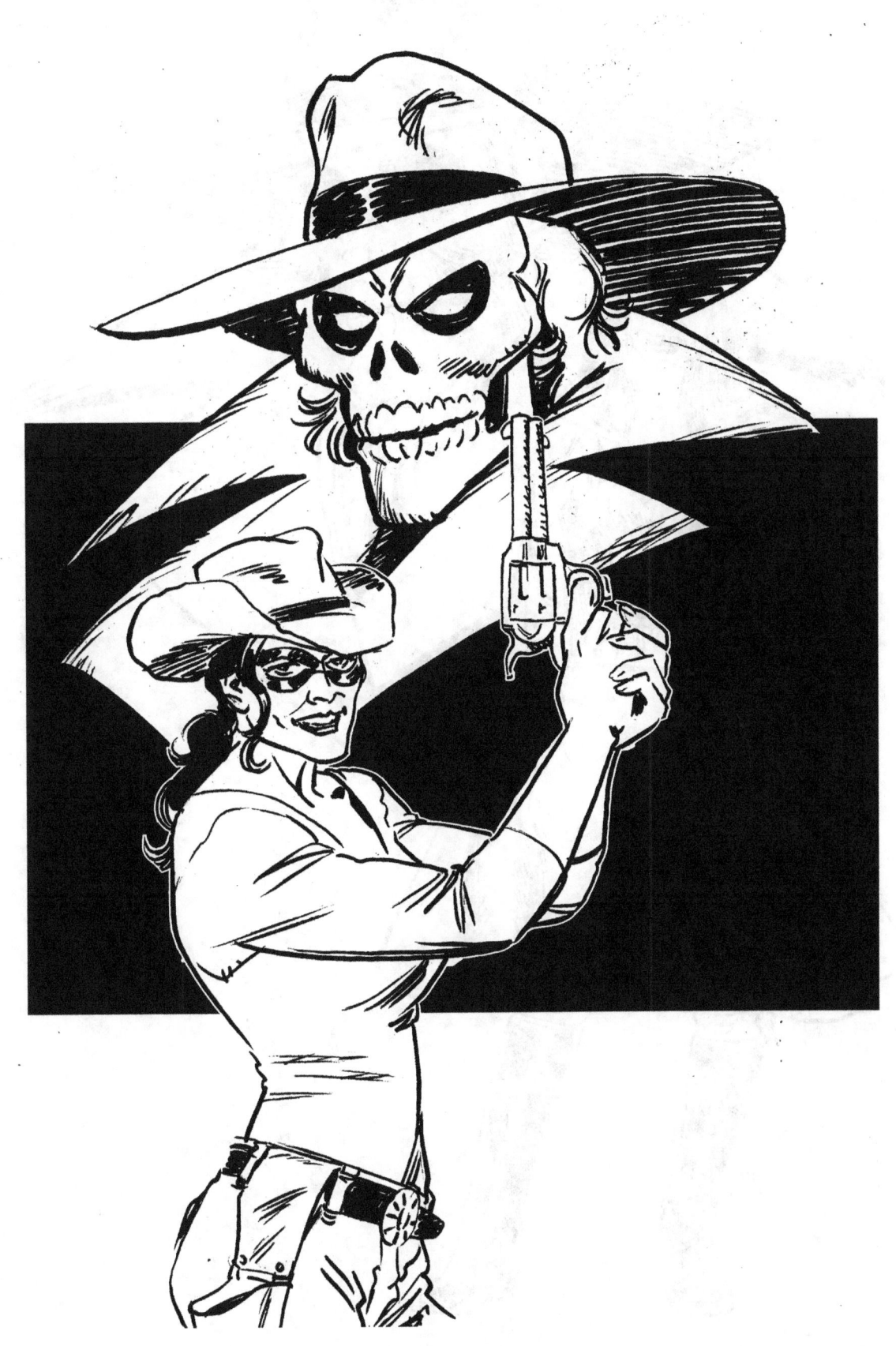

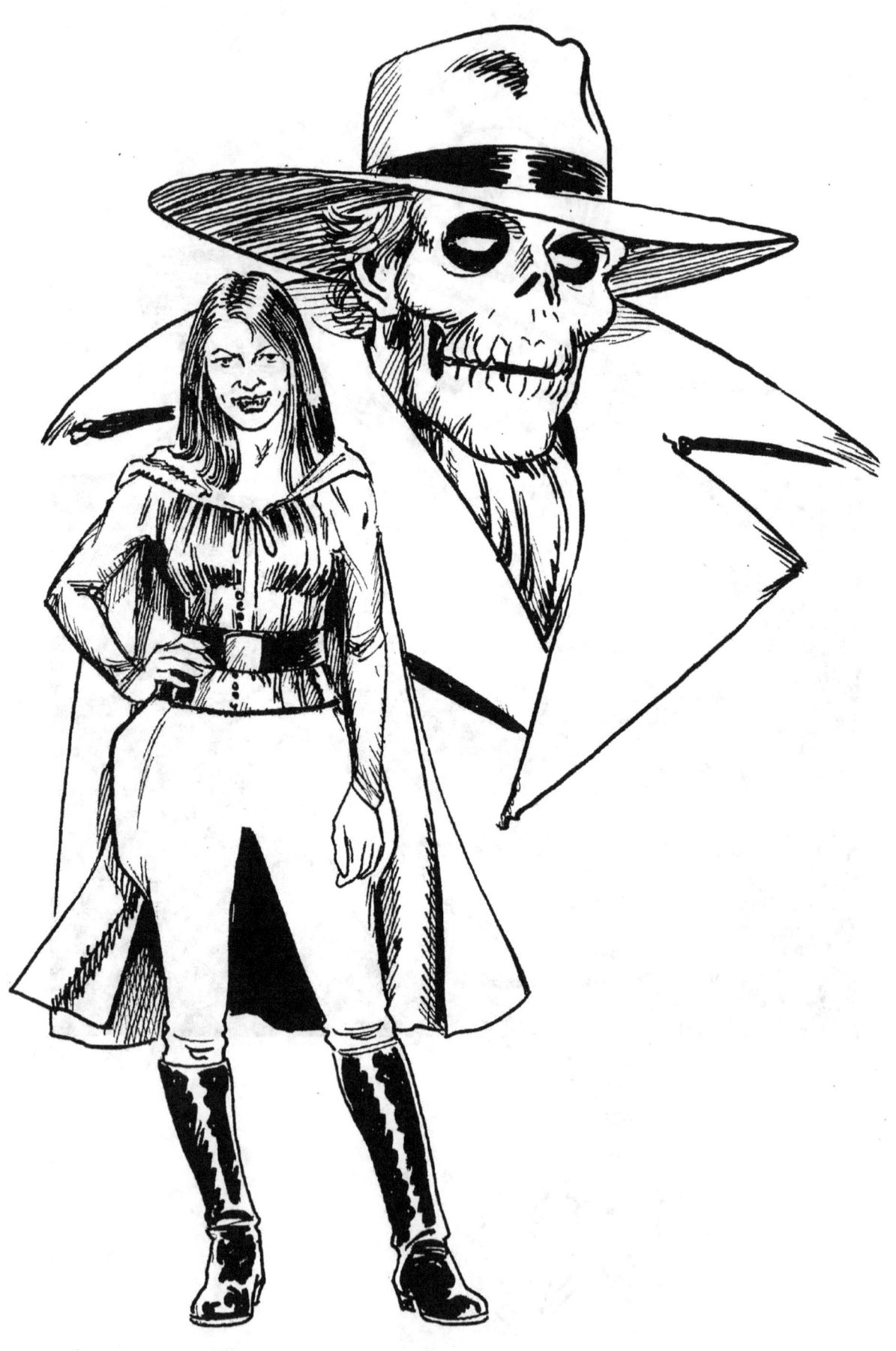

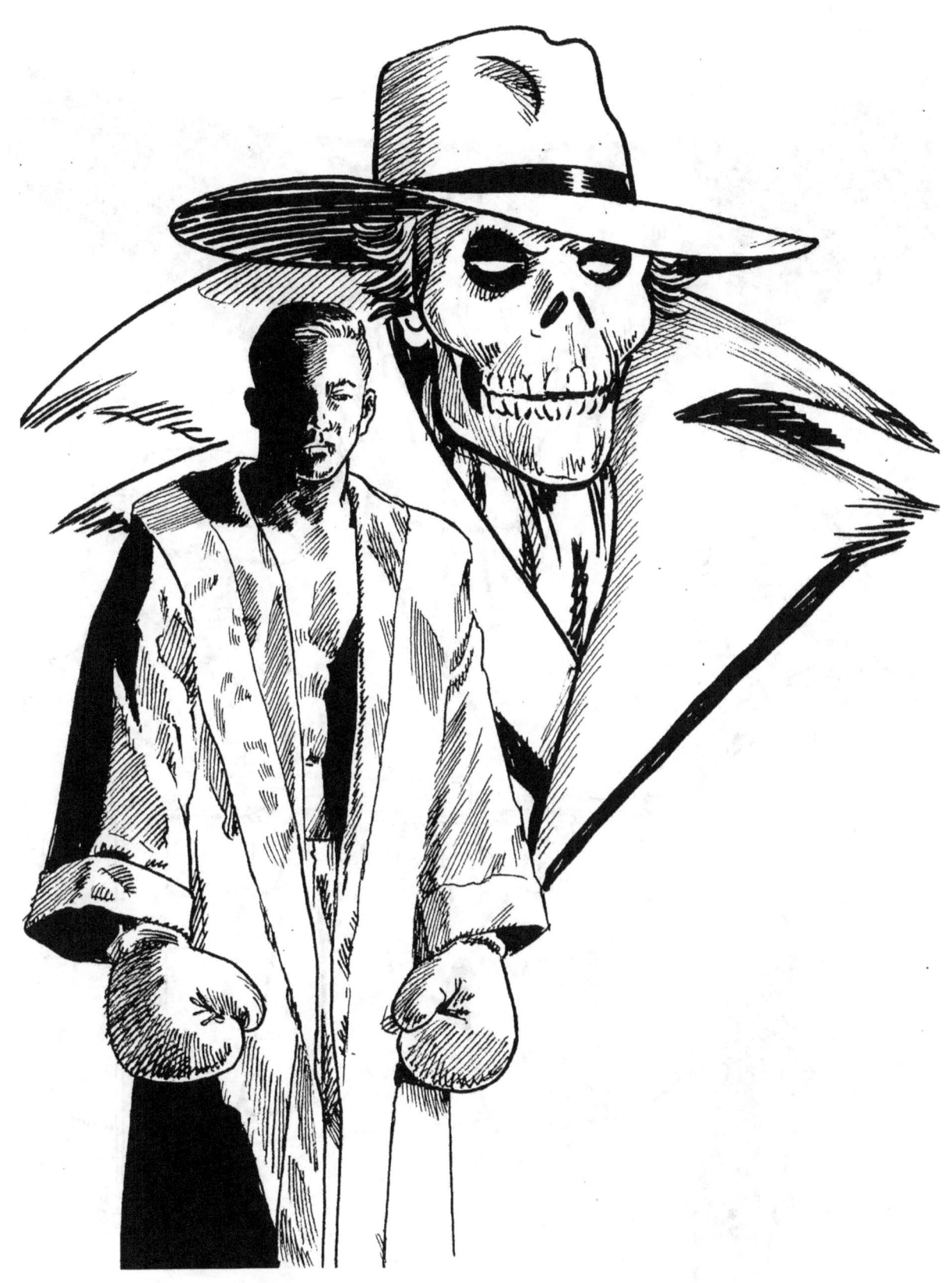

35

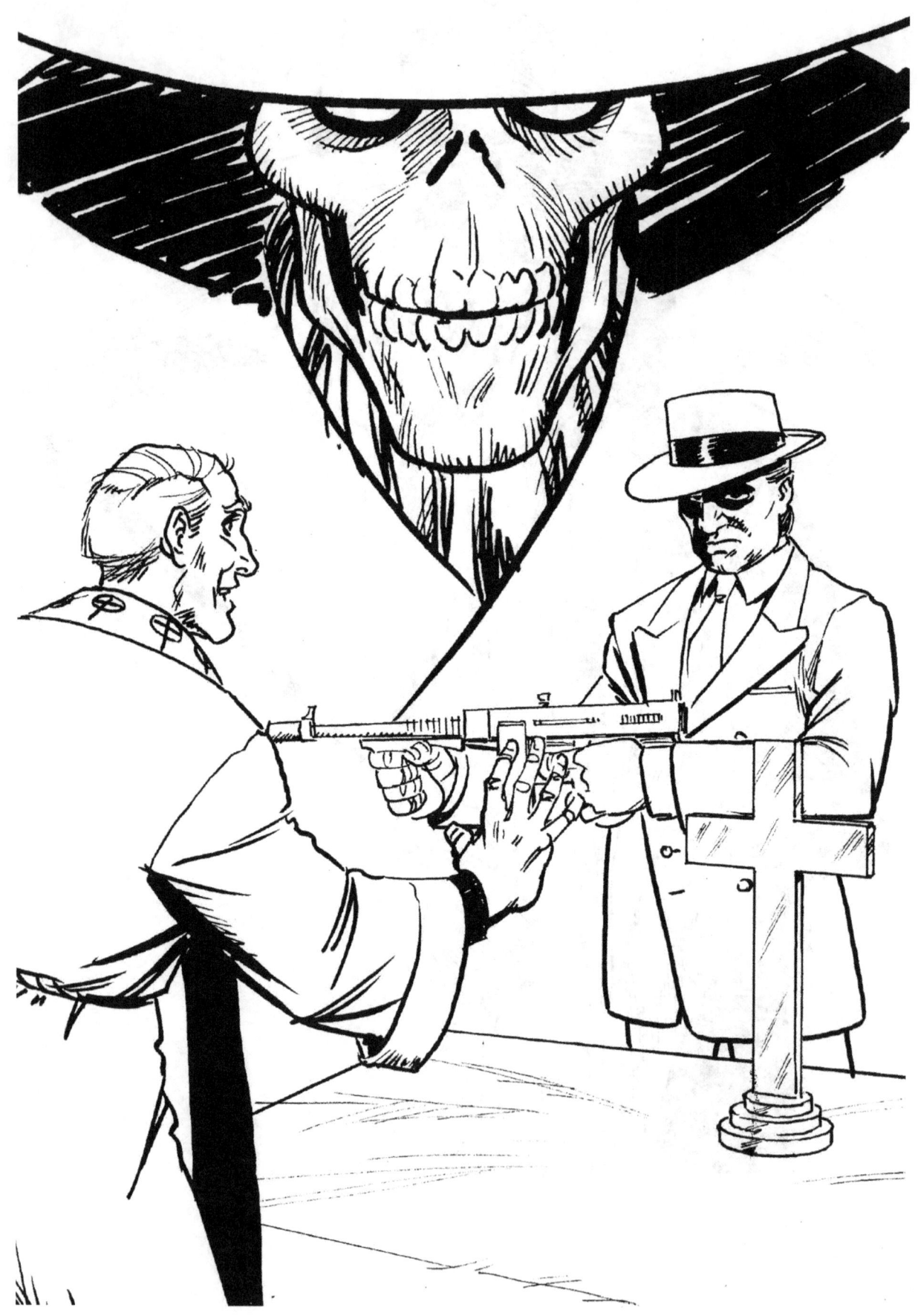

CHAPTER 2
THE GOOD GUYS

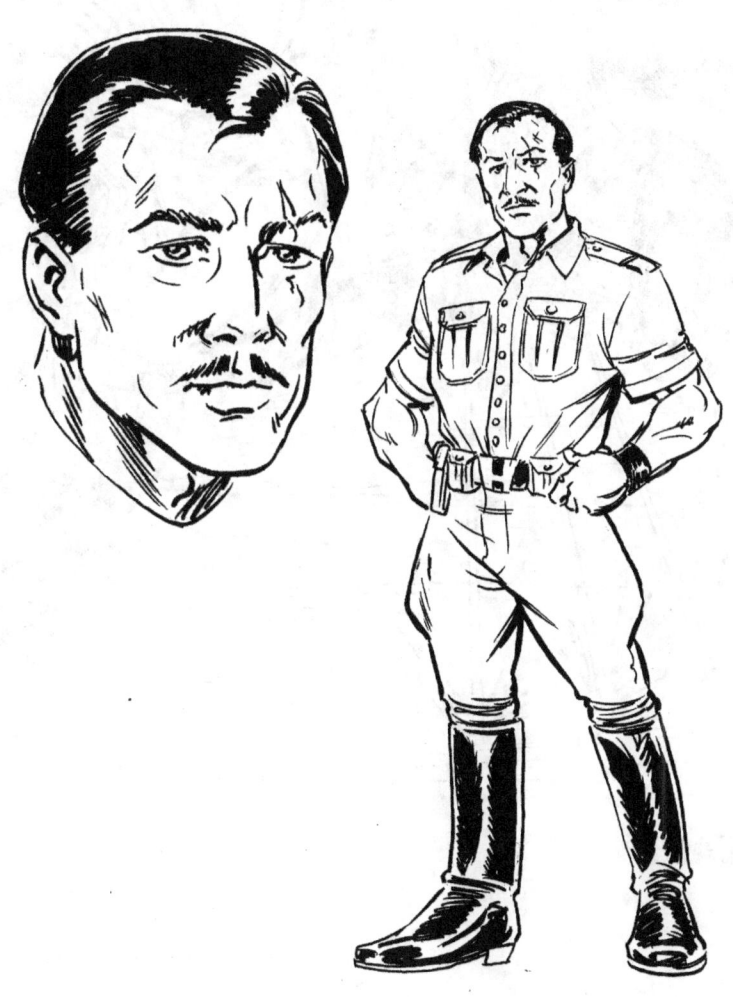

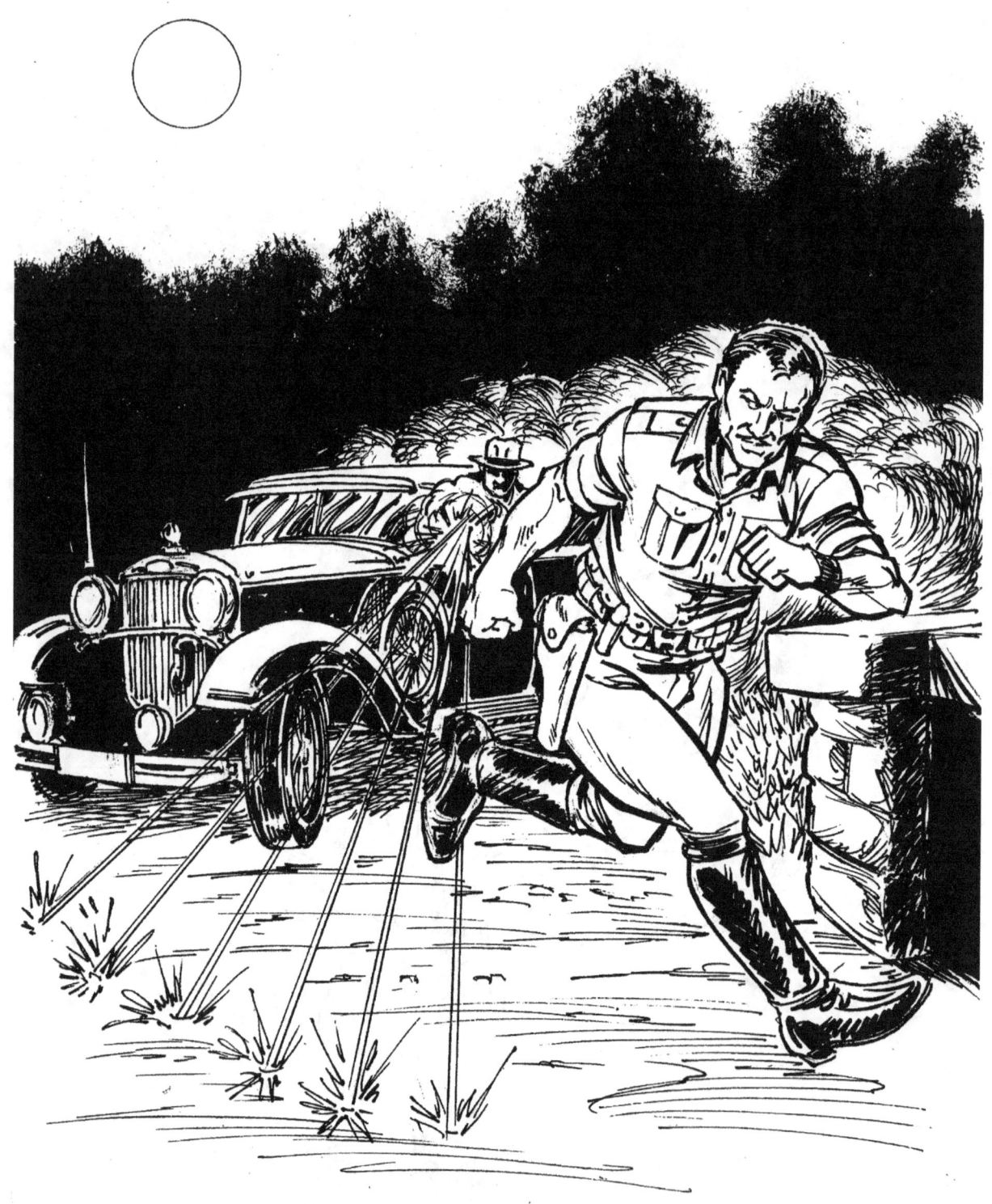

CAPTAIN HAZZARD

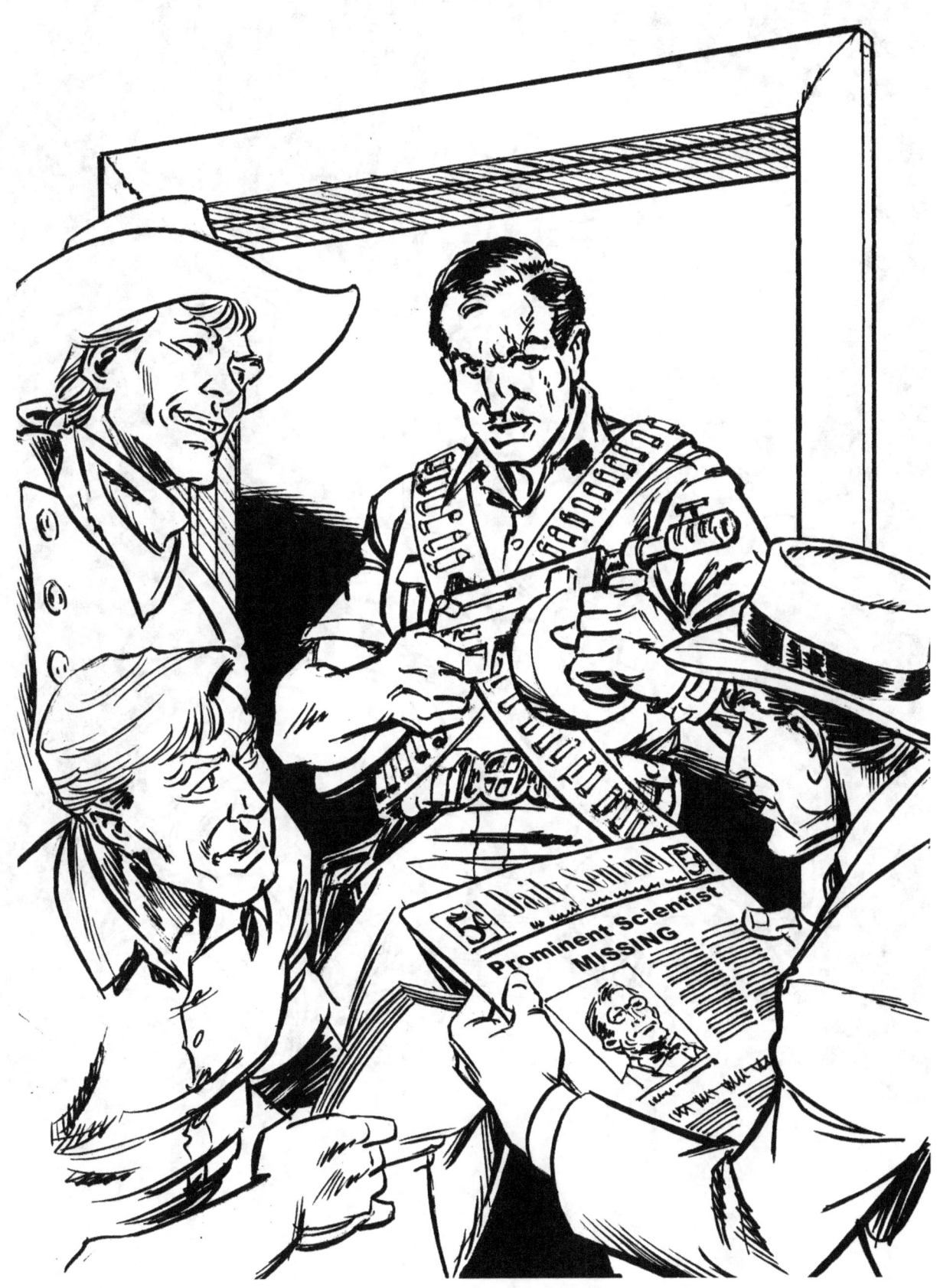

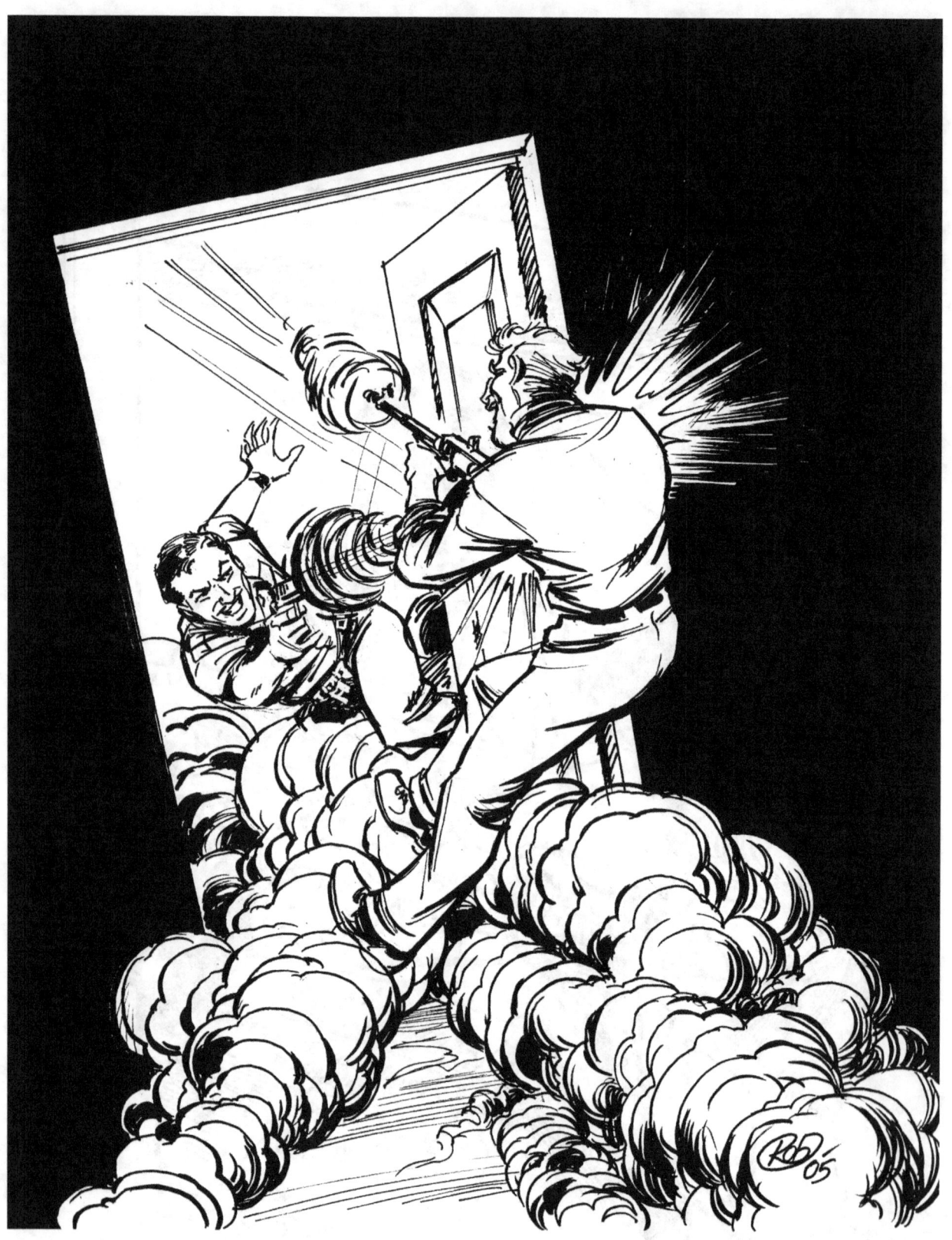

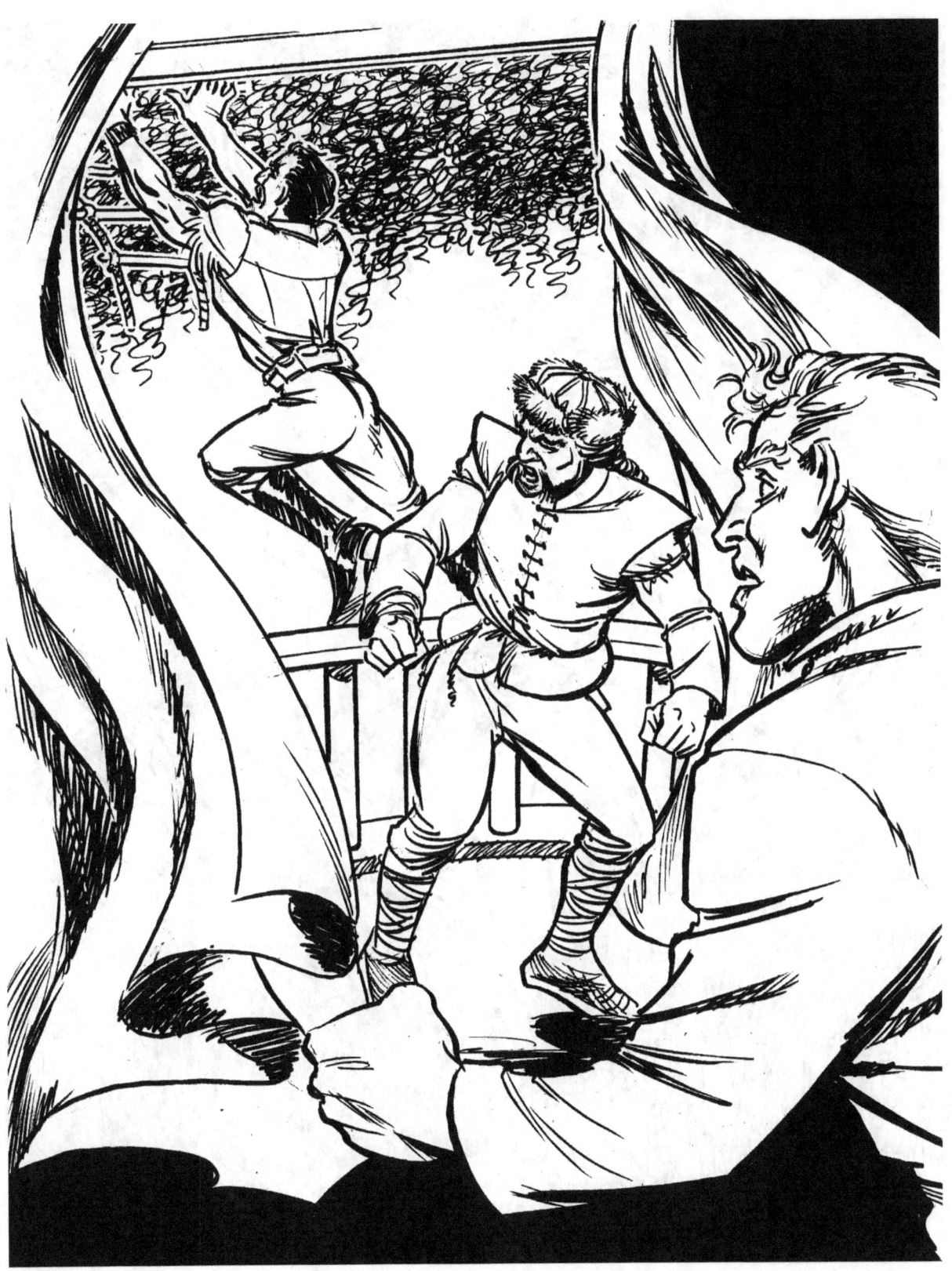

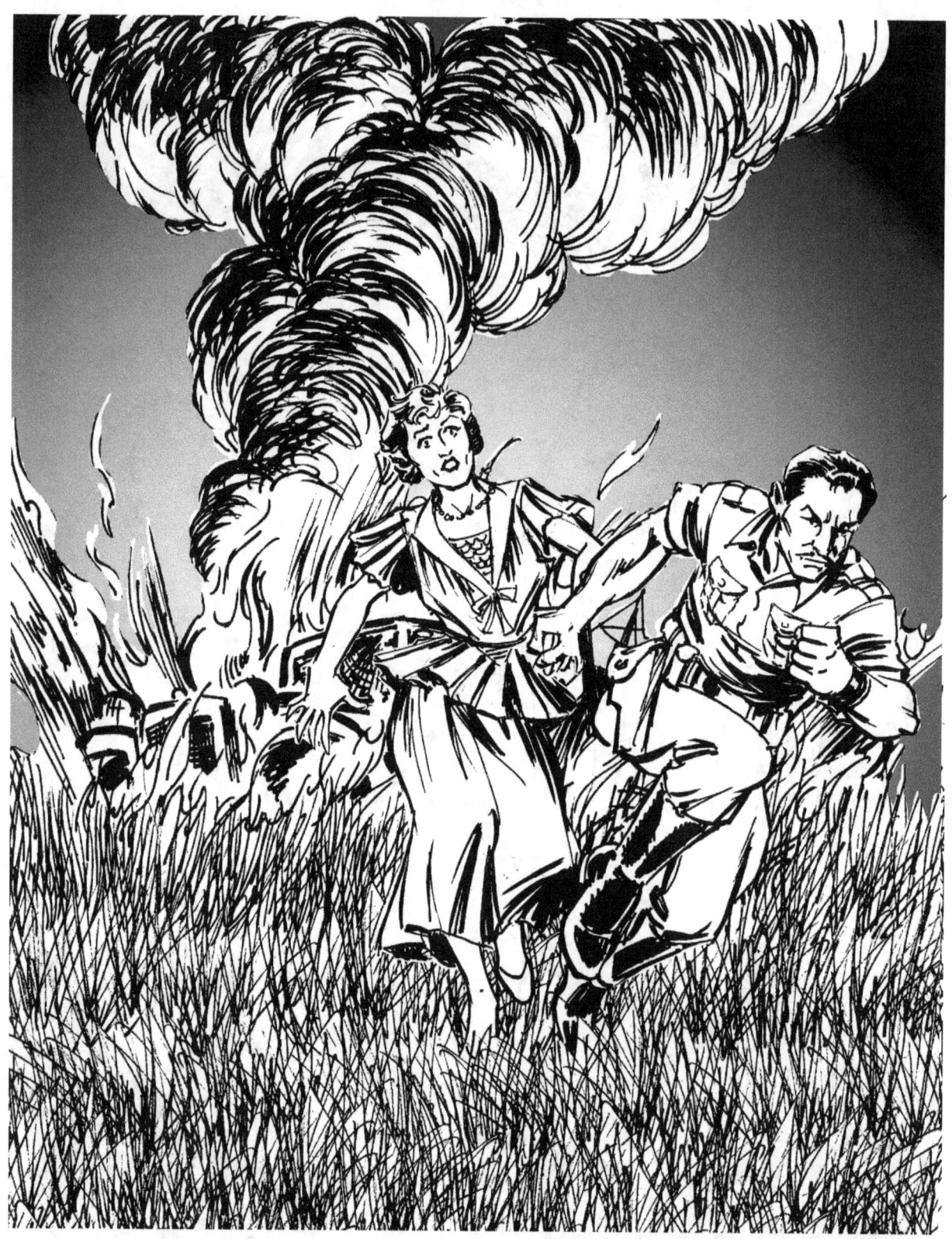

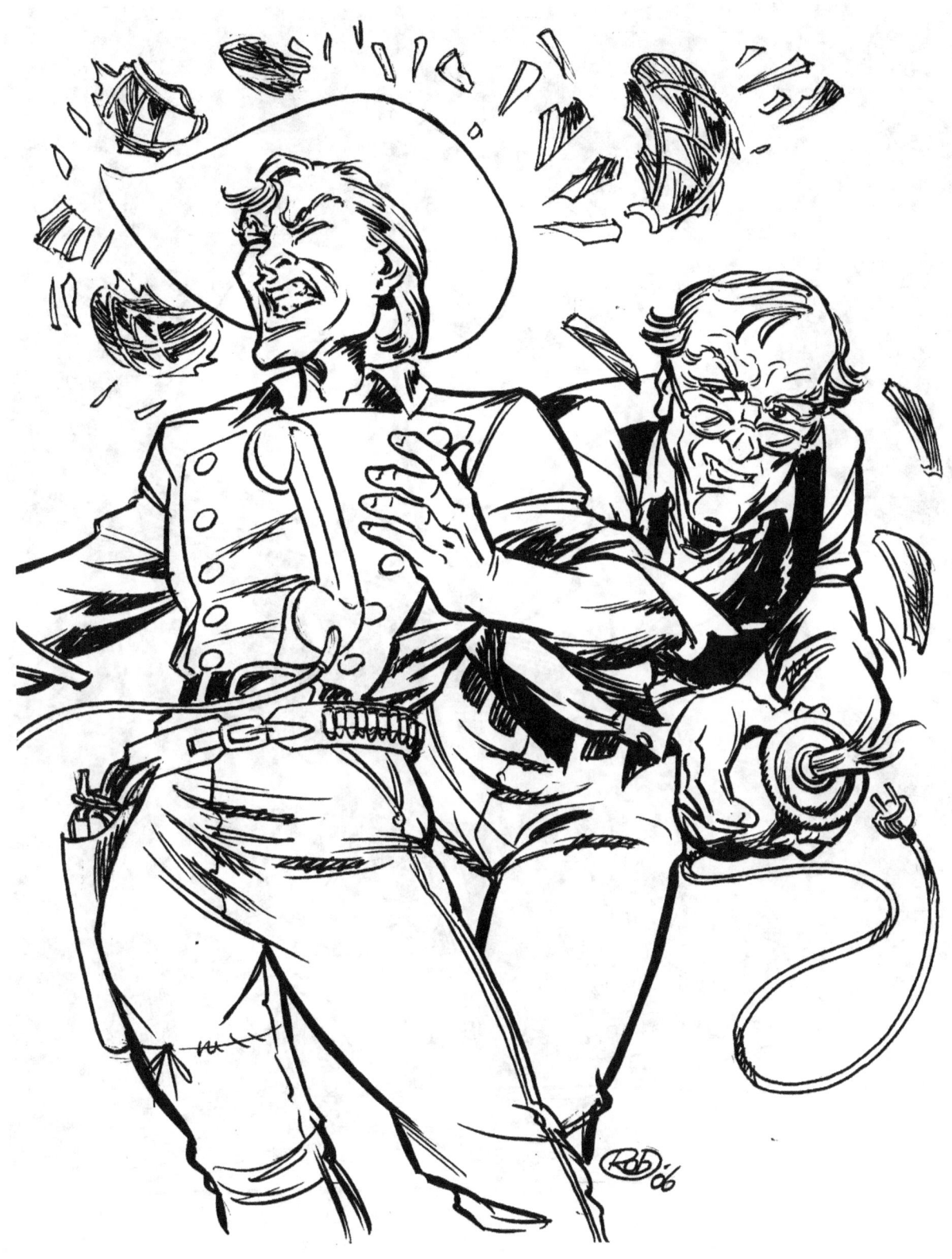

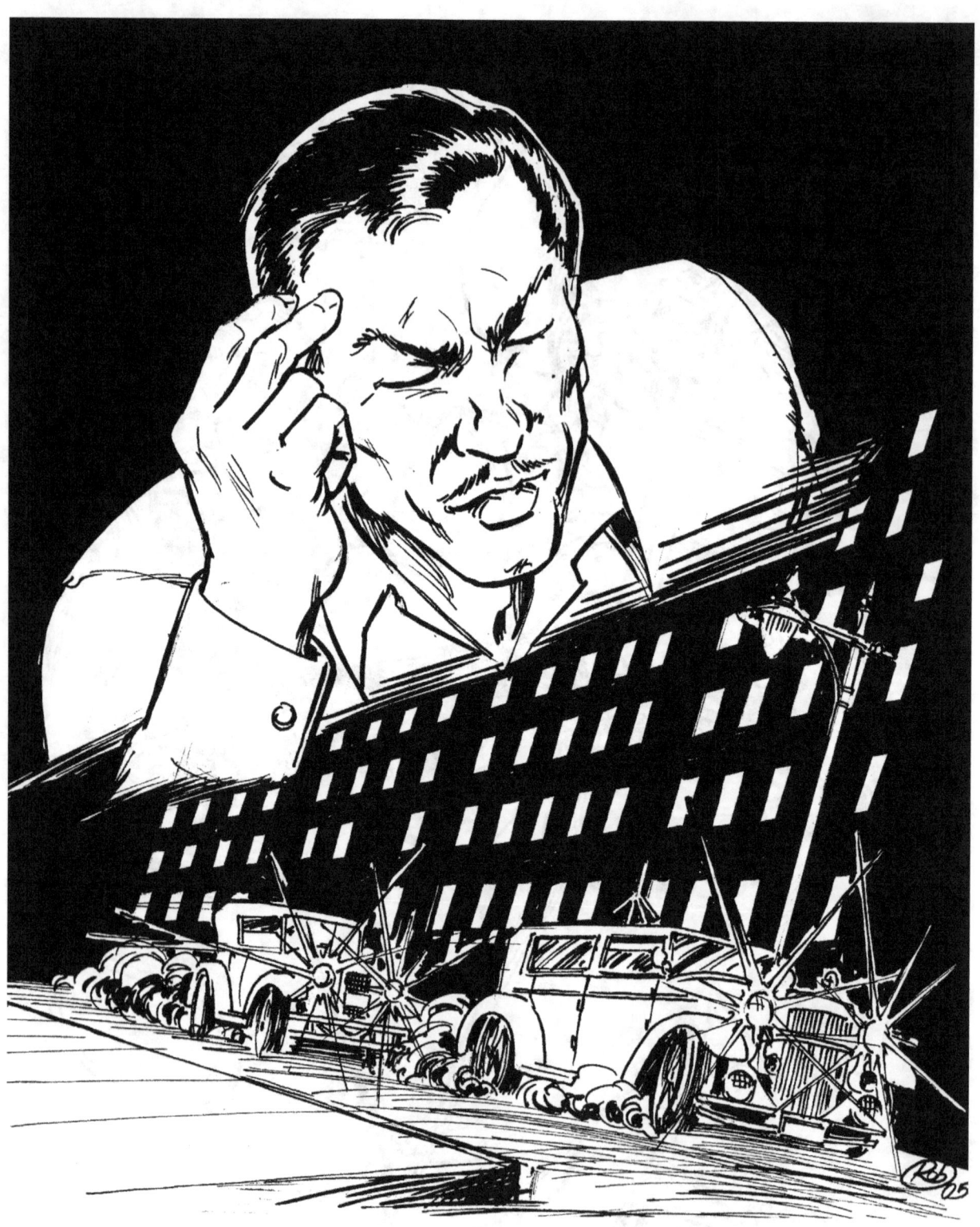

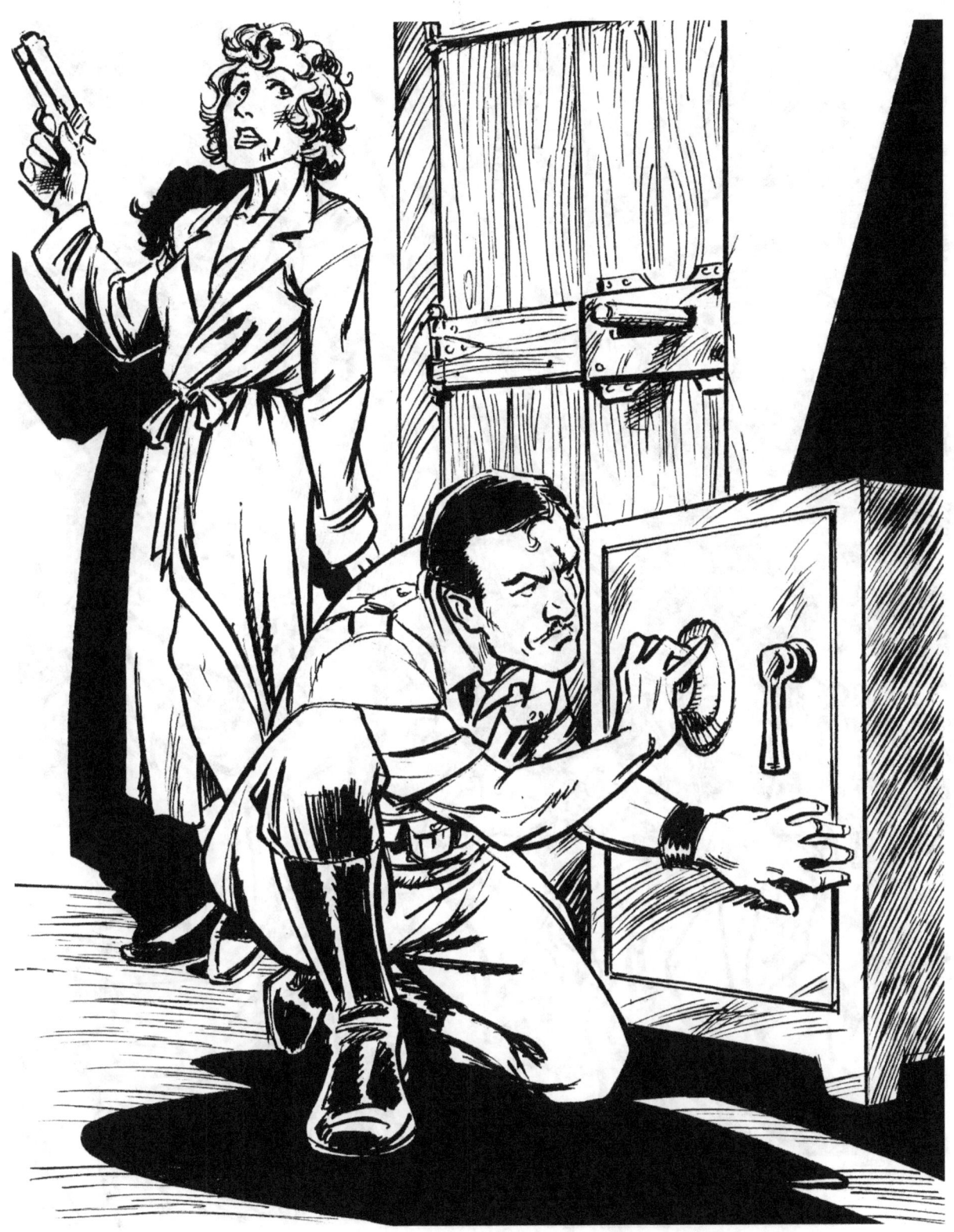

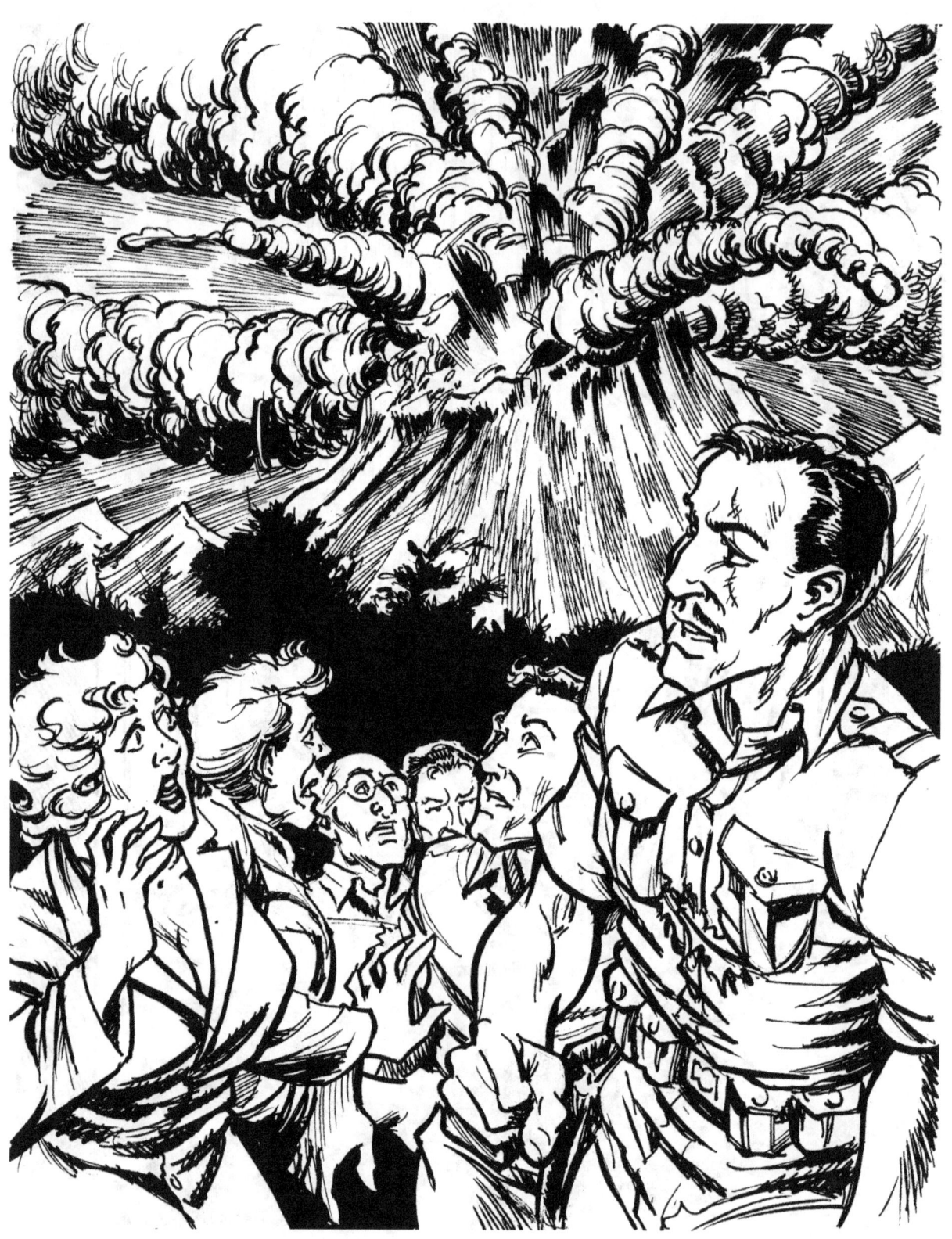

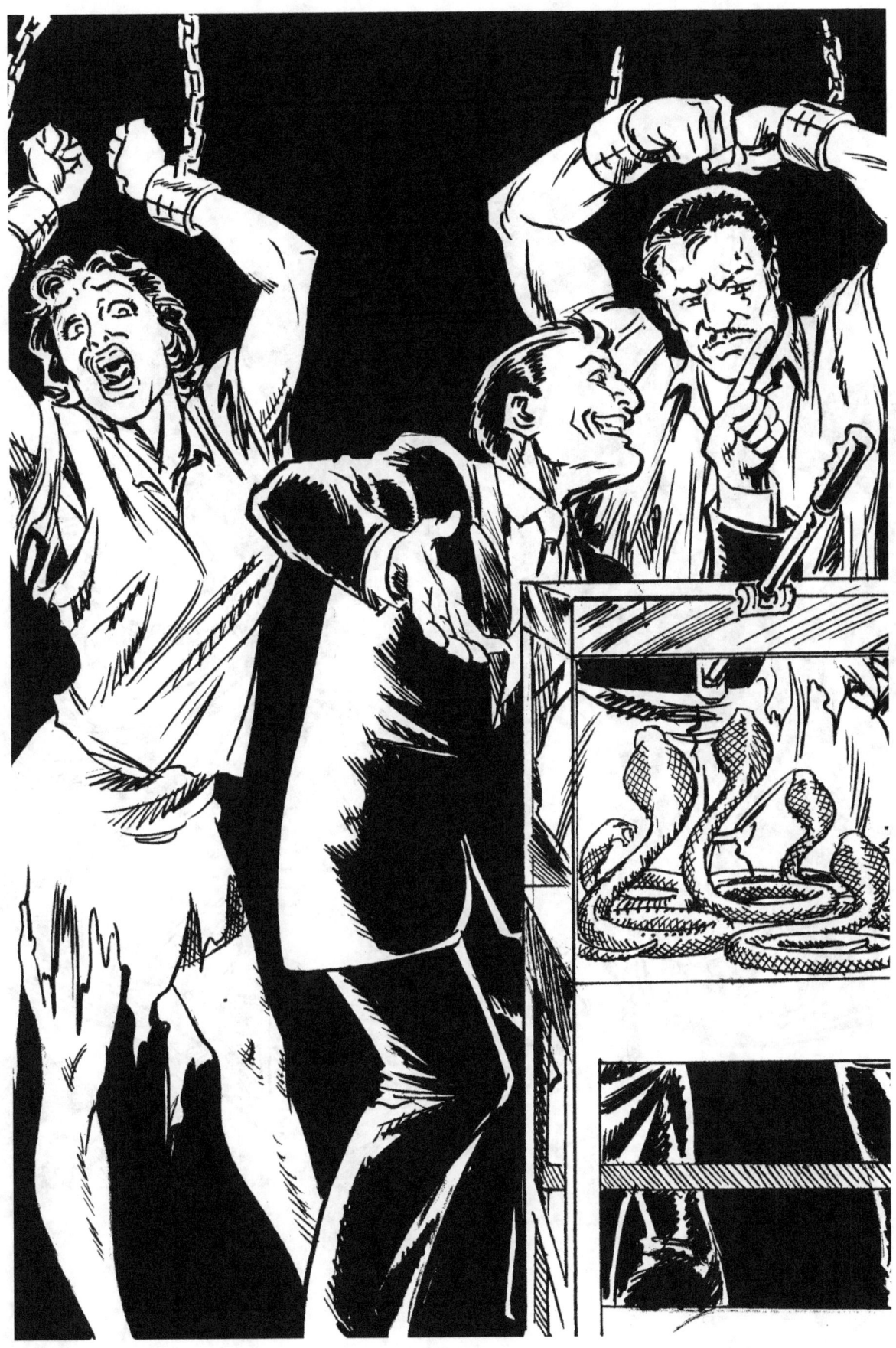

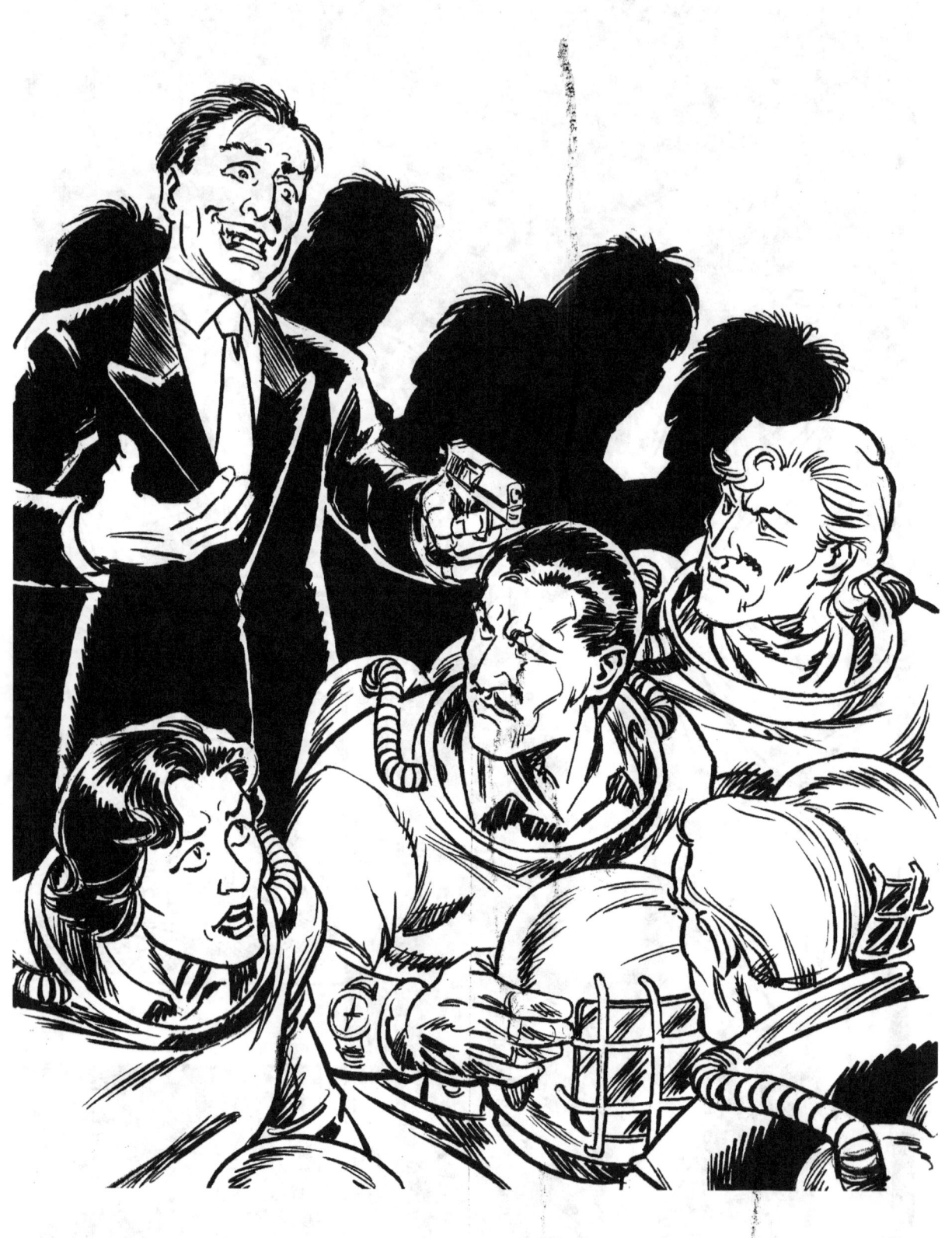

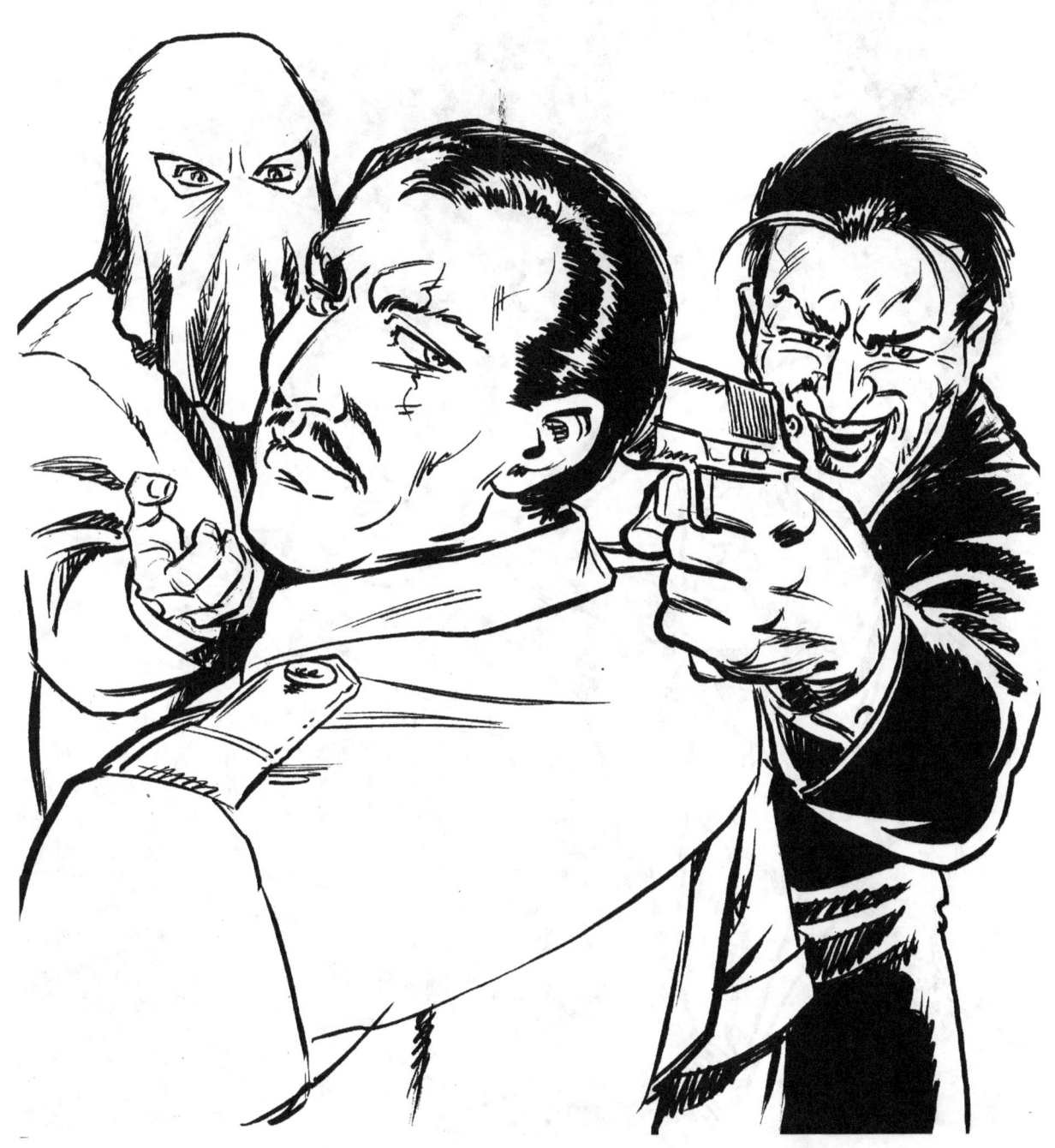

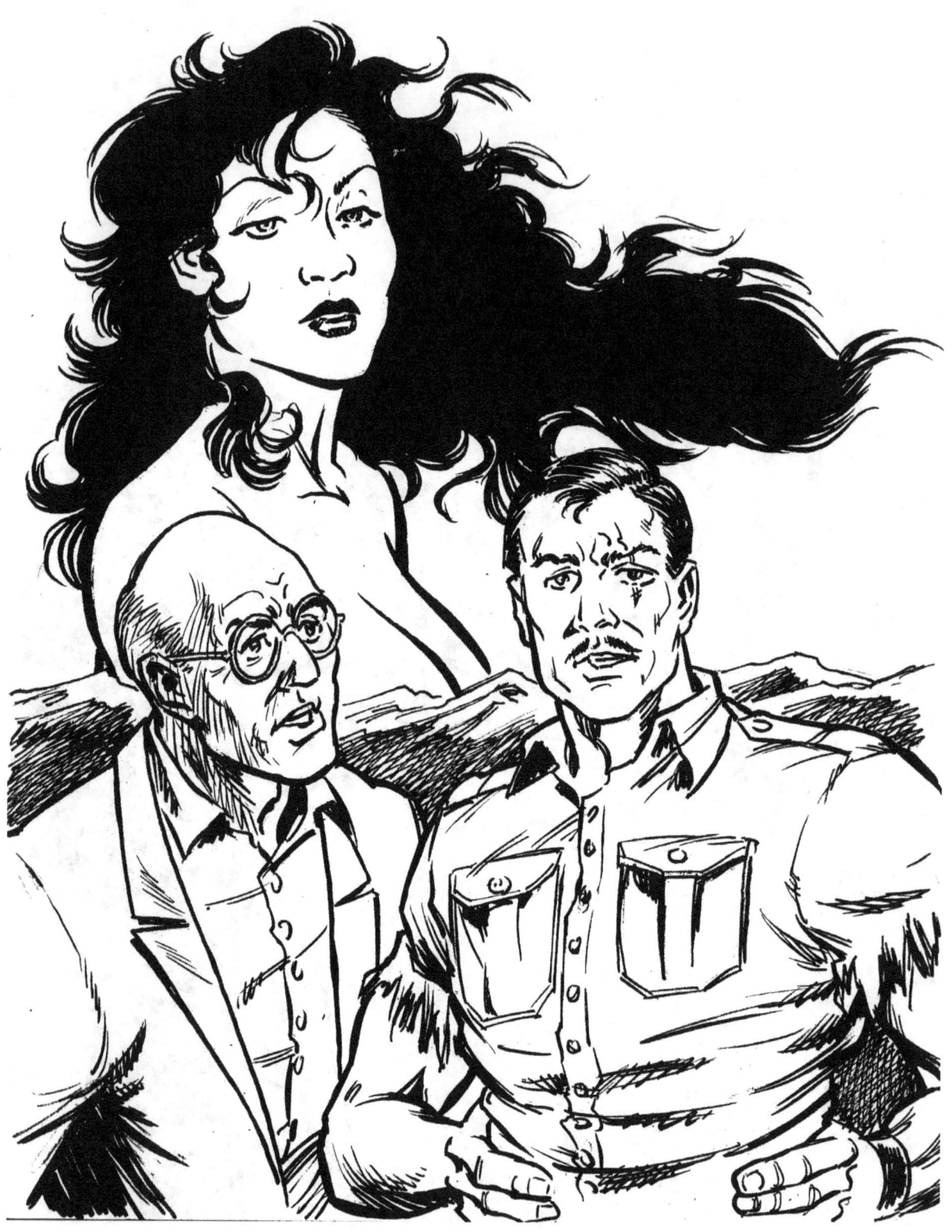

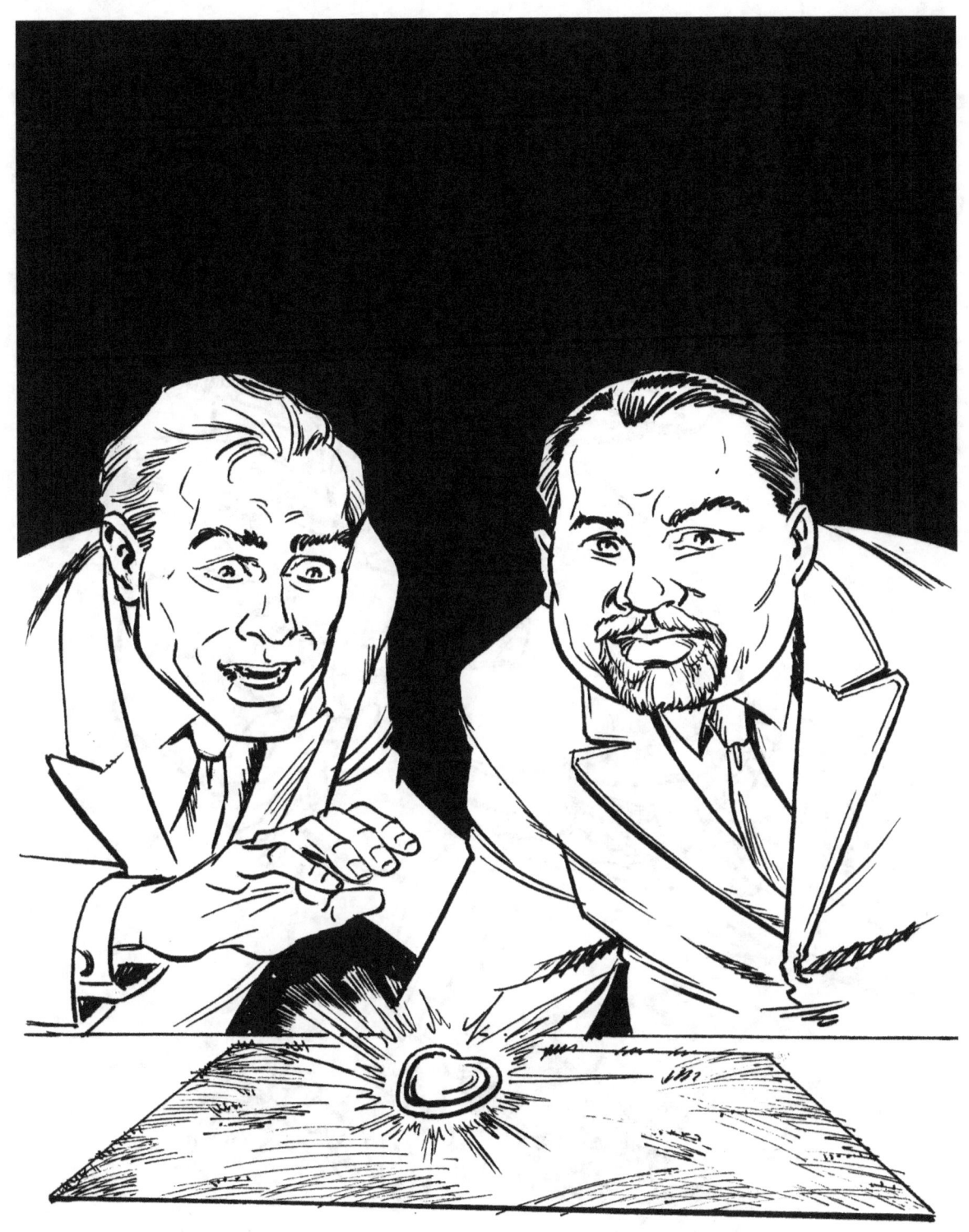

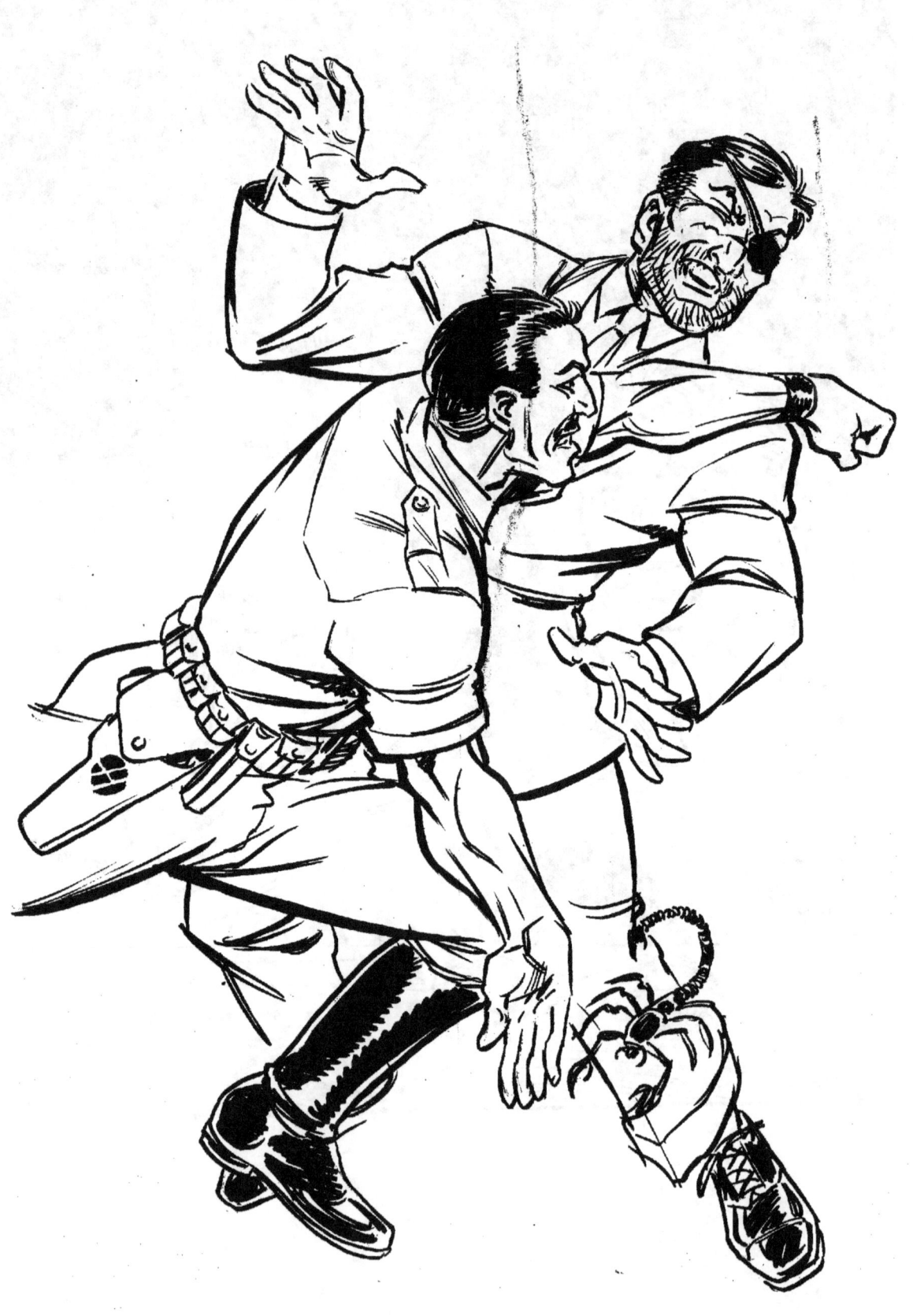

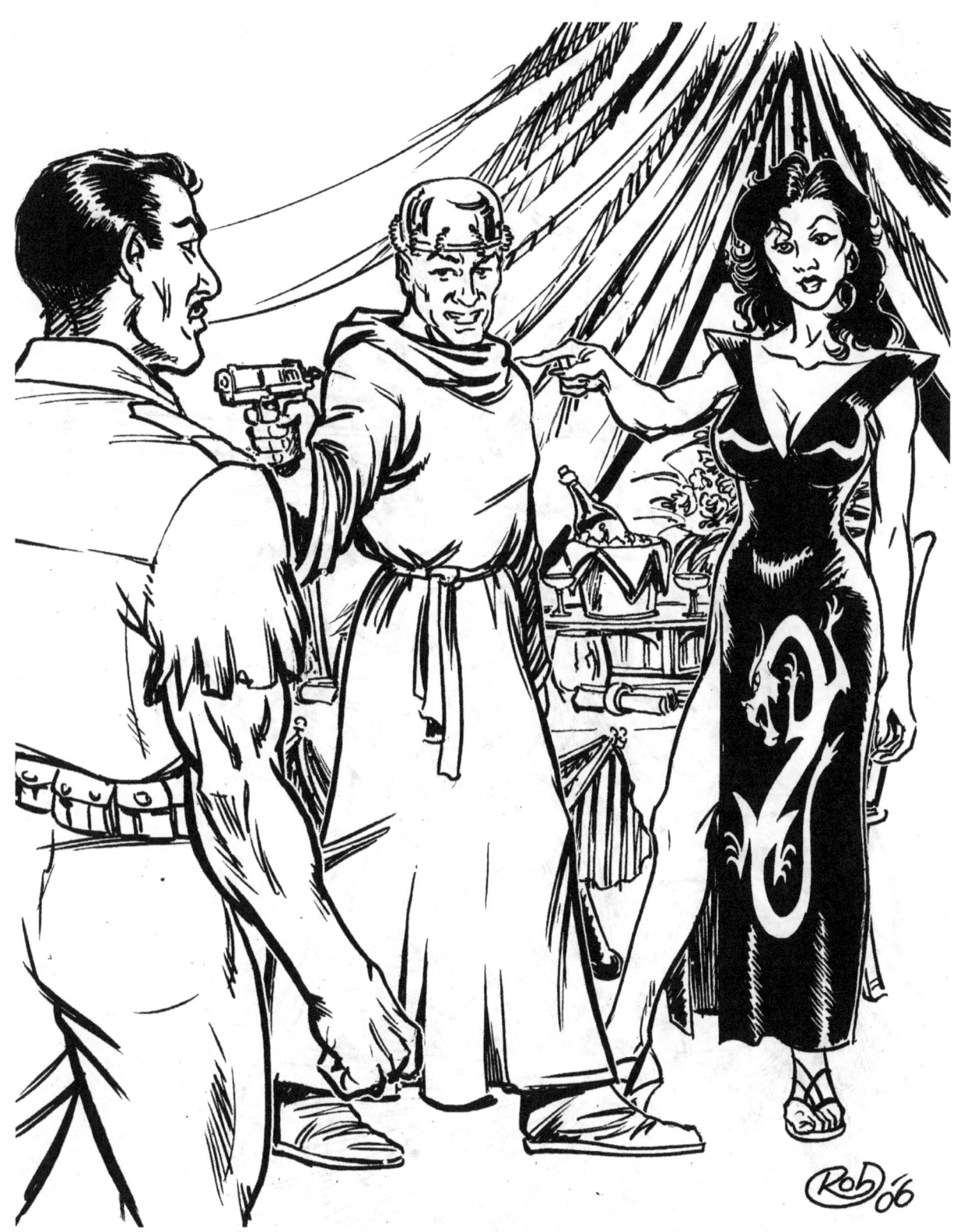

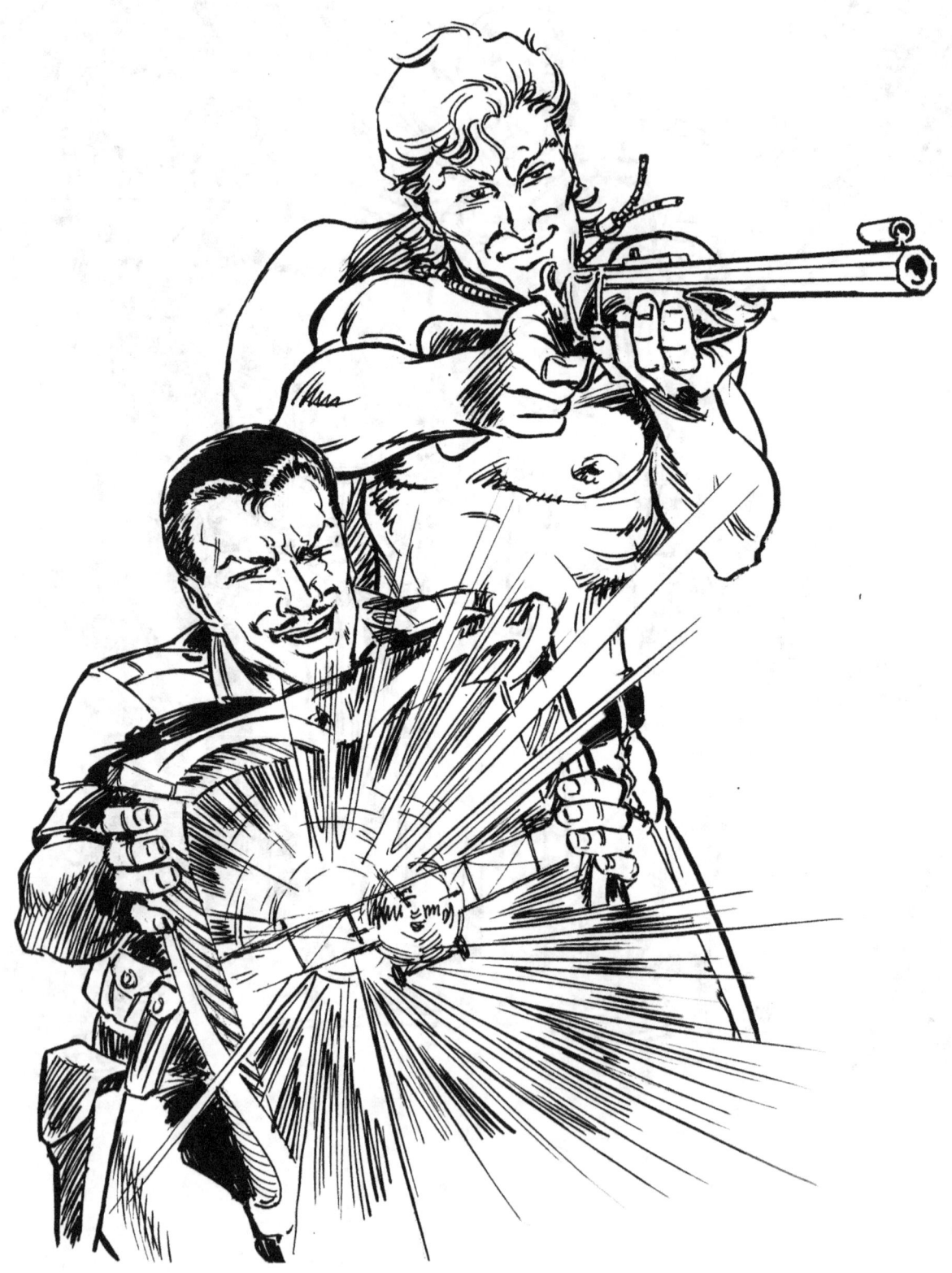

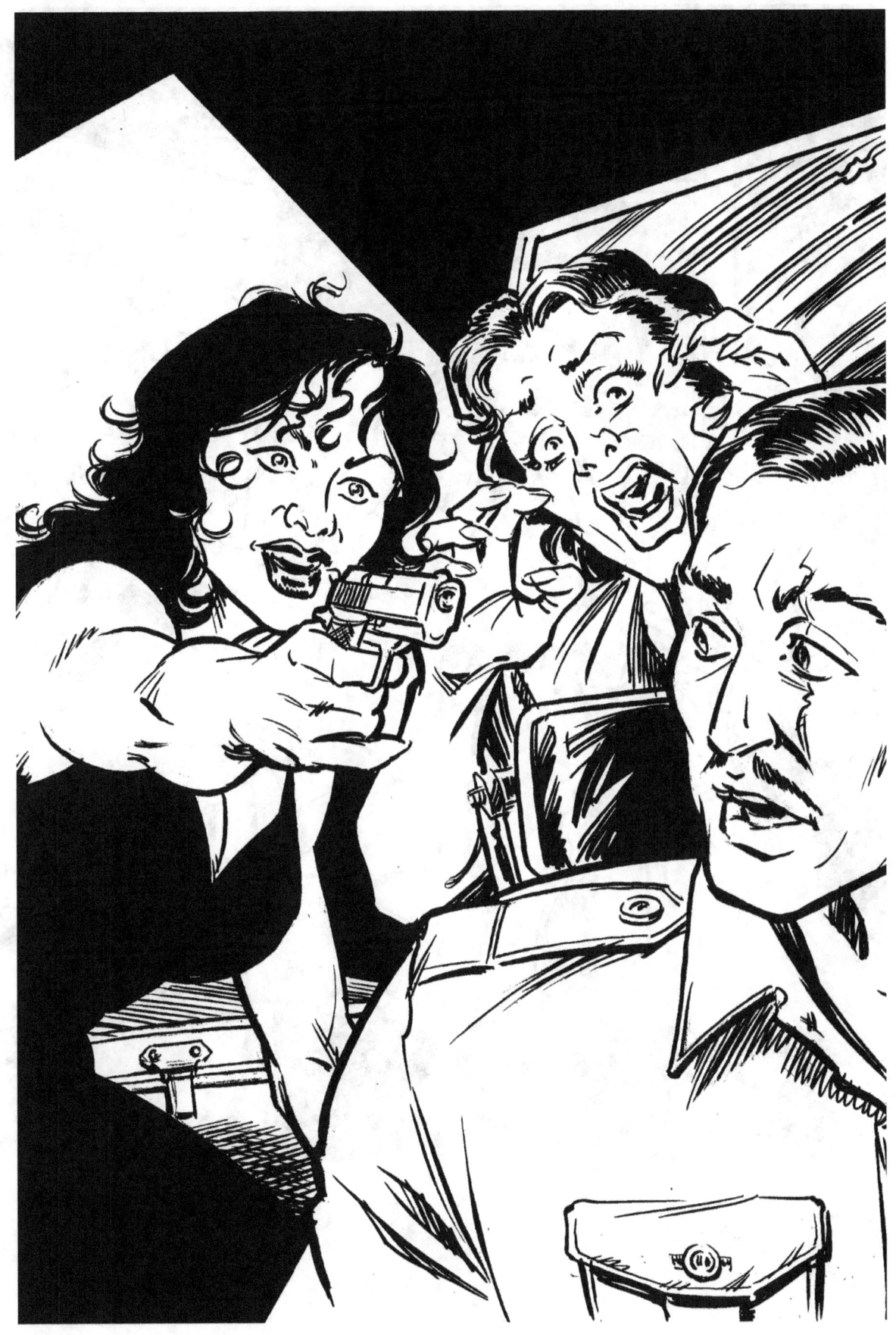

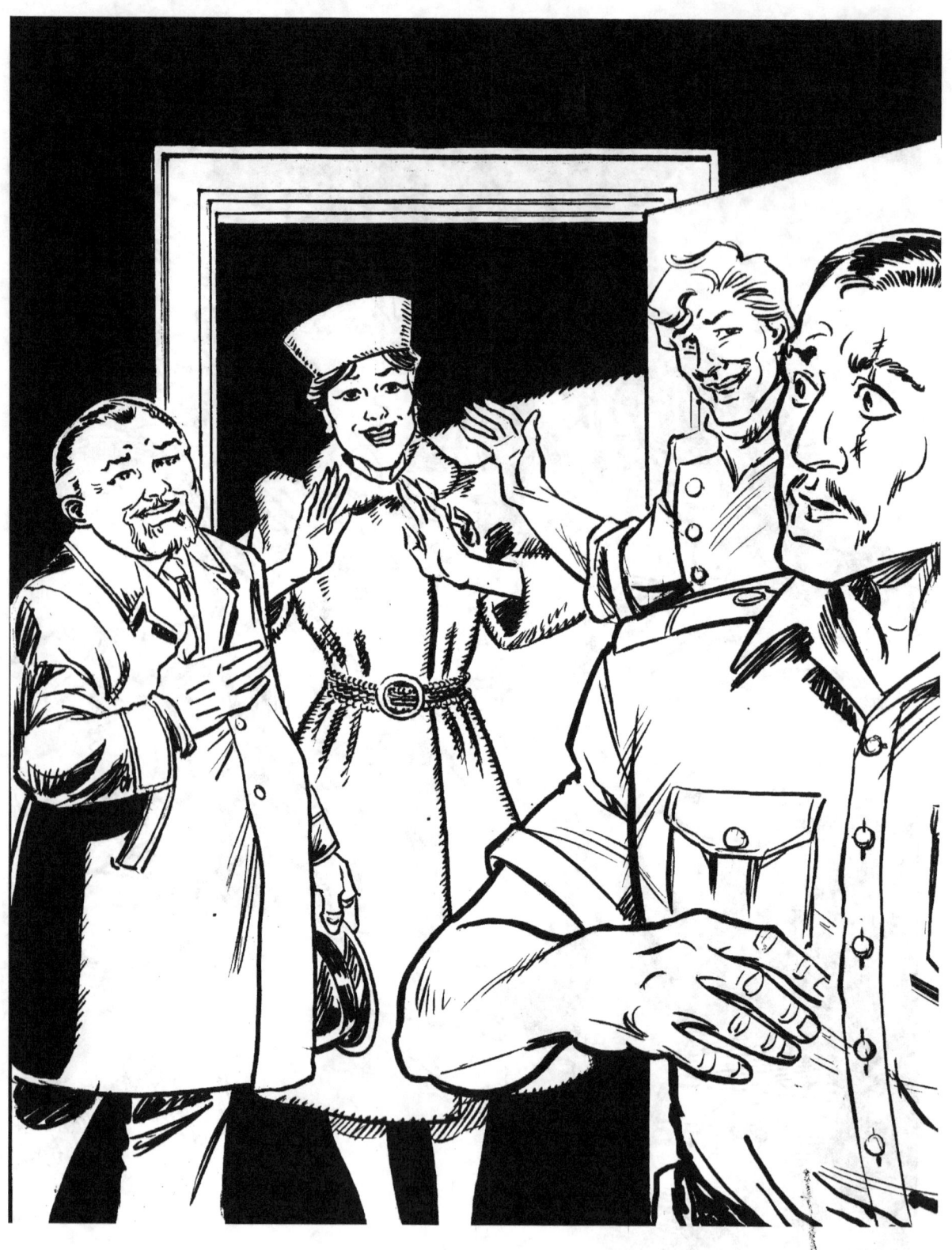

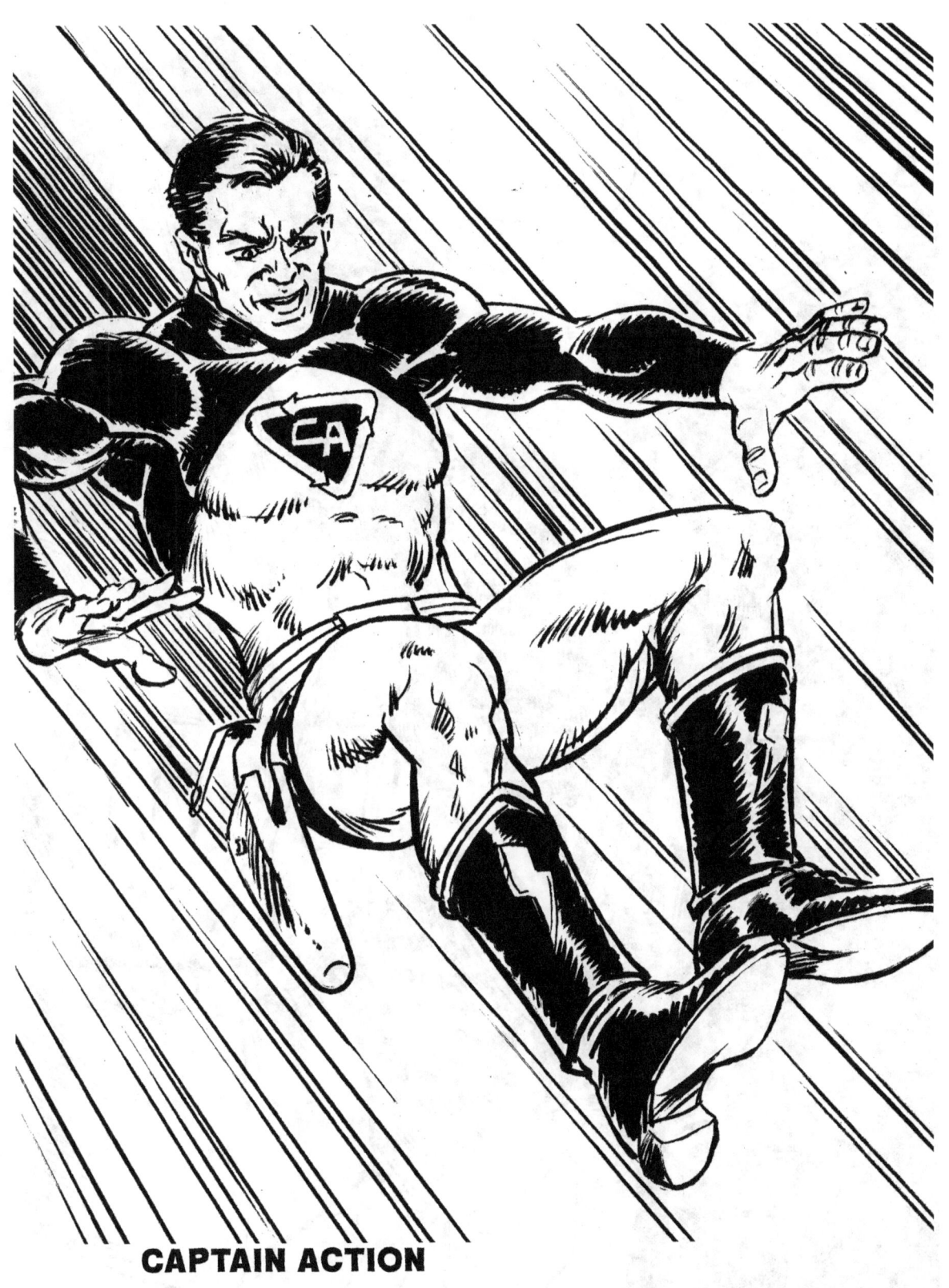

CAPTAIN ACTION

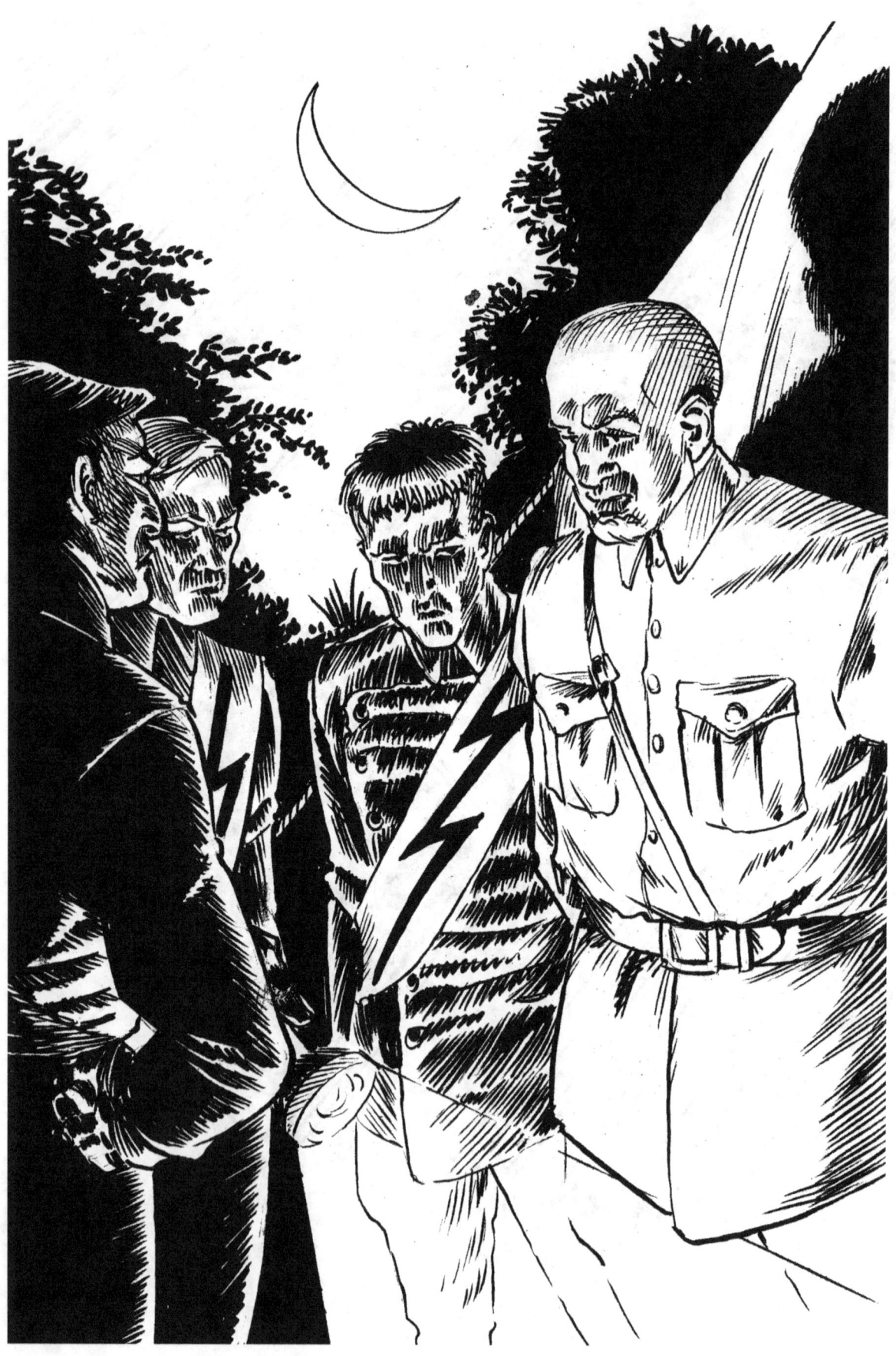

58

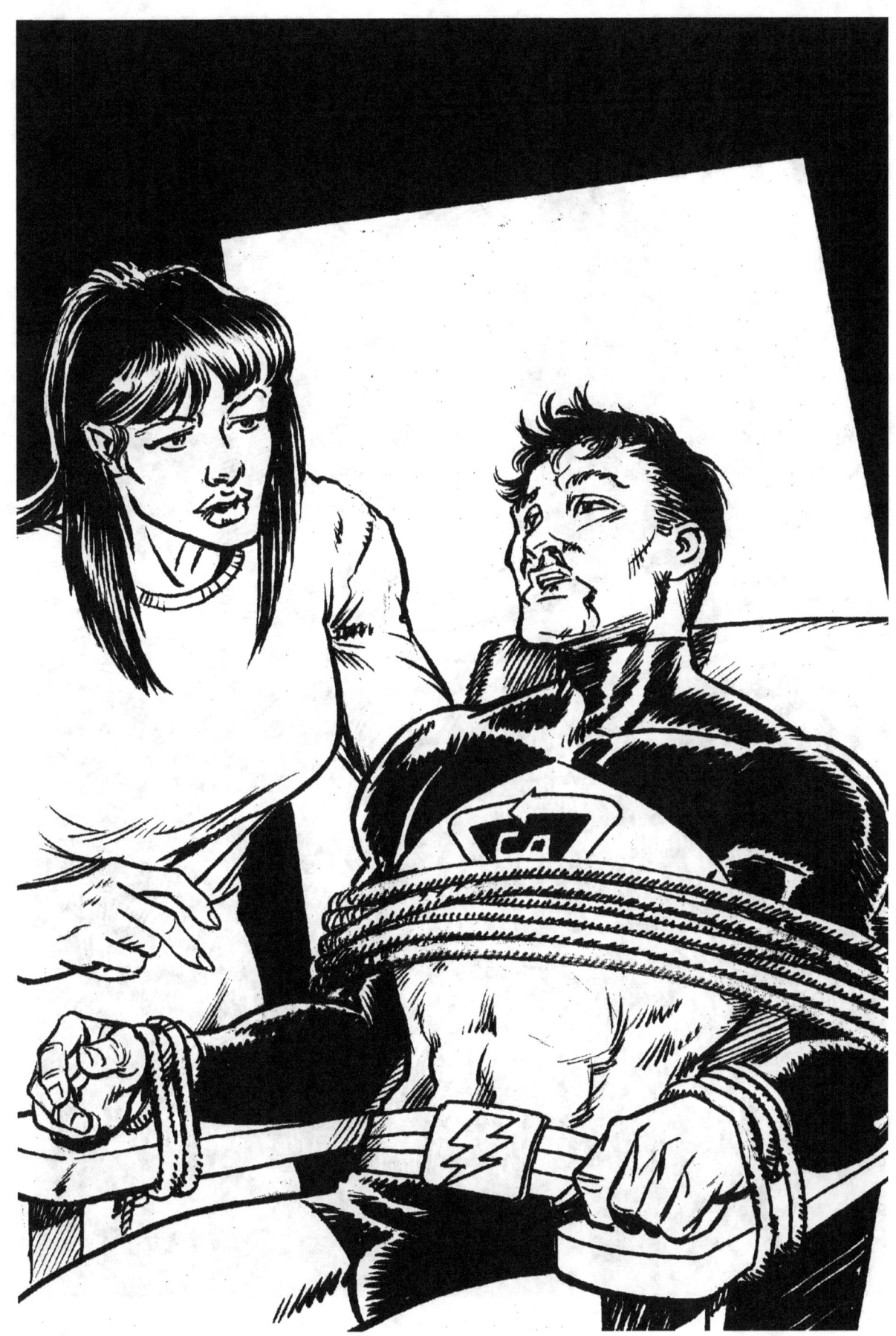

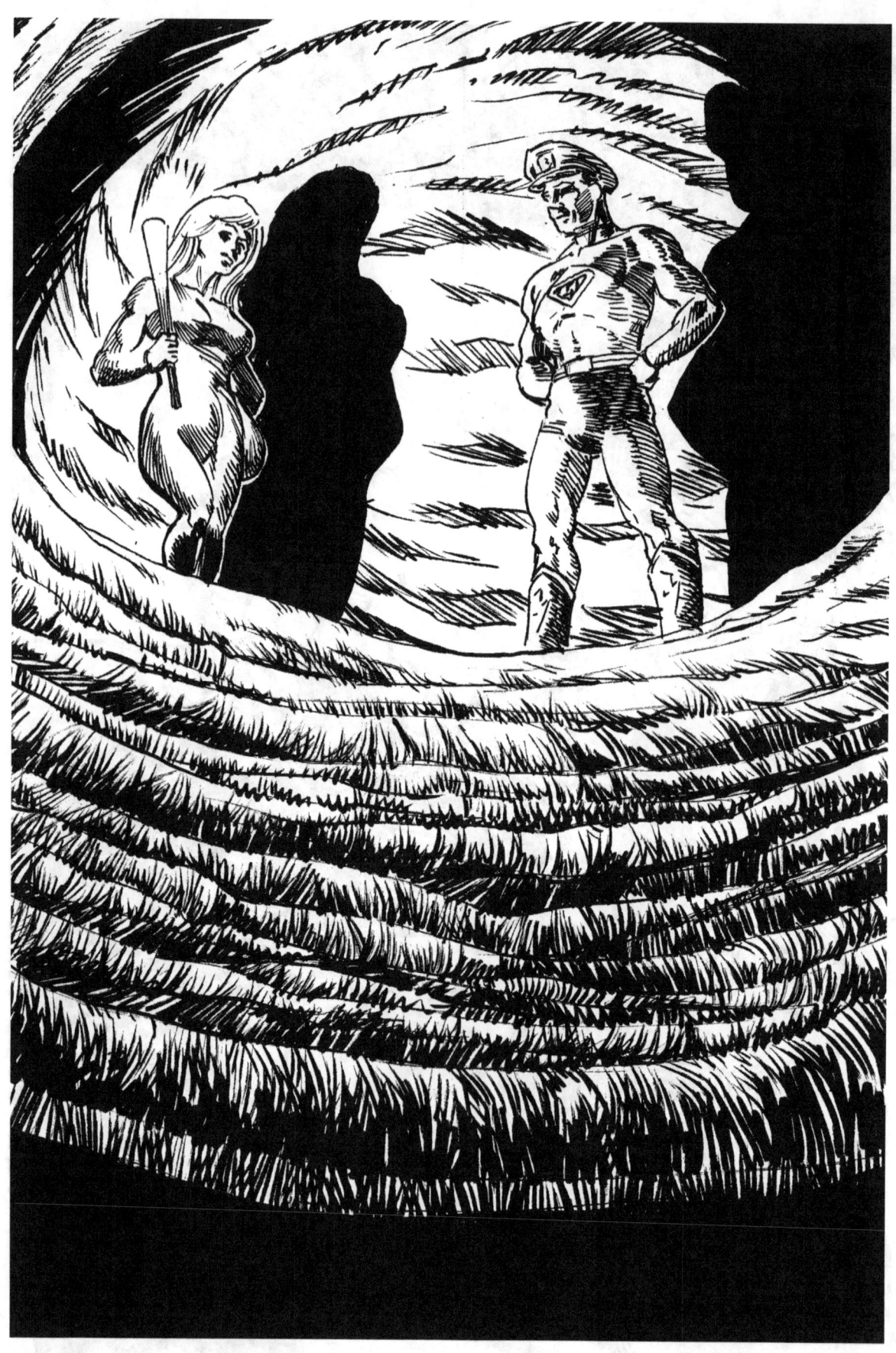

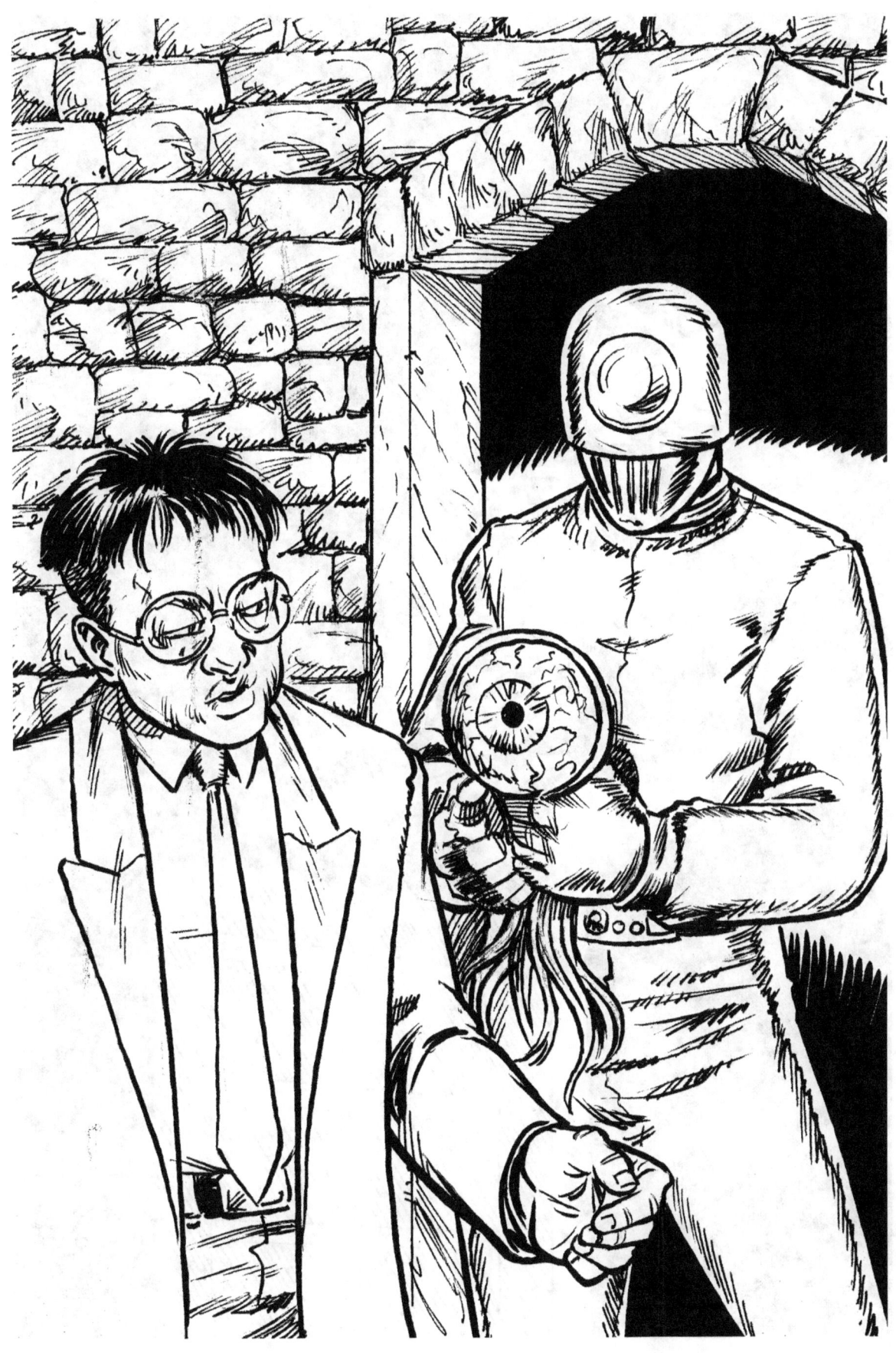

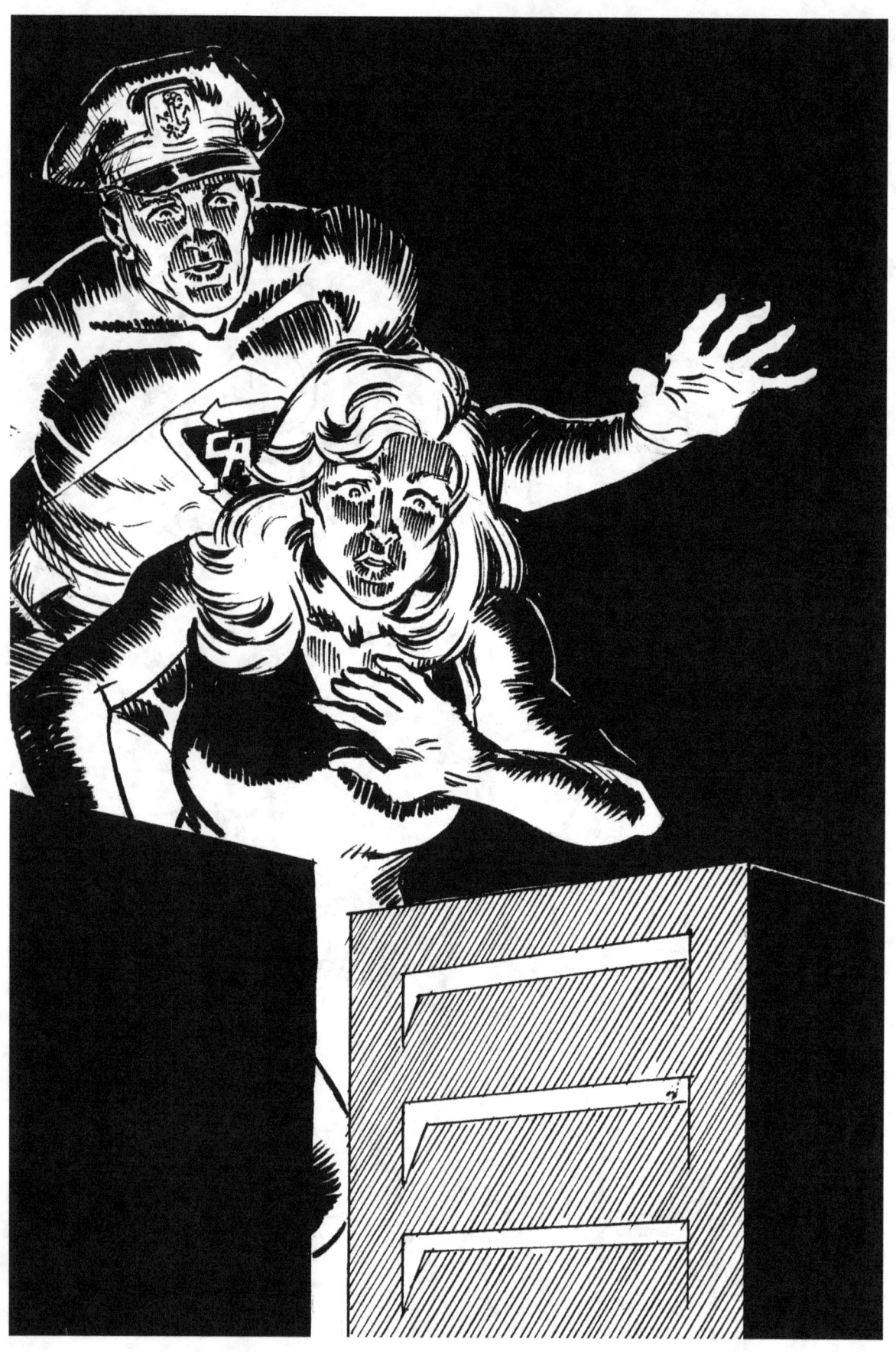

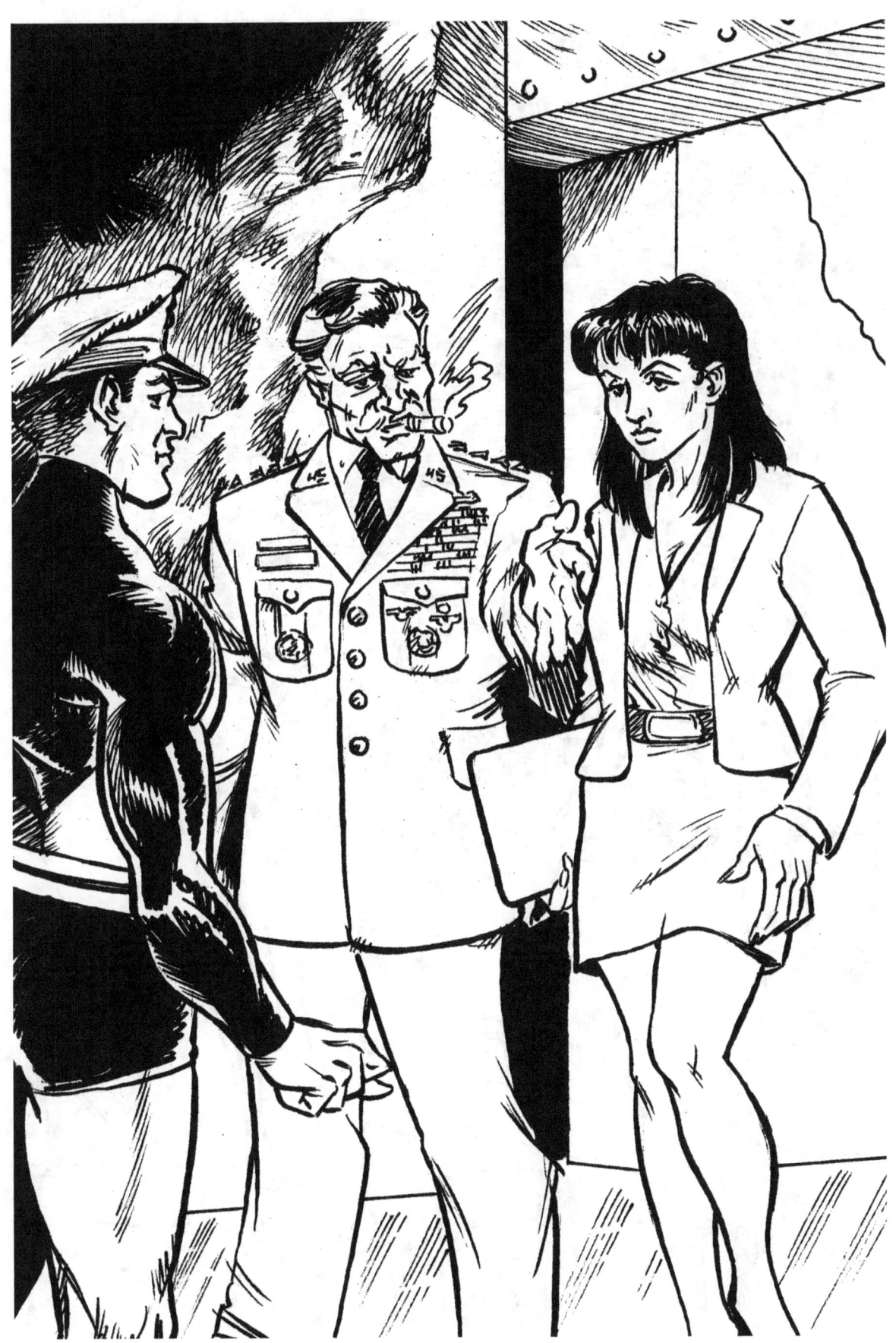

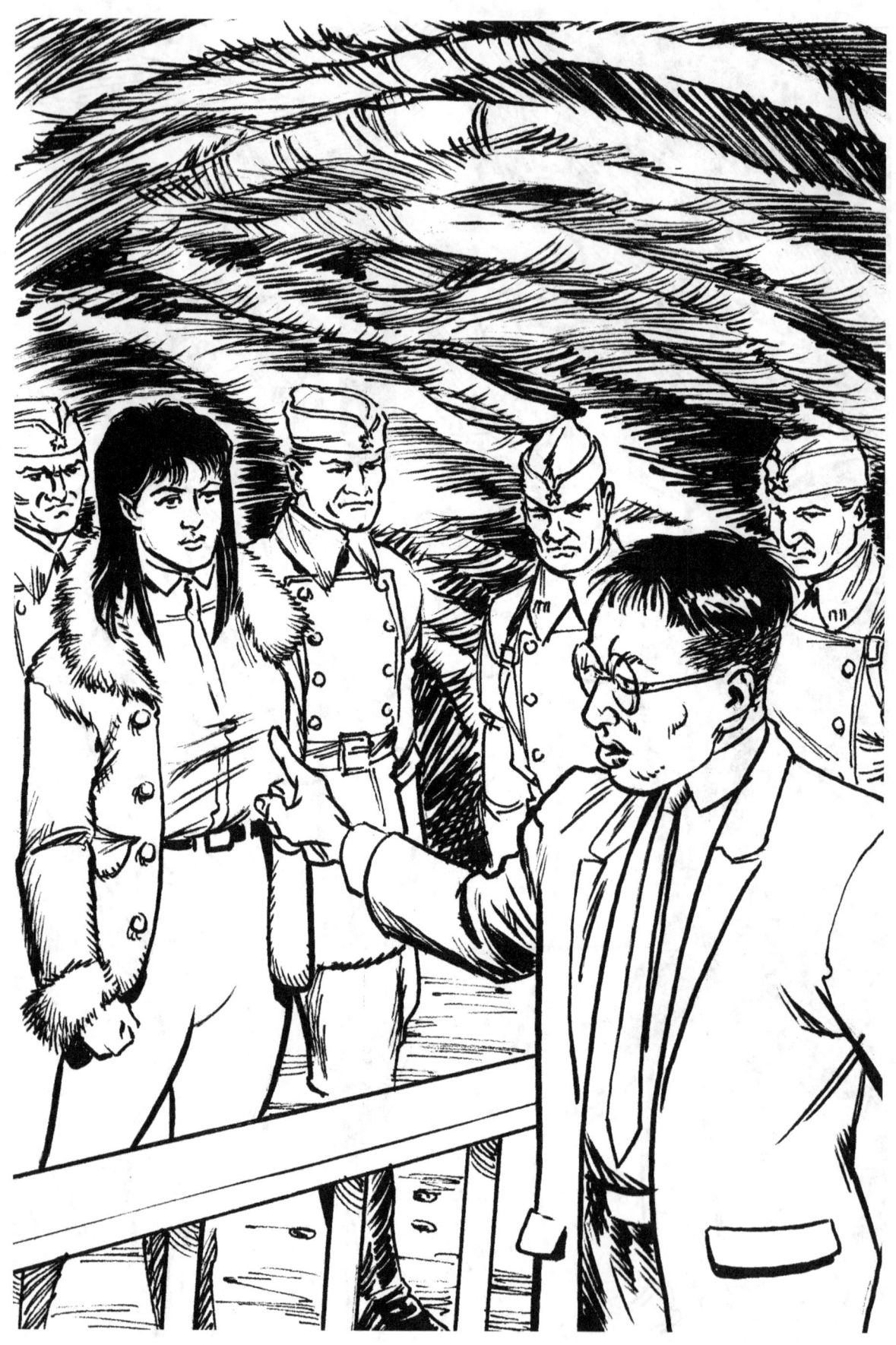

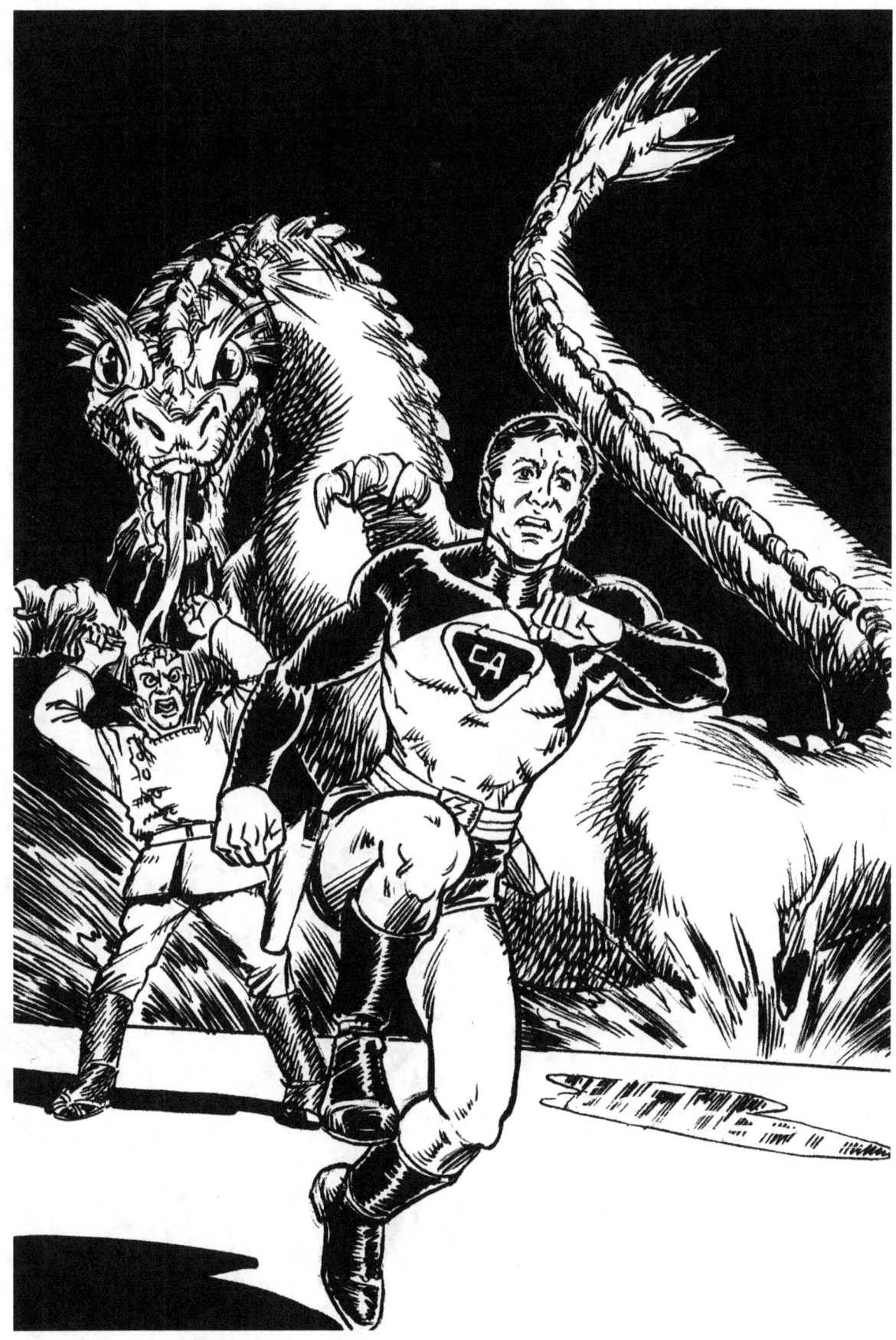

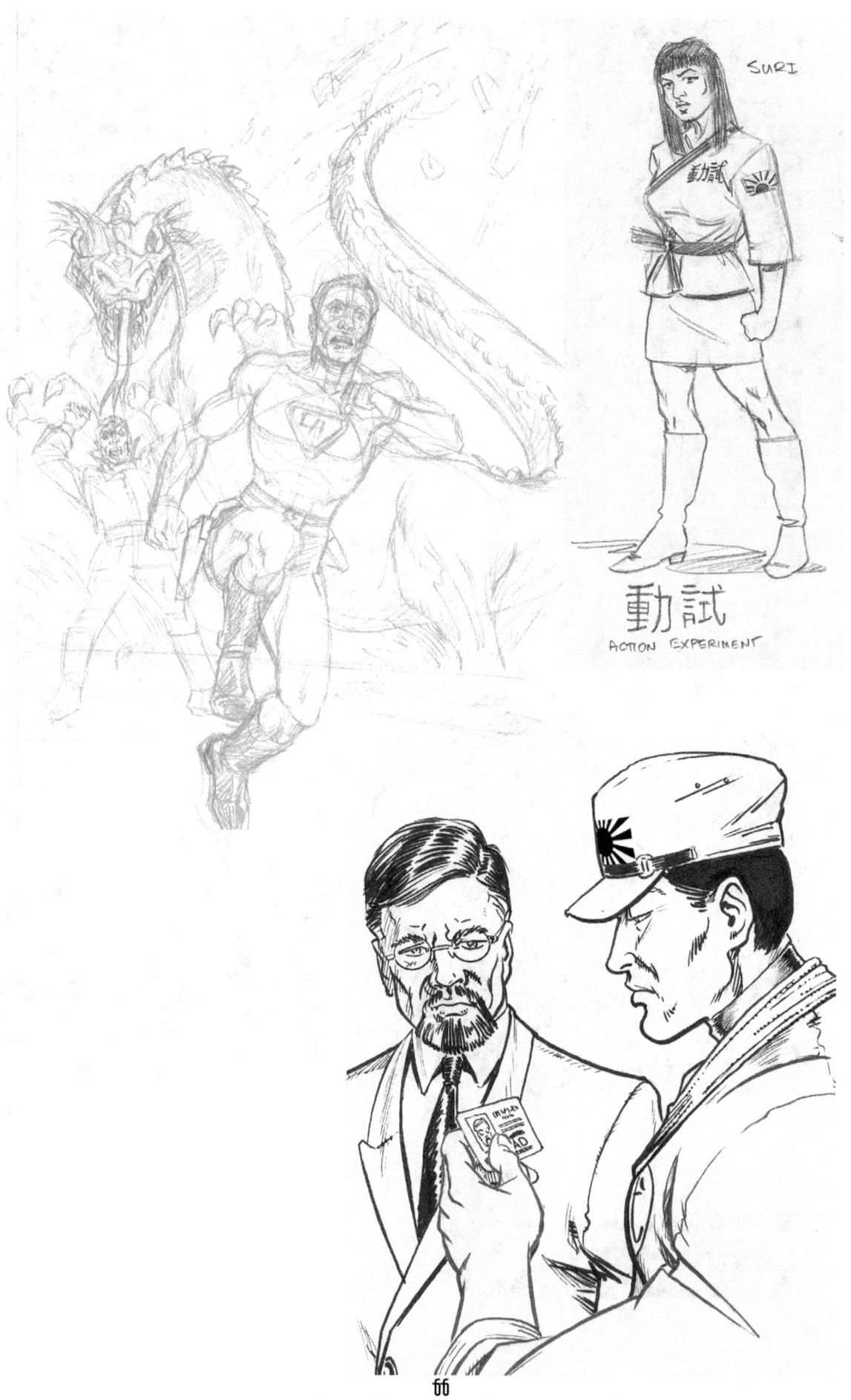

SURI

動試
ACTION EXPERIMENT

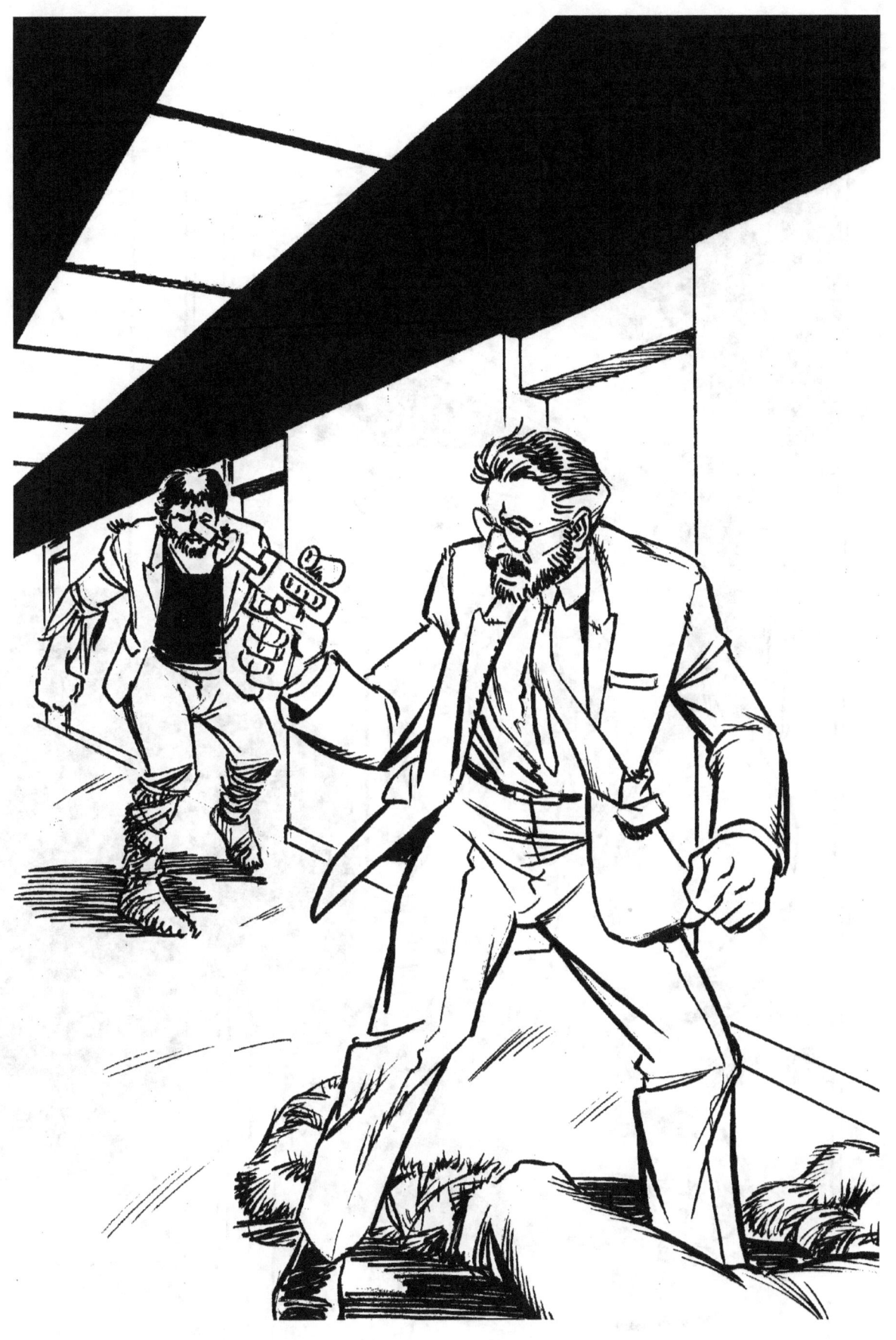

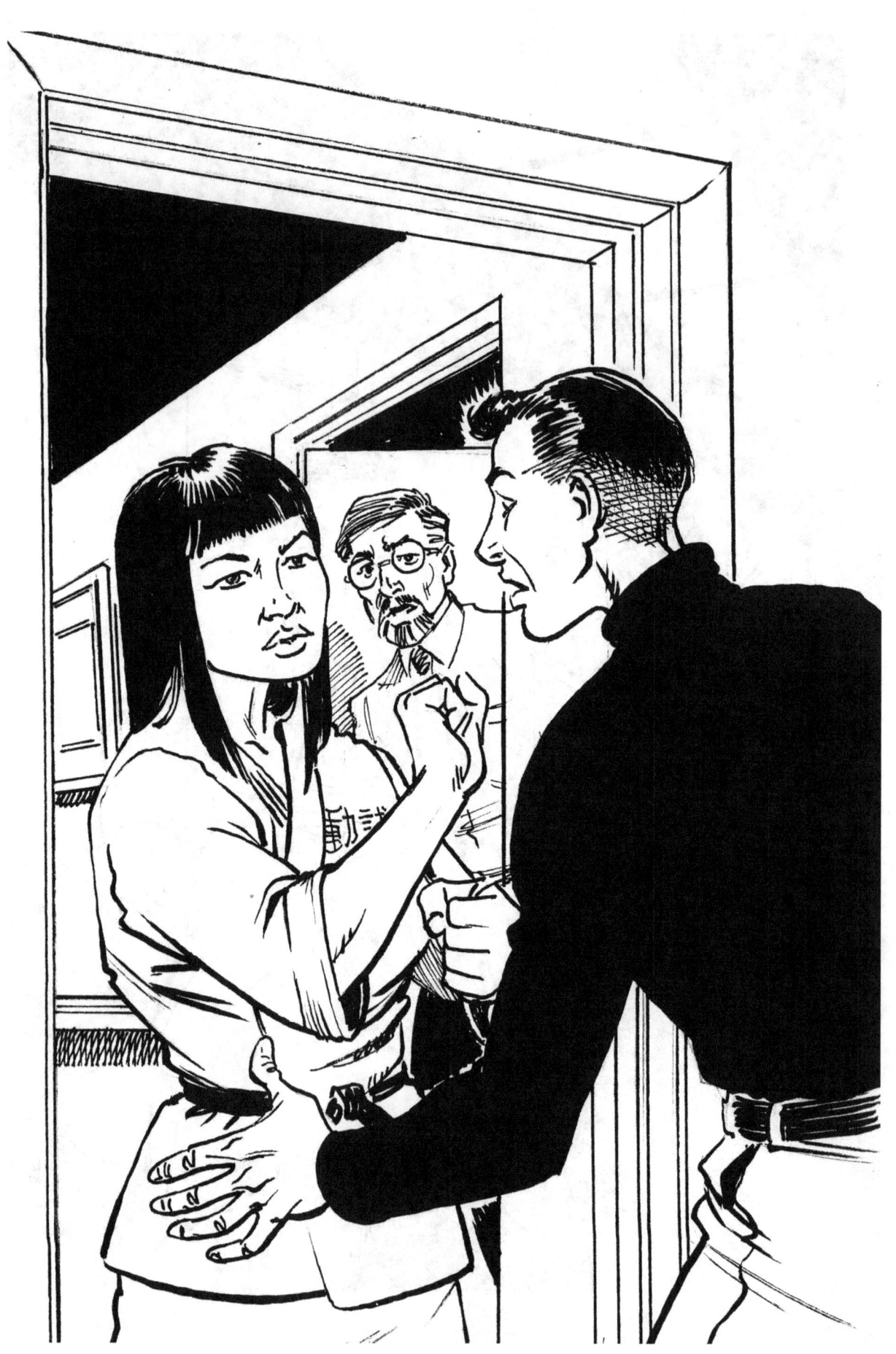

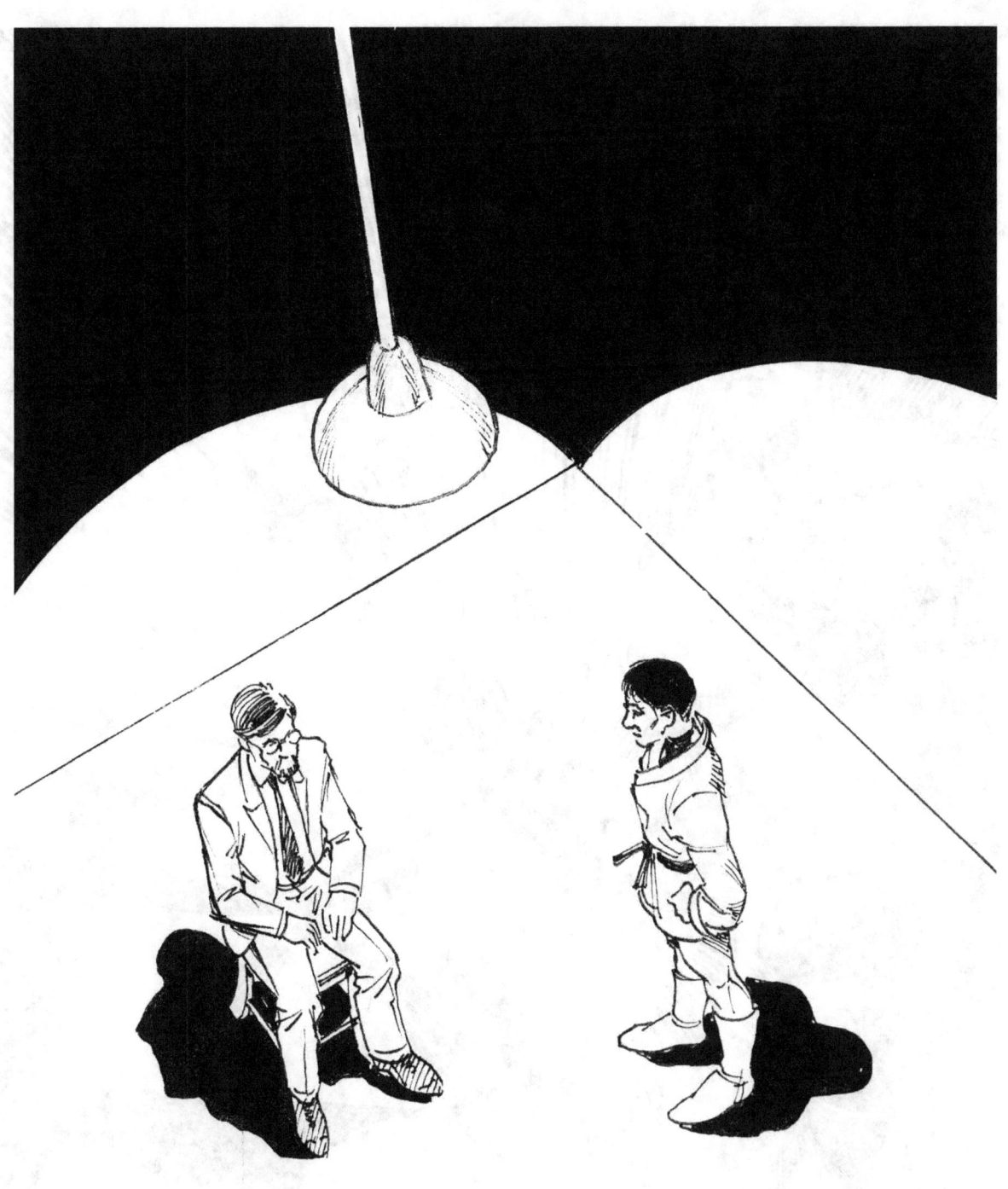

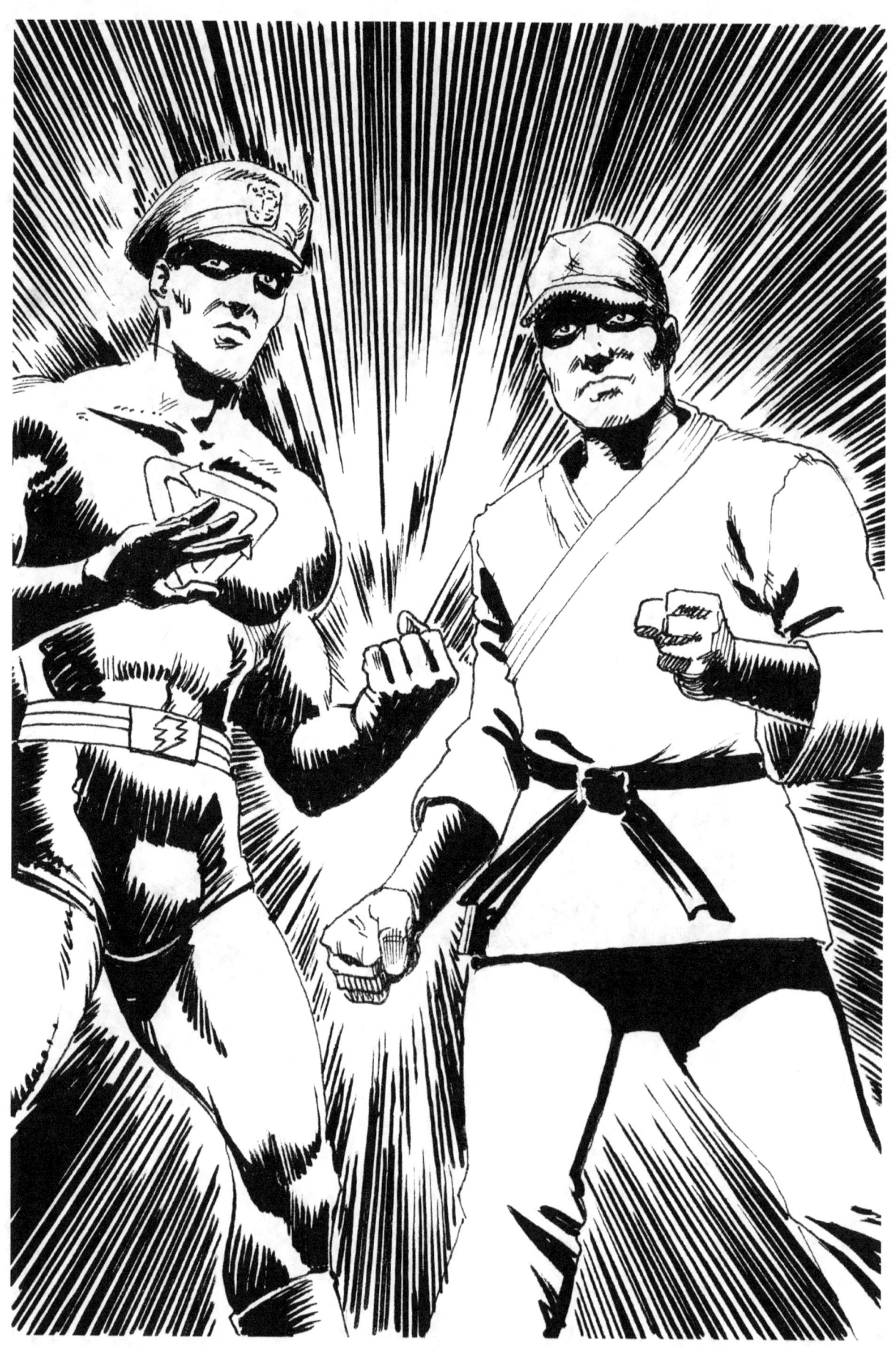

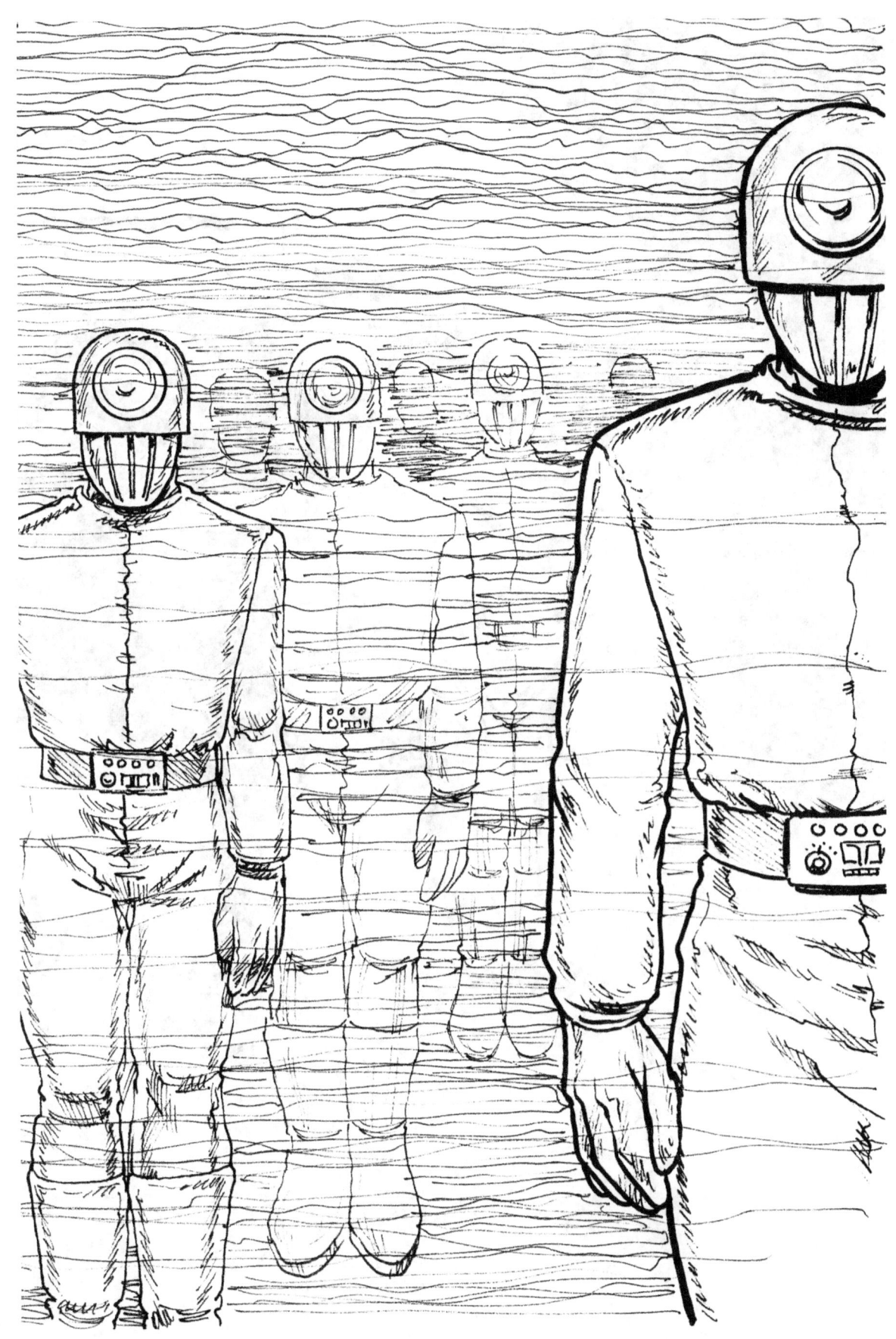

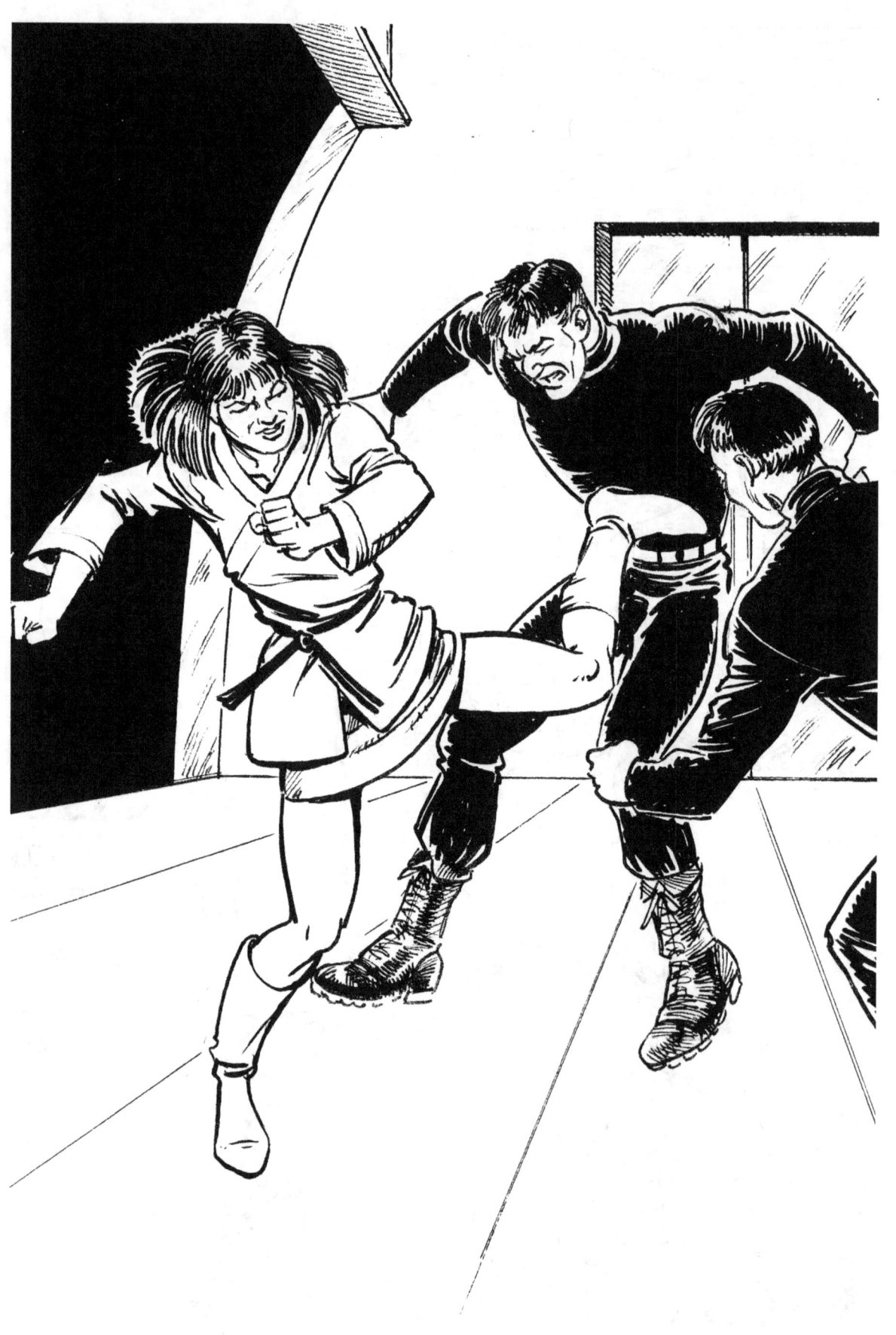

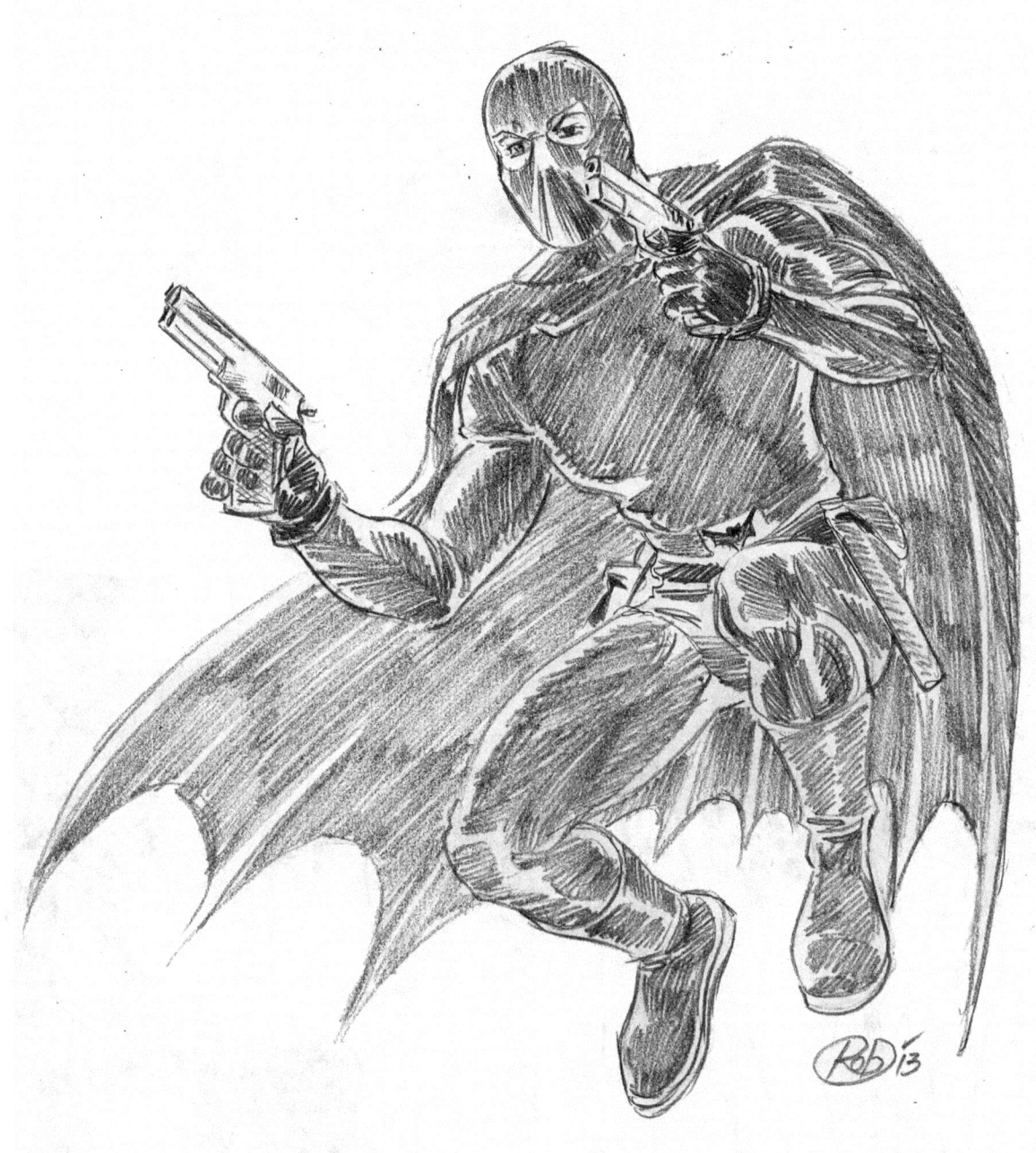

THE BLACK BAT

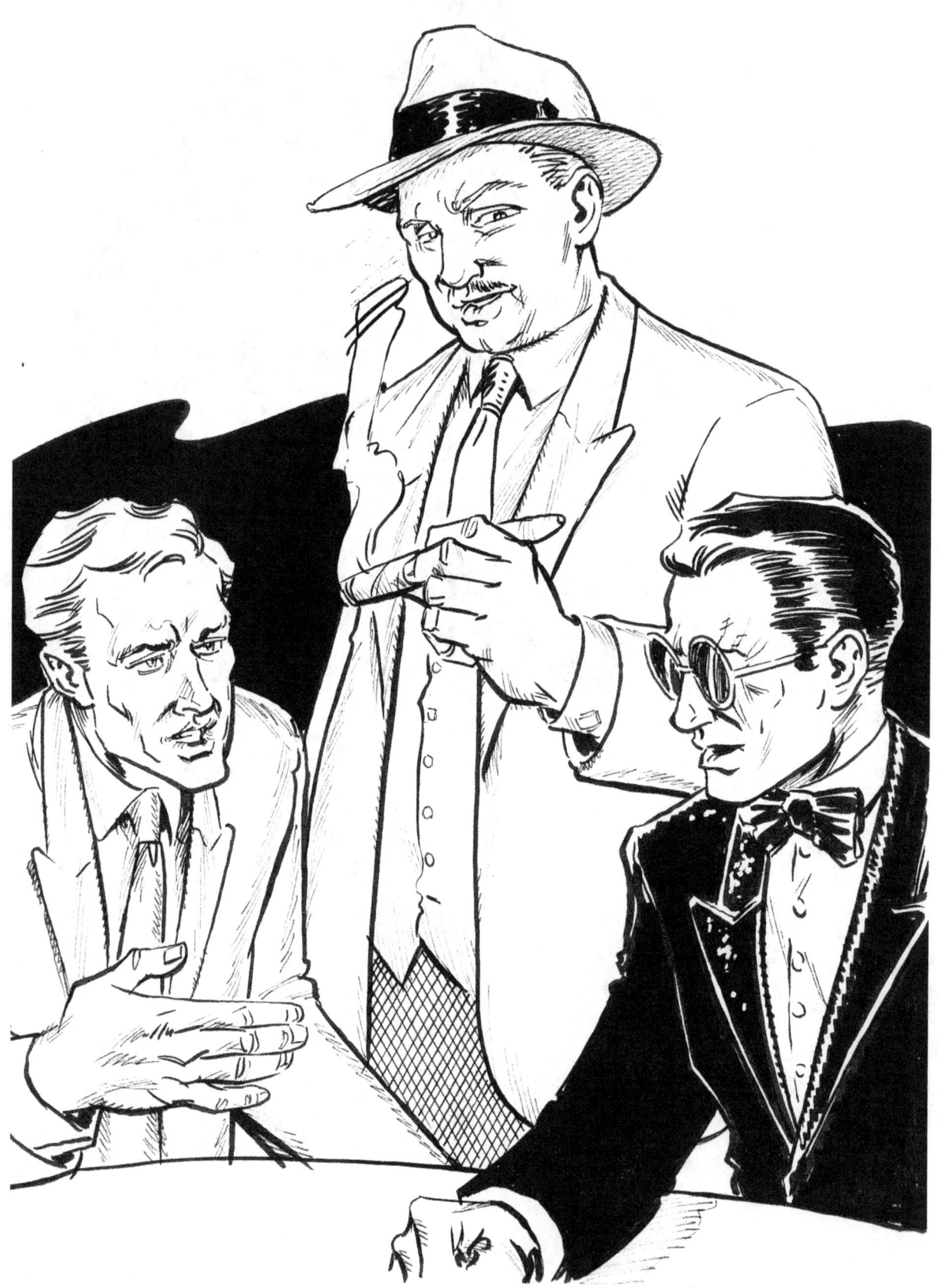

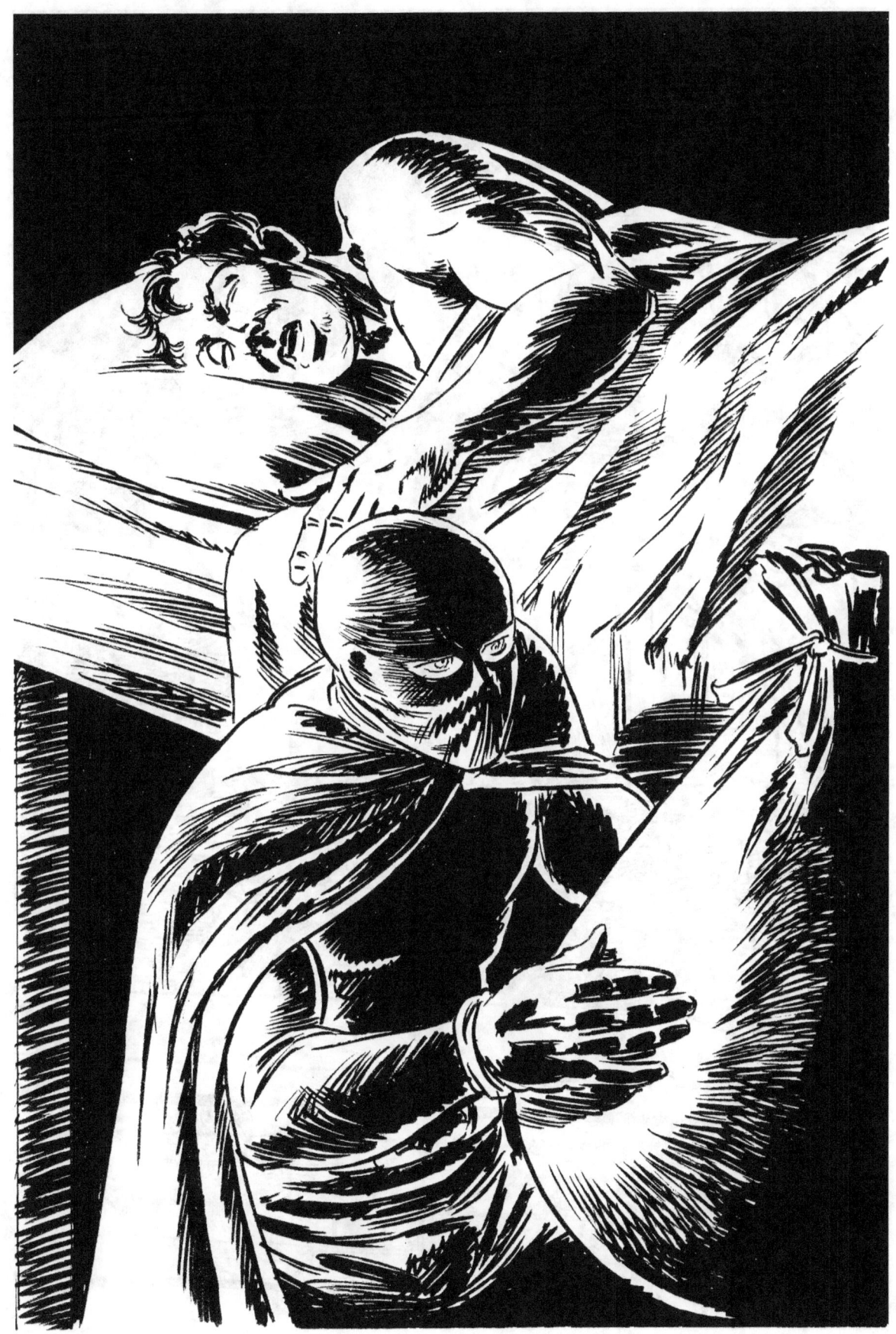

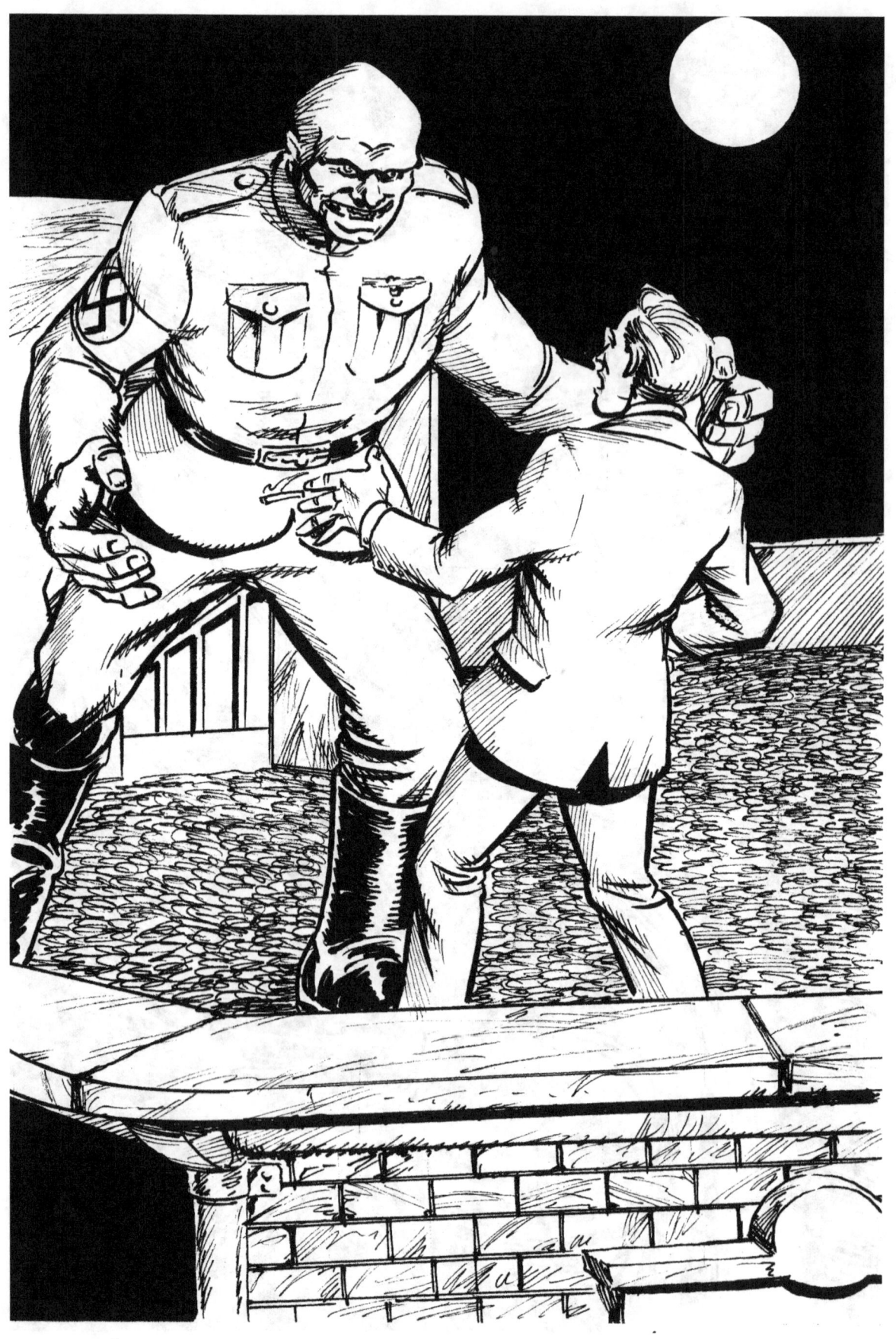

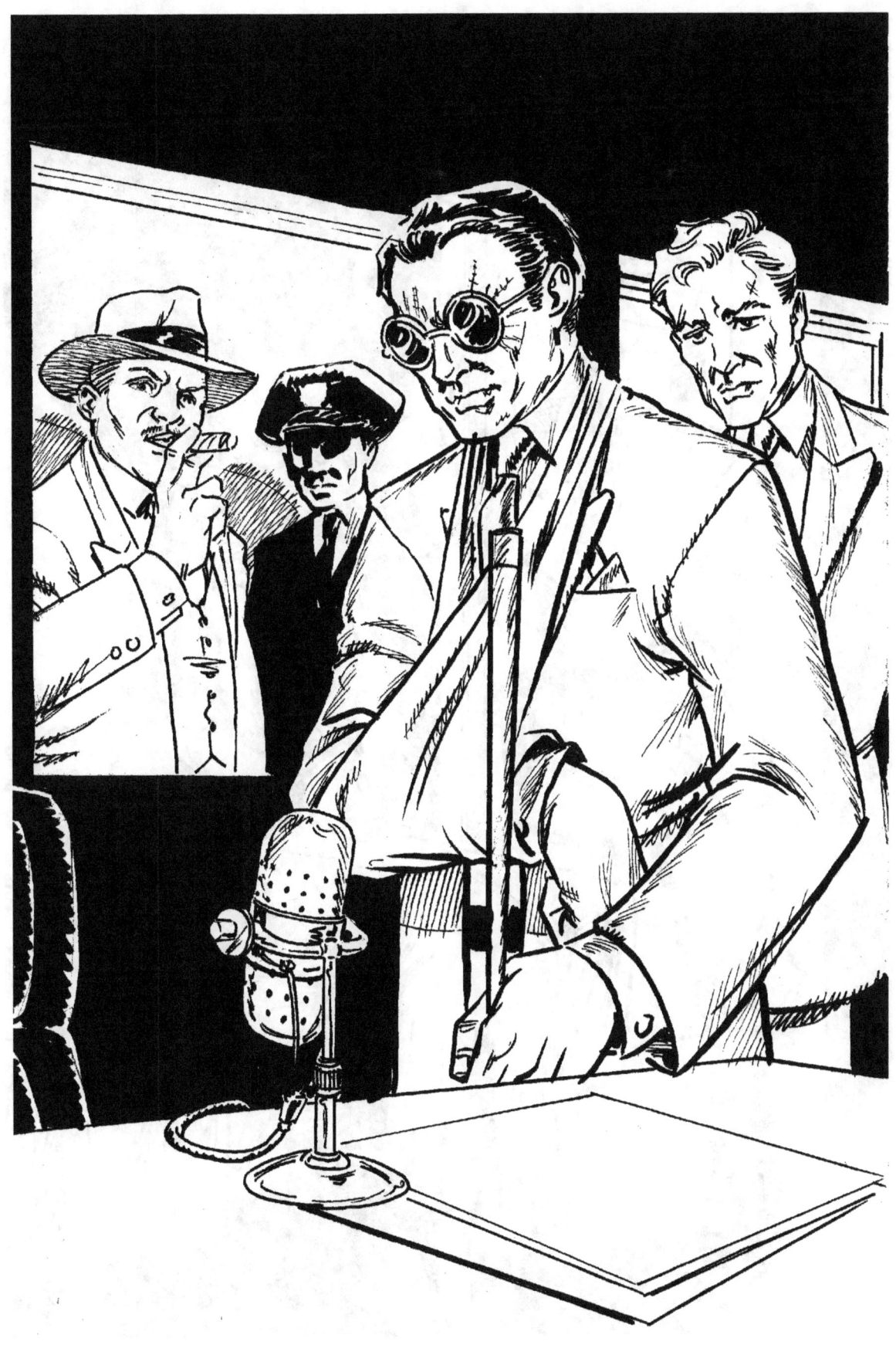

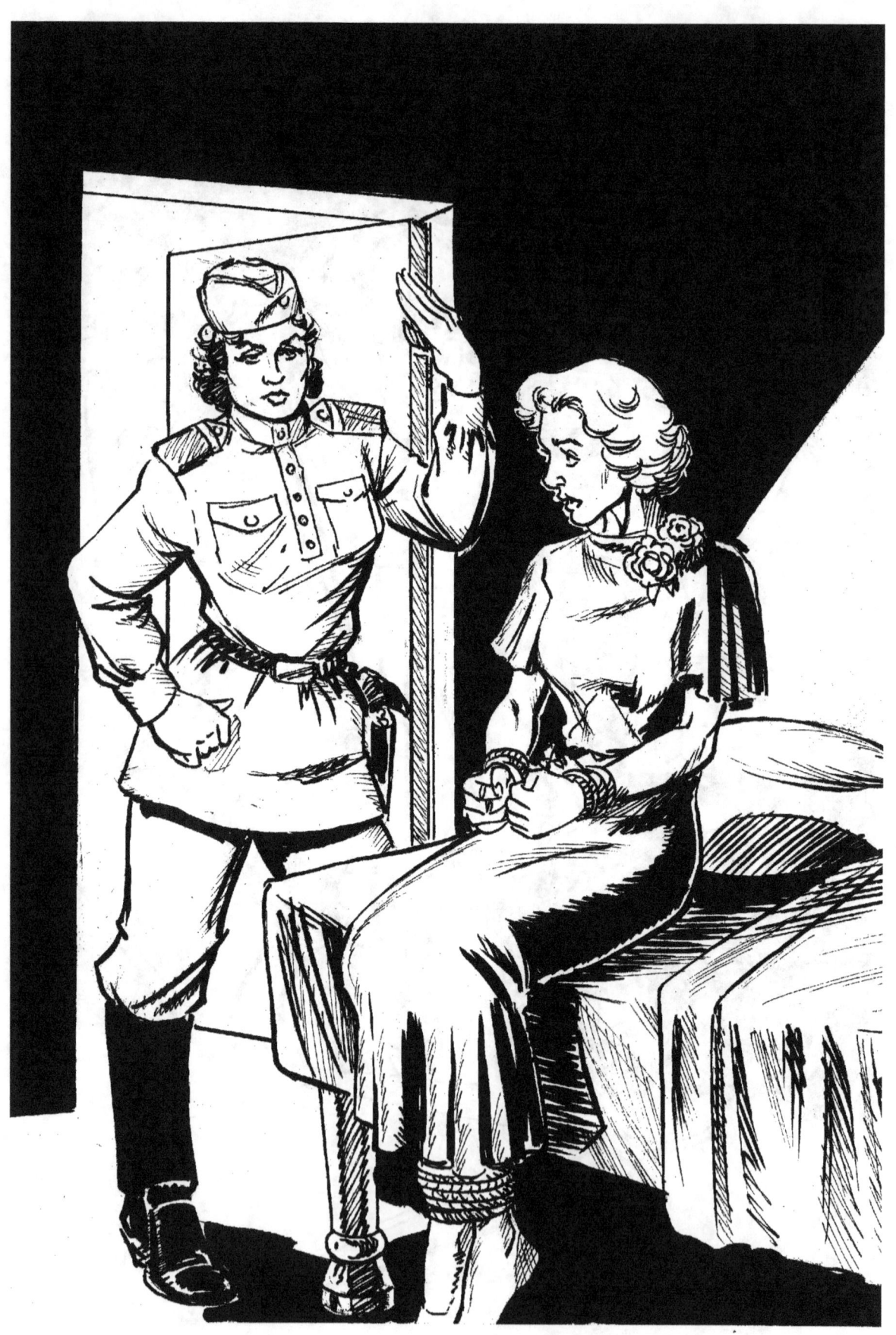

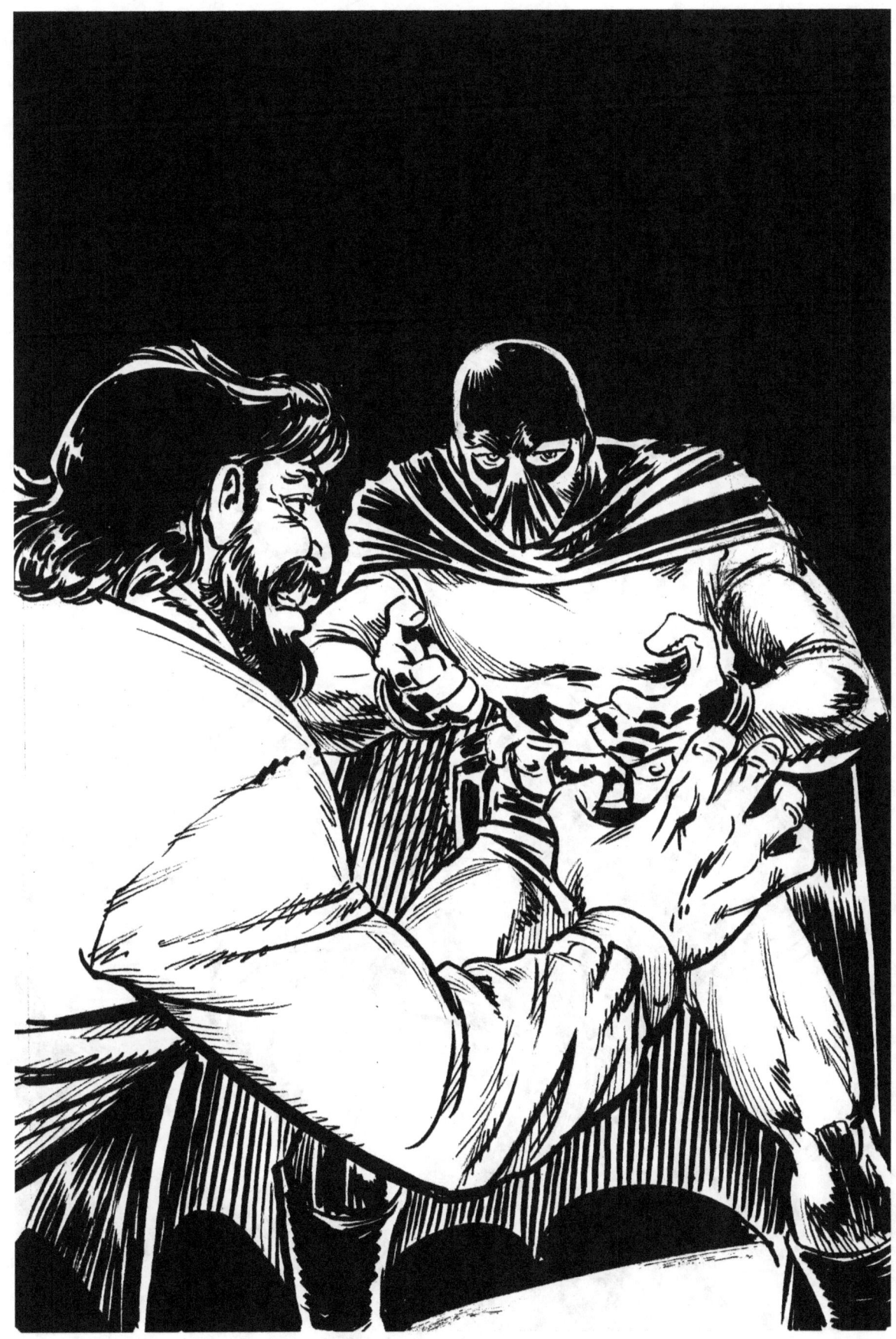

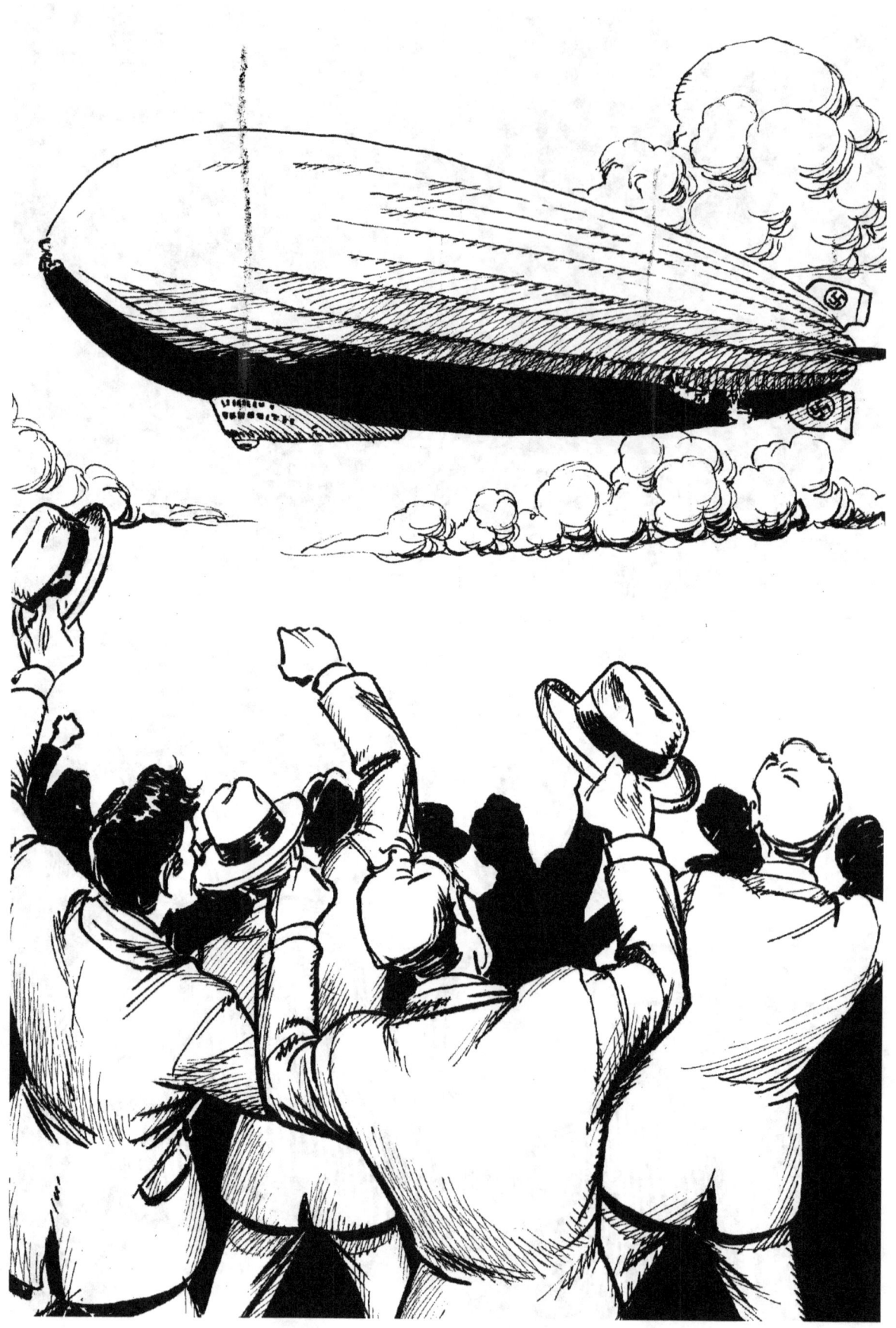

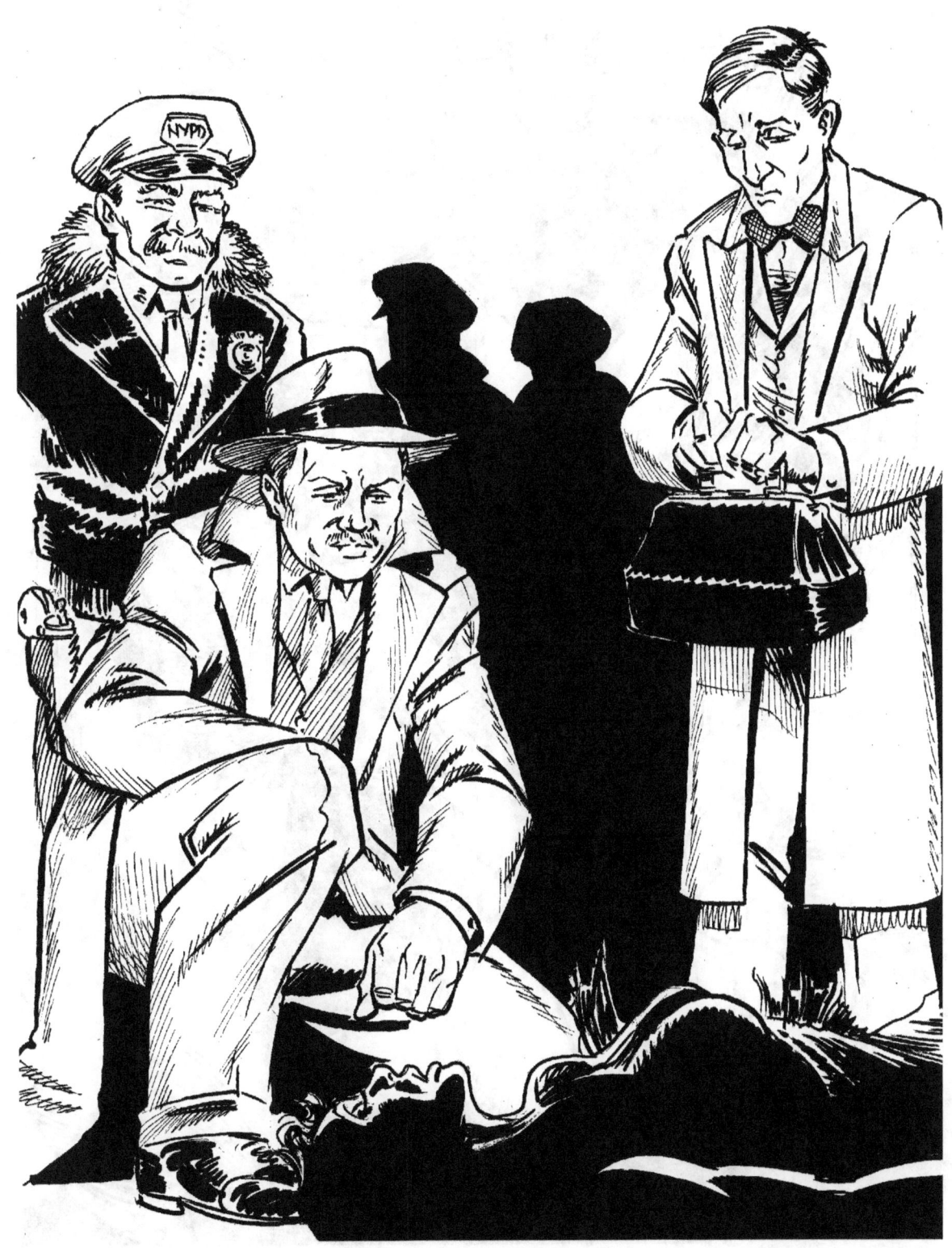

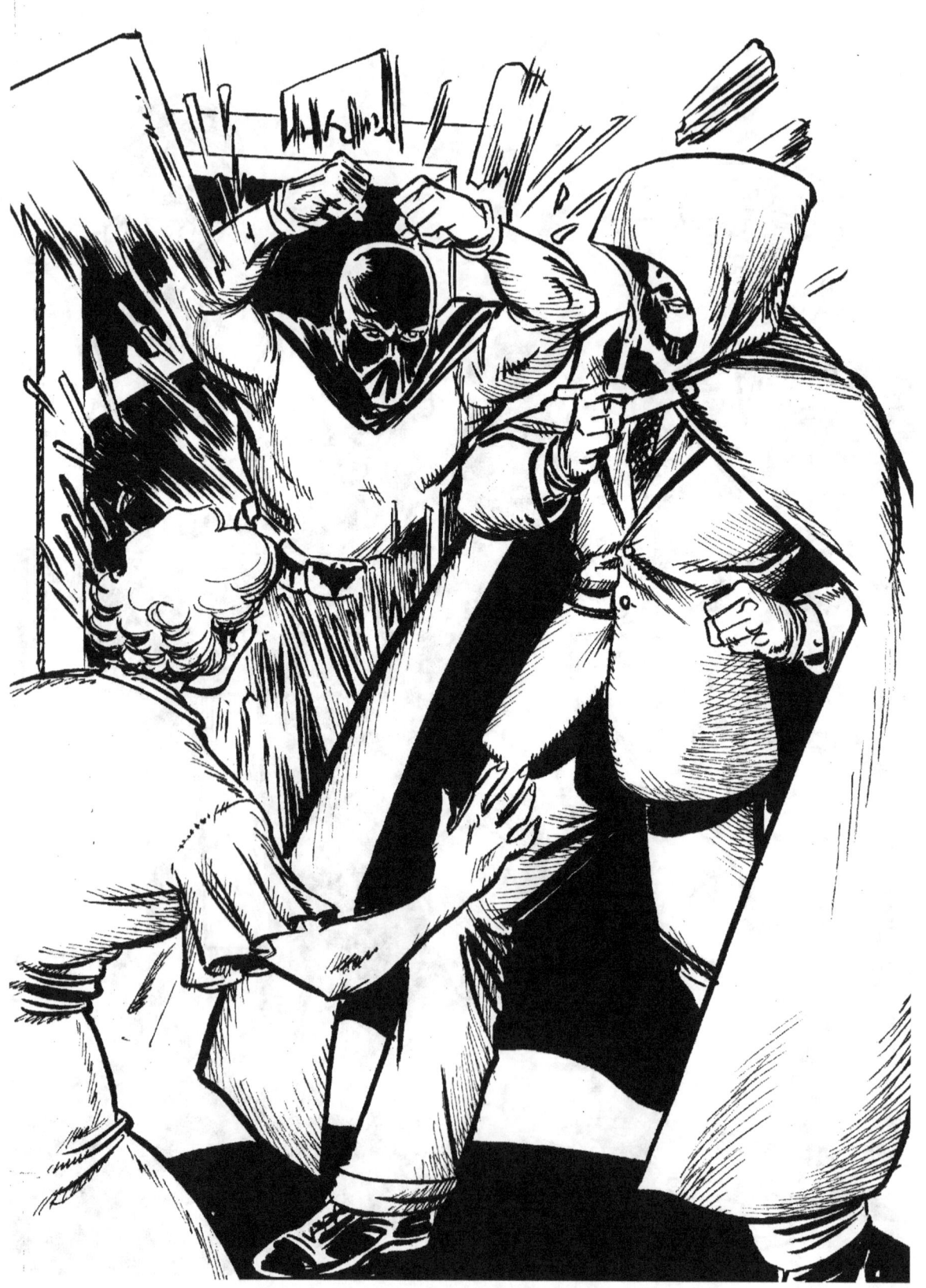

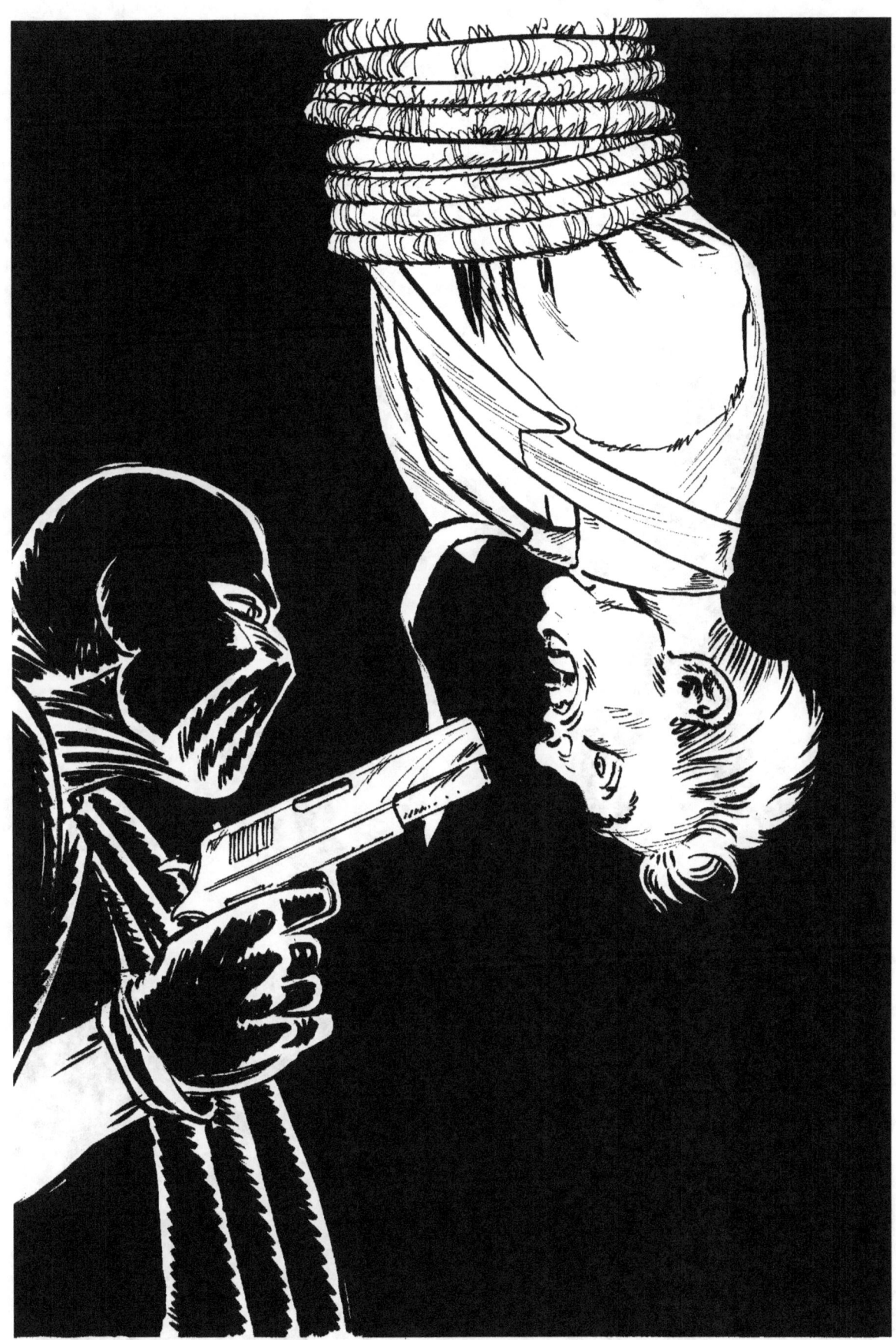

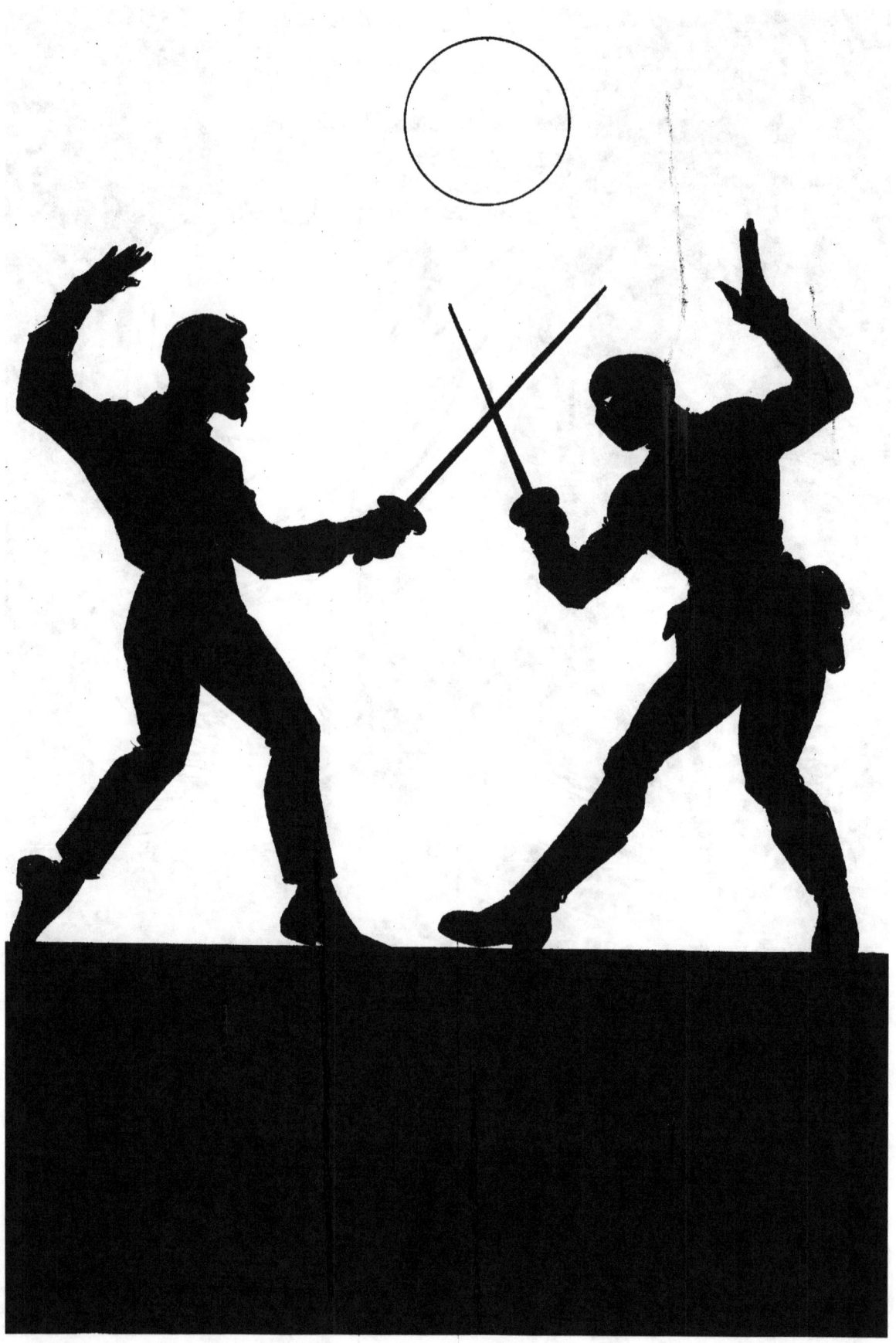

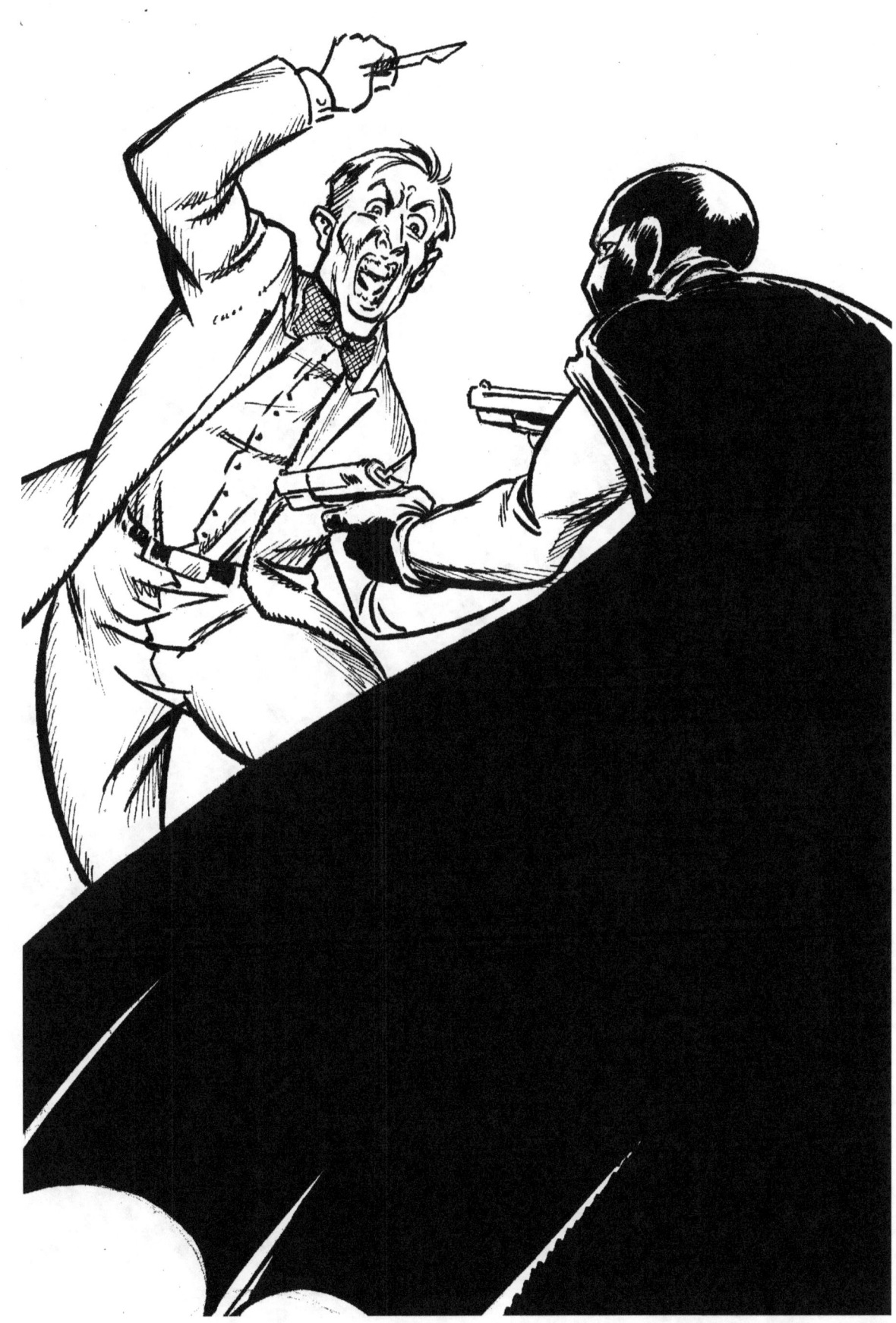

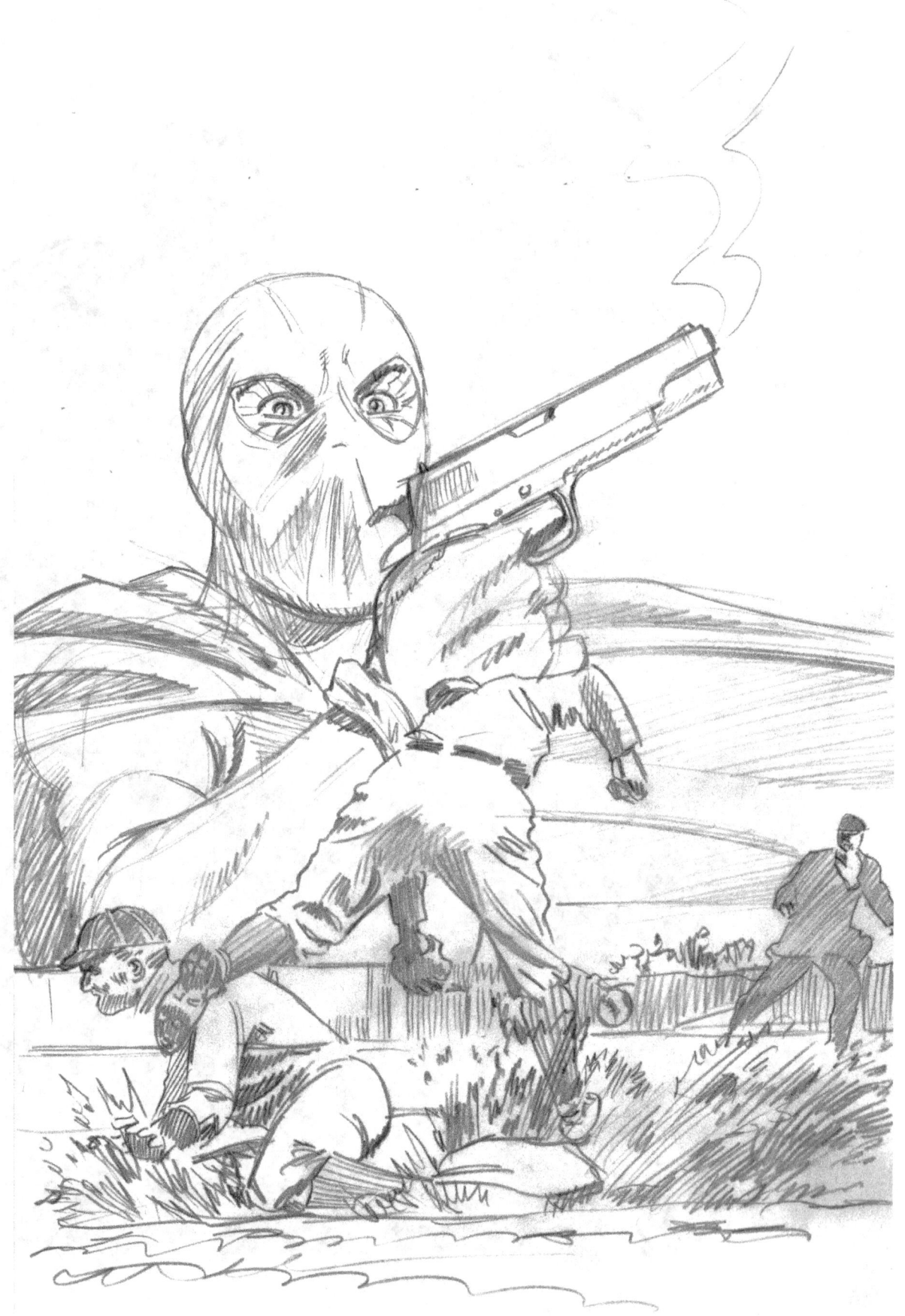

CHAPTER 3
THE SUPER SPIES

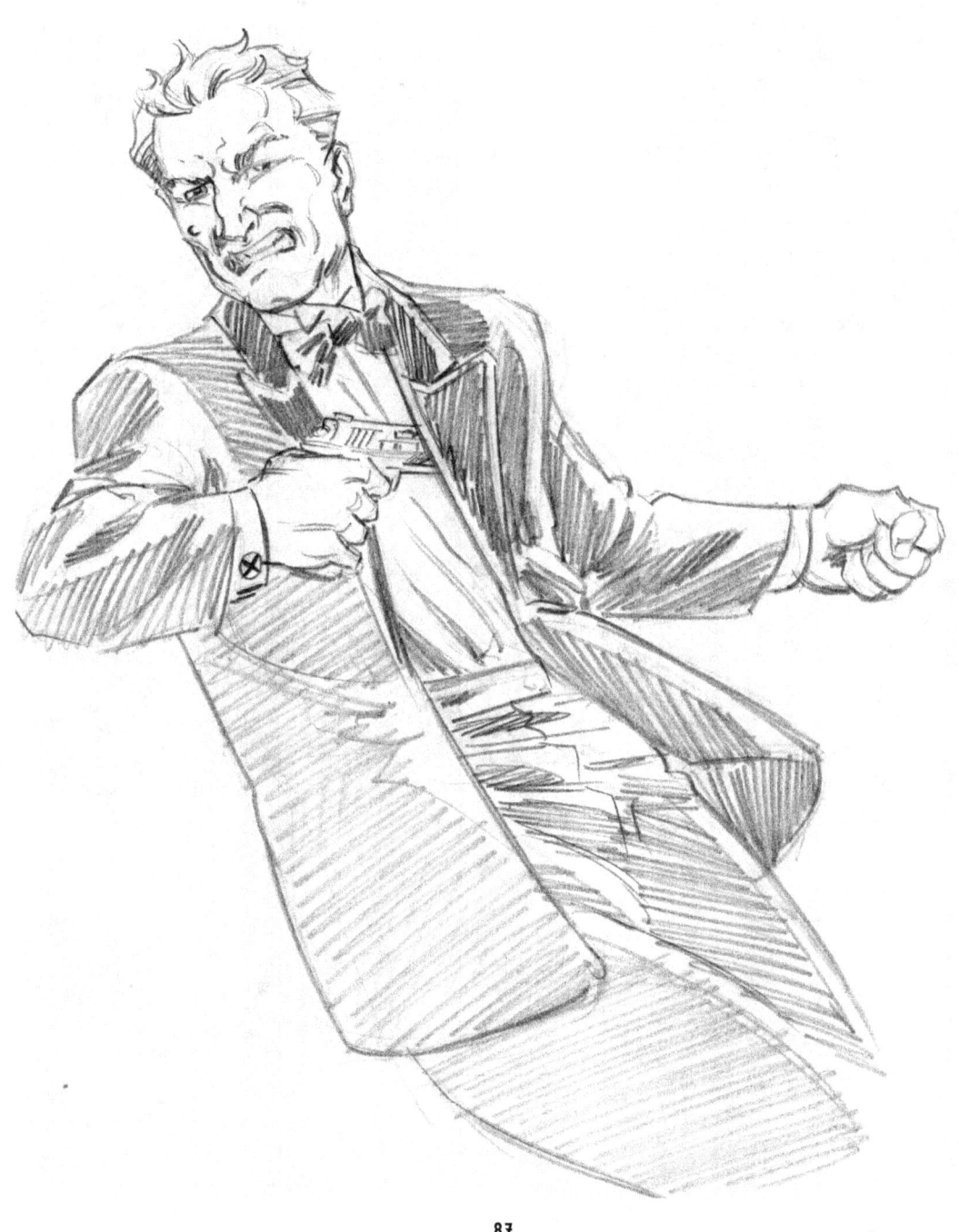

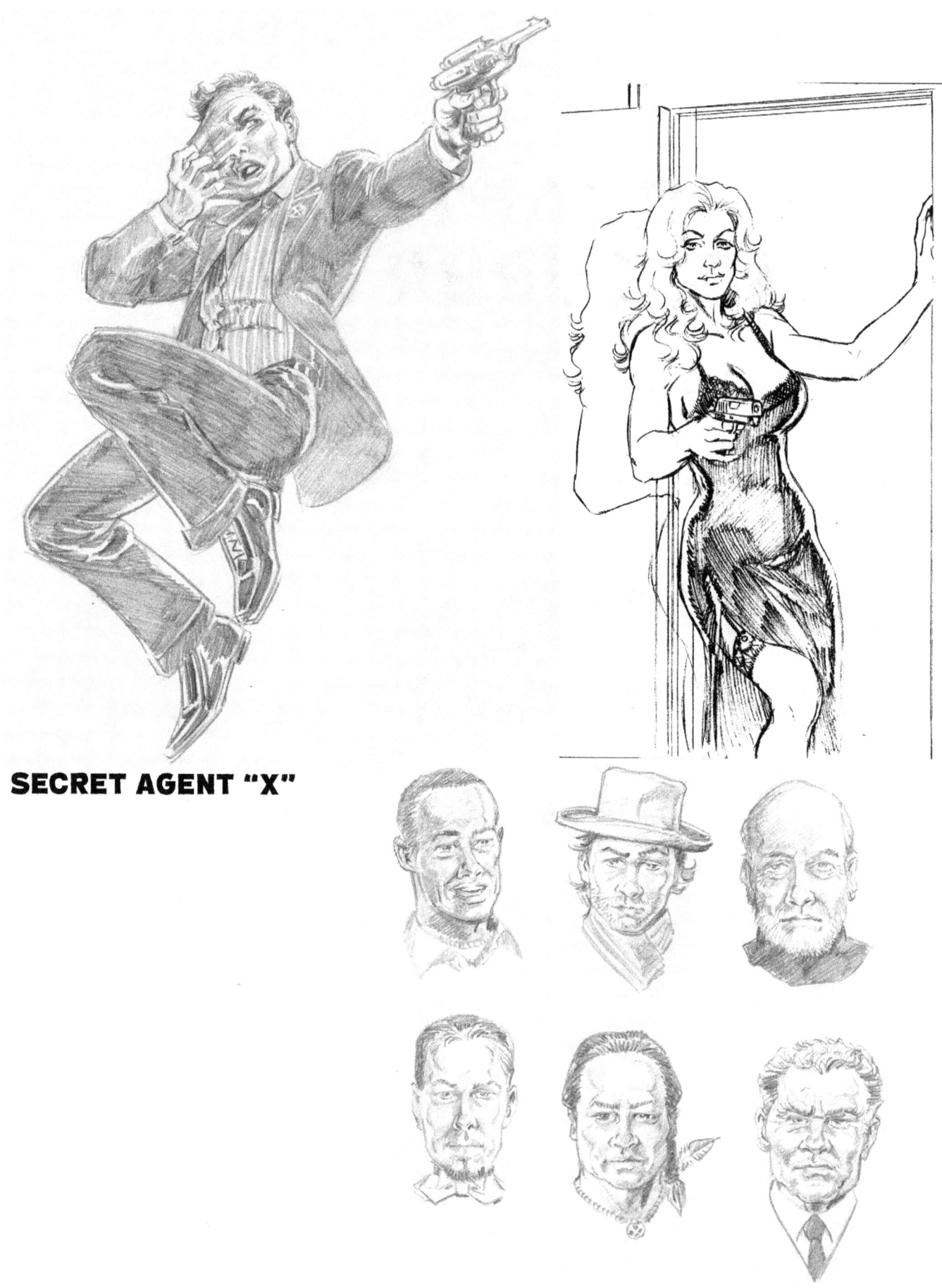

SECRET AGENT "X"

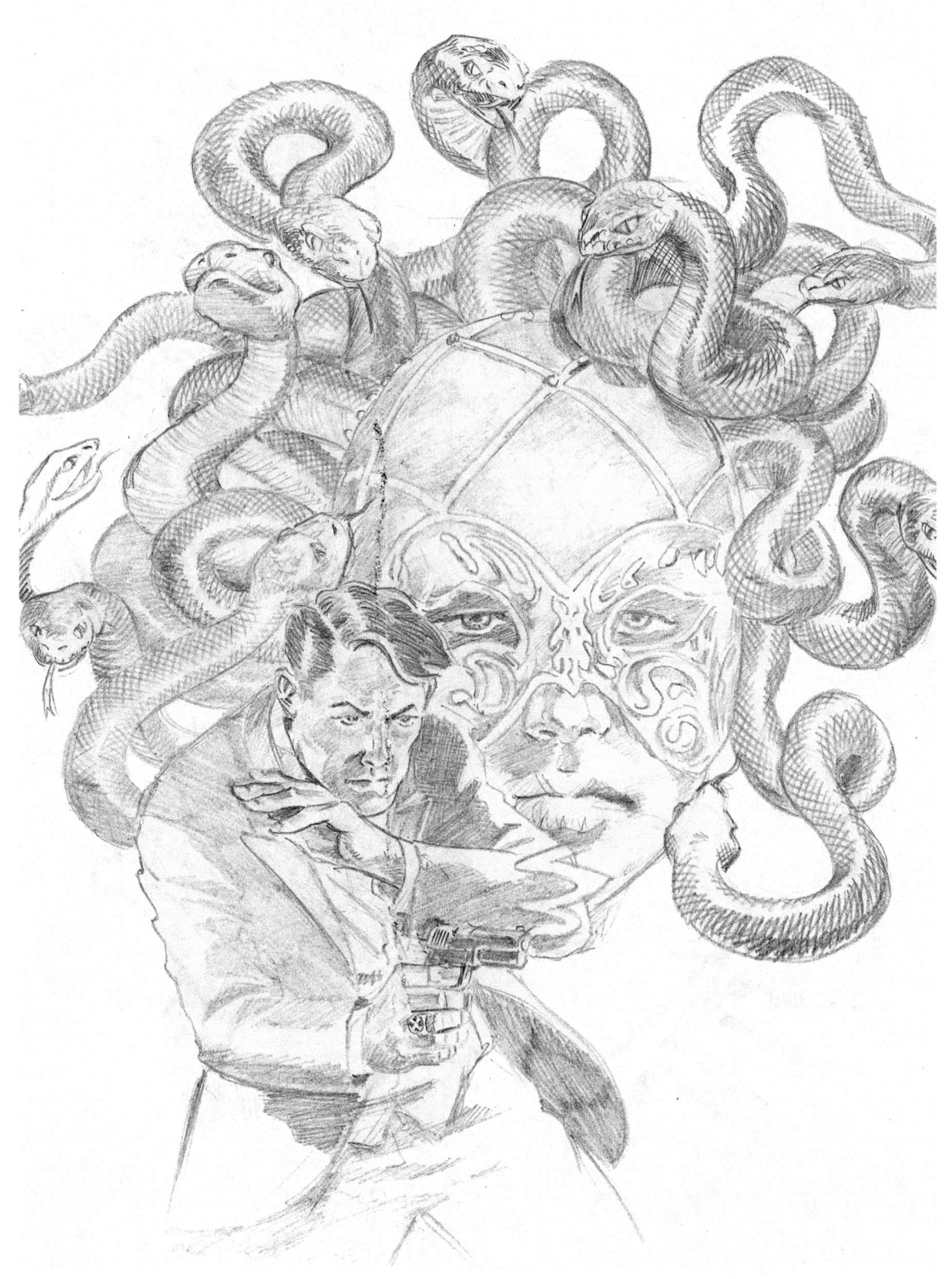

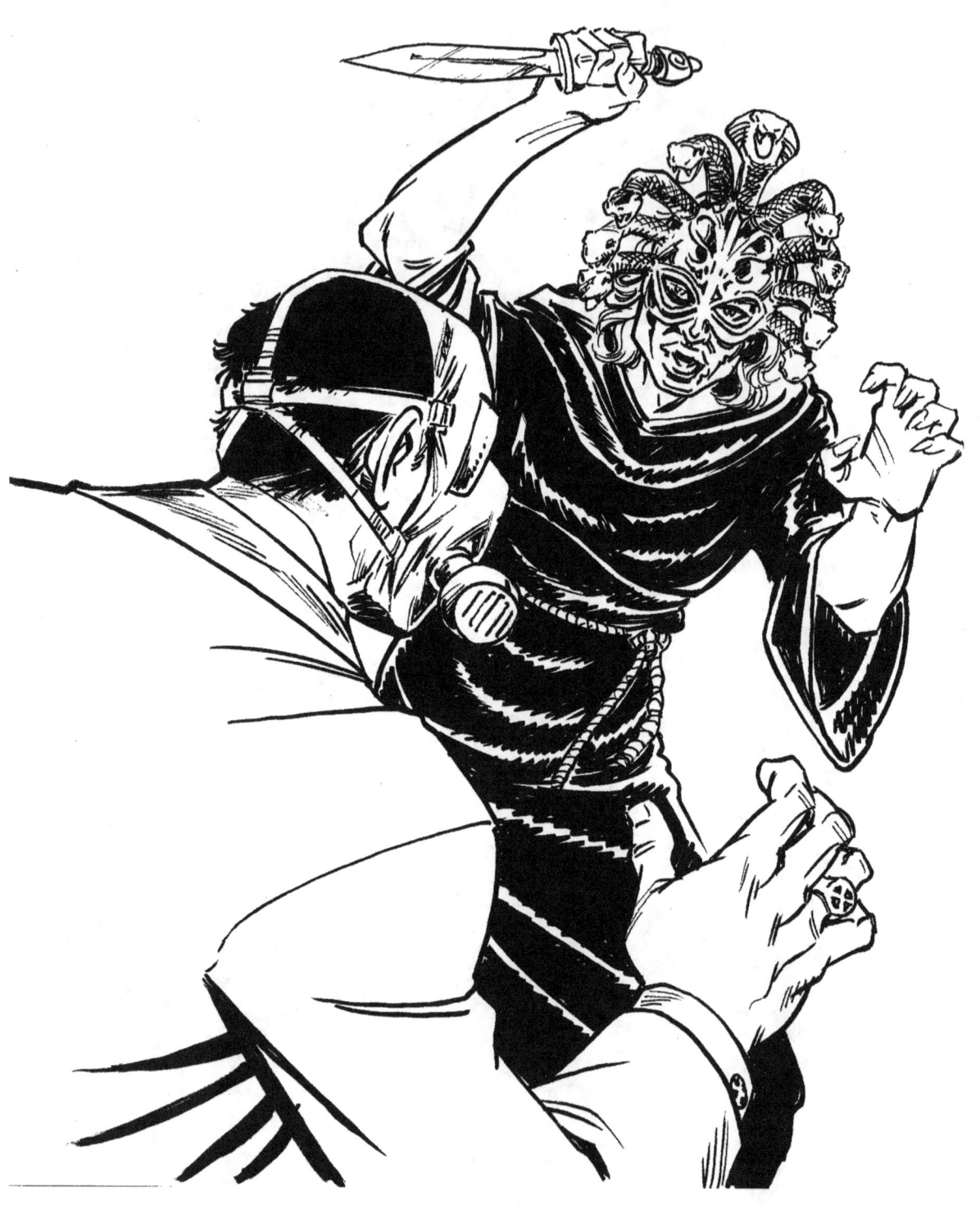

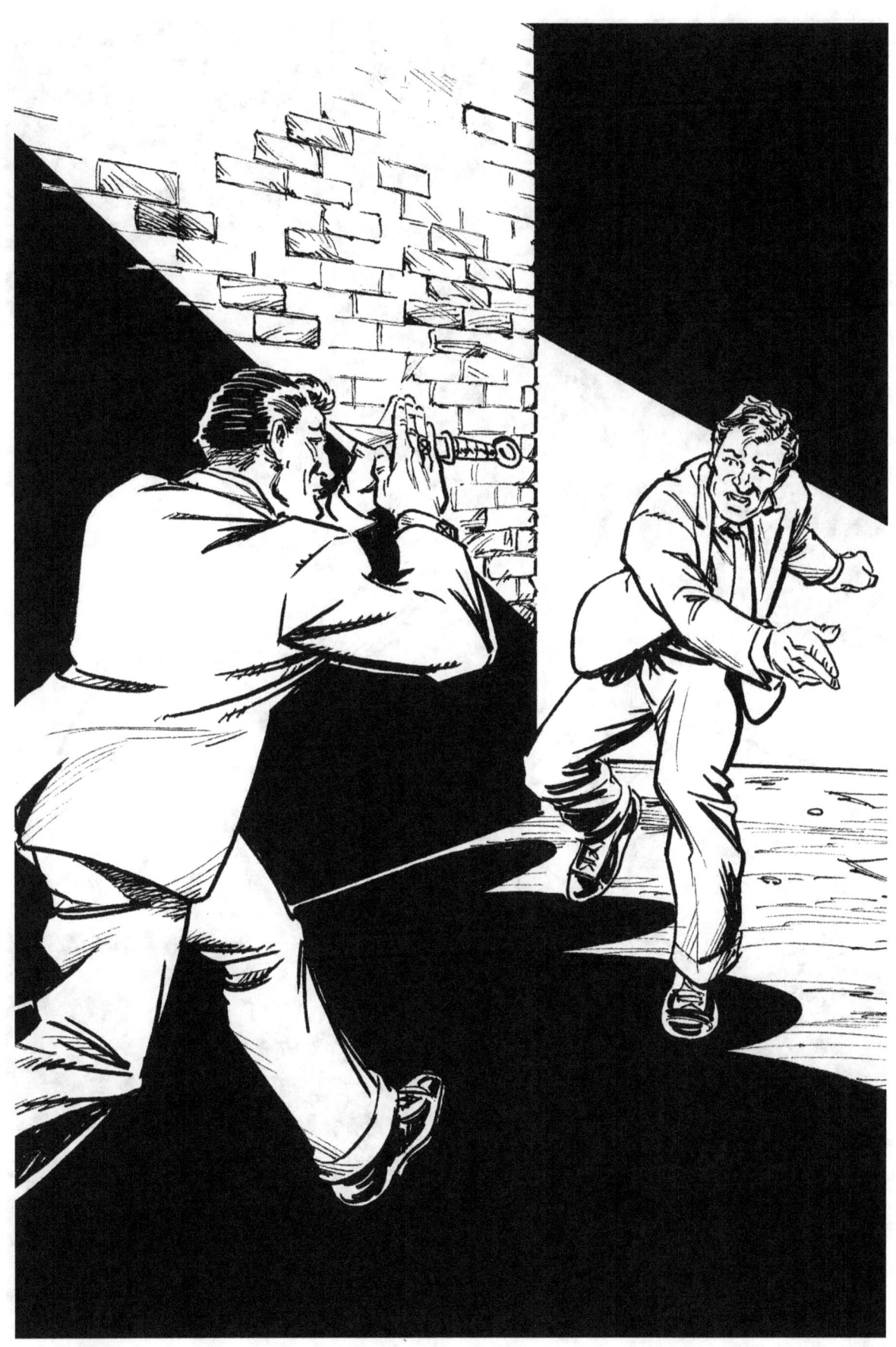

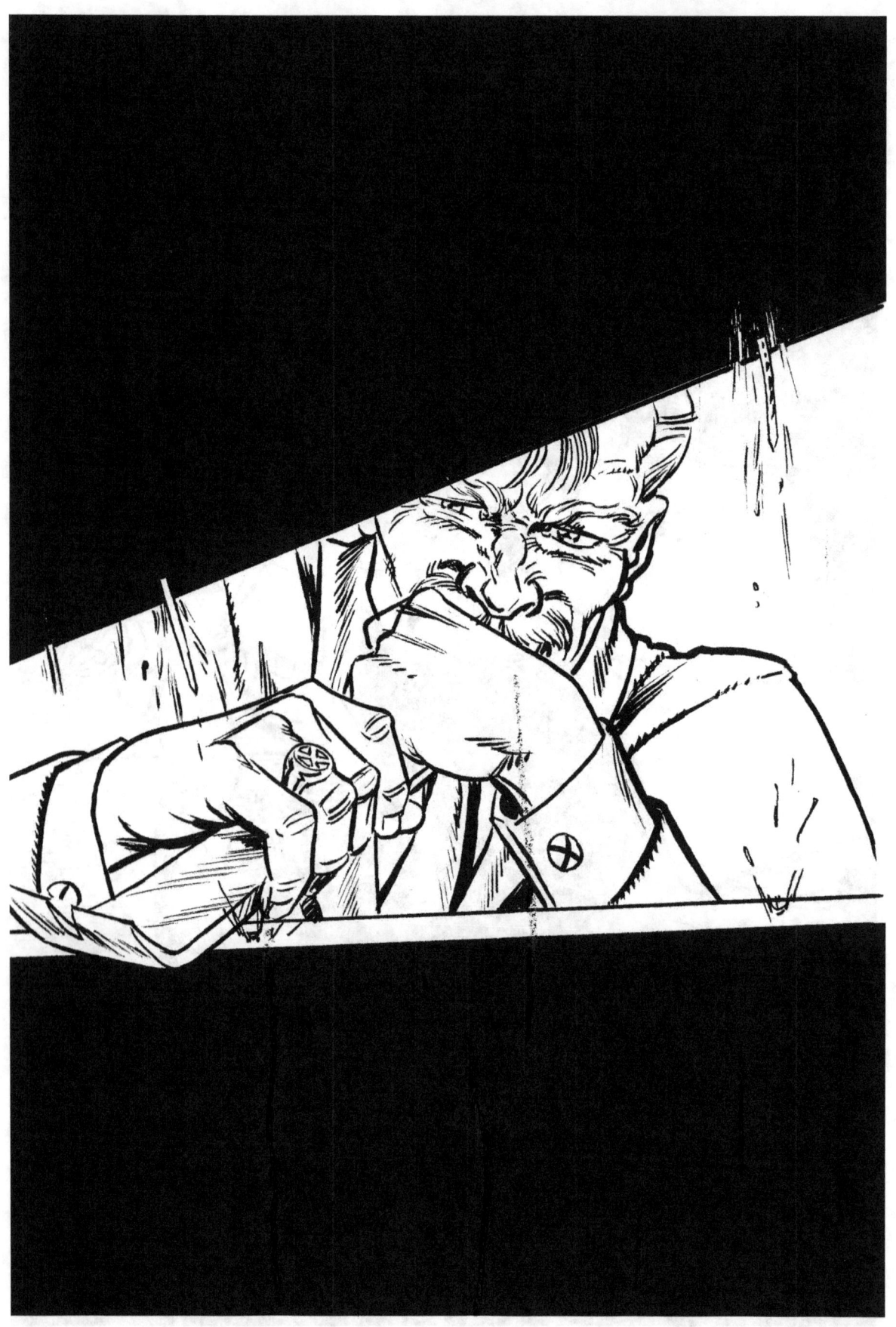

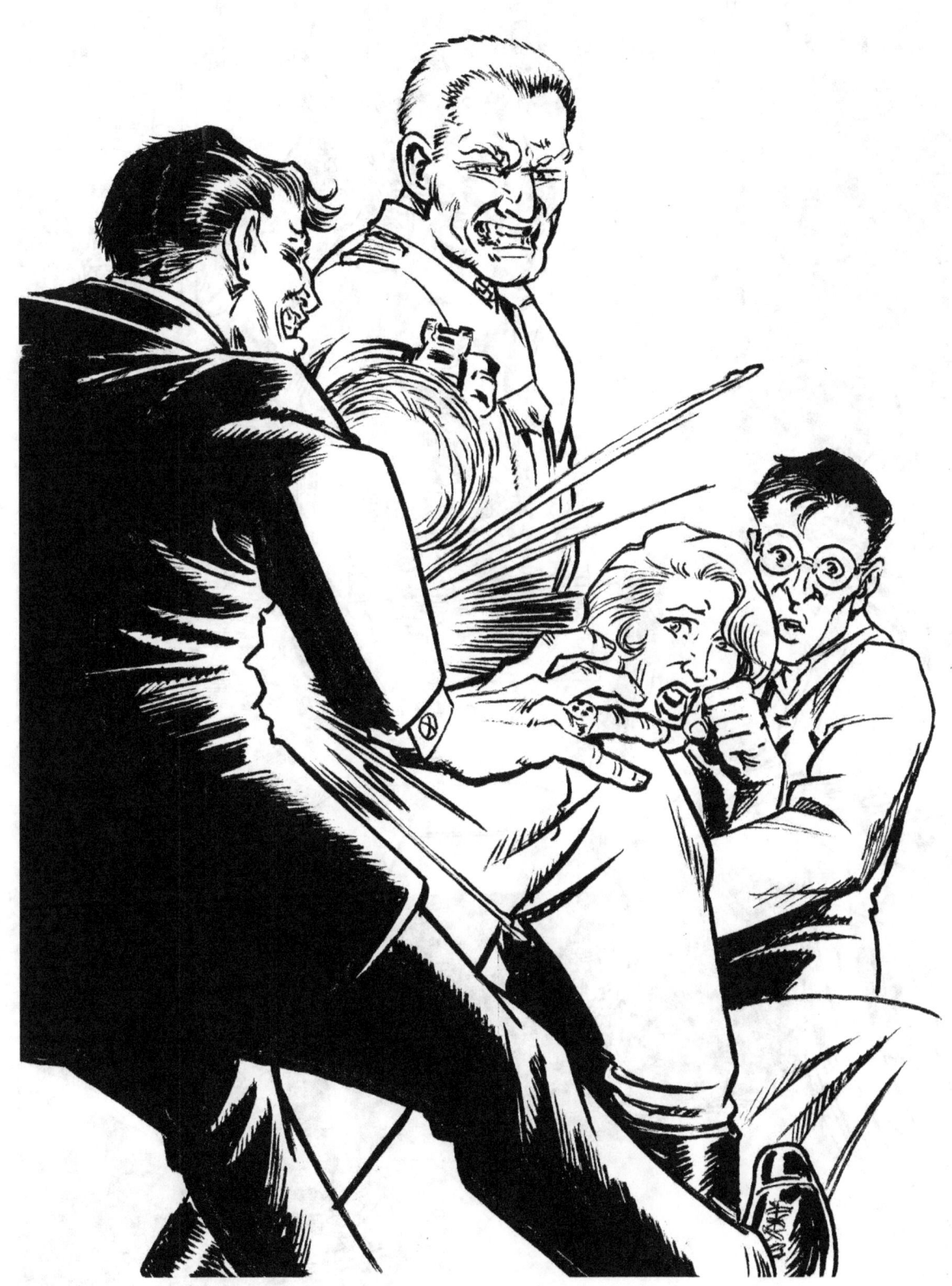

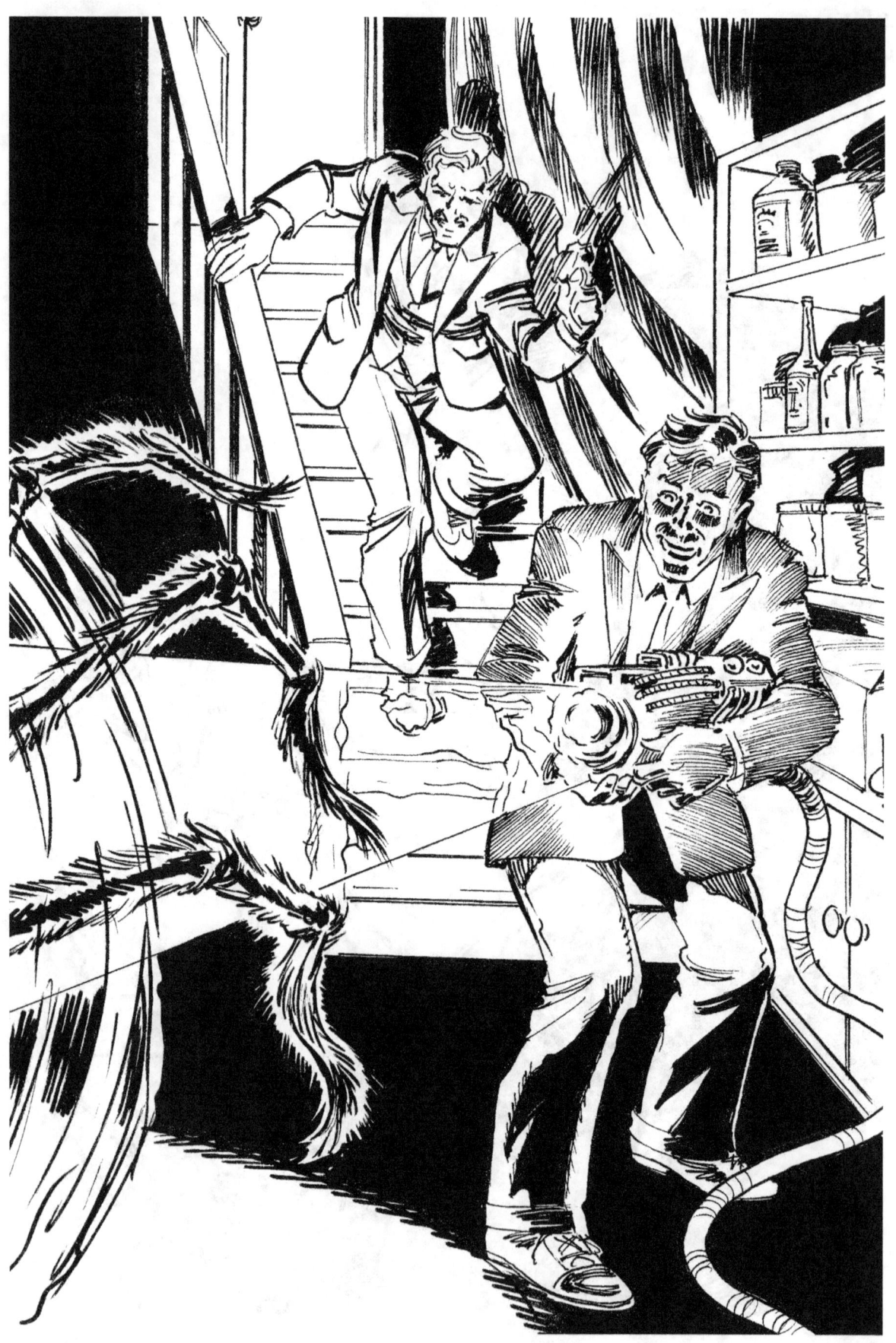

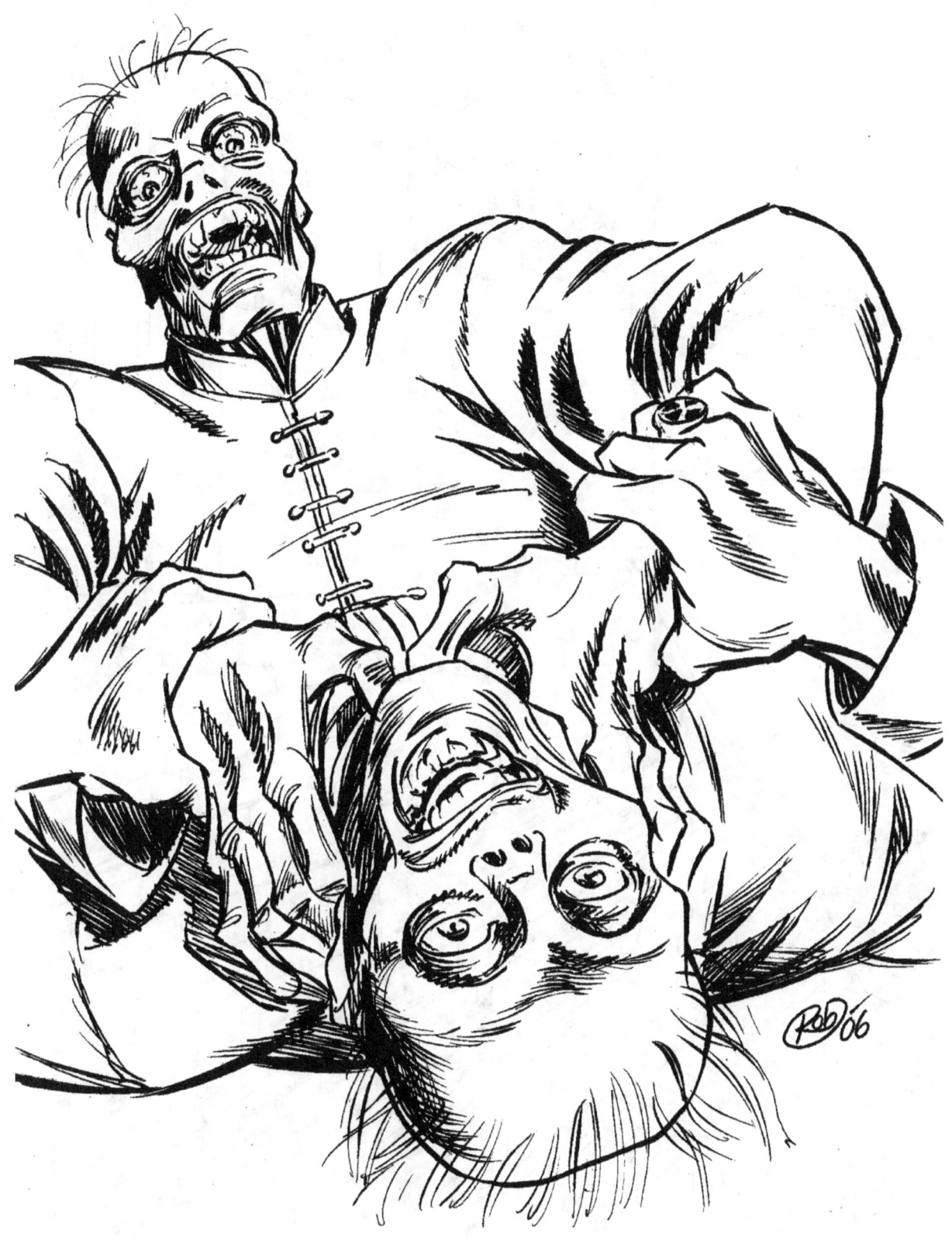

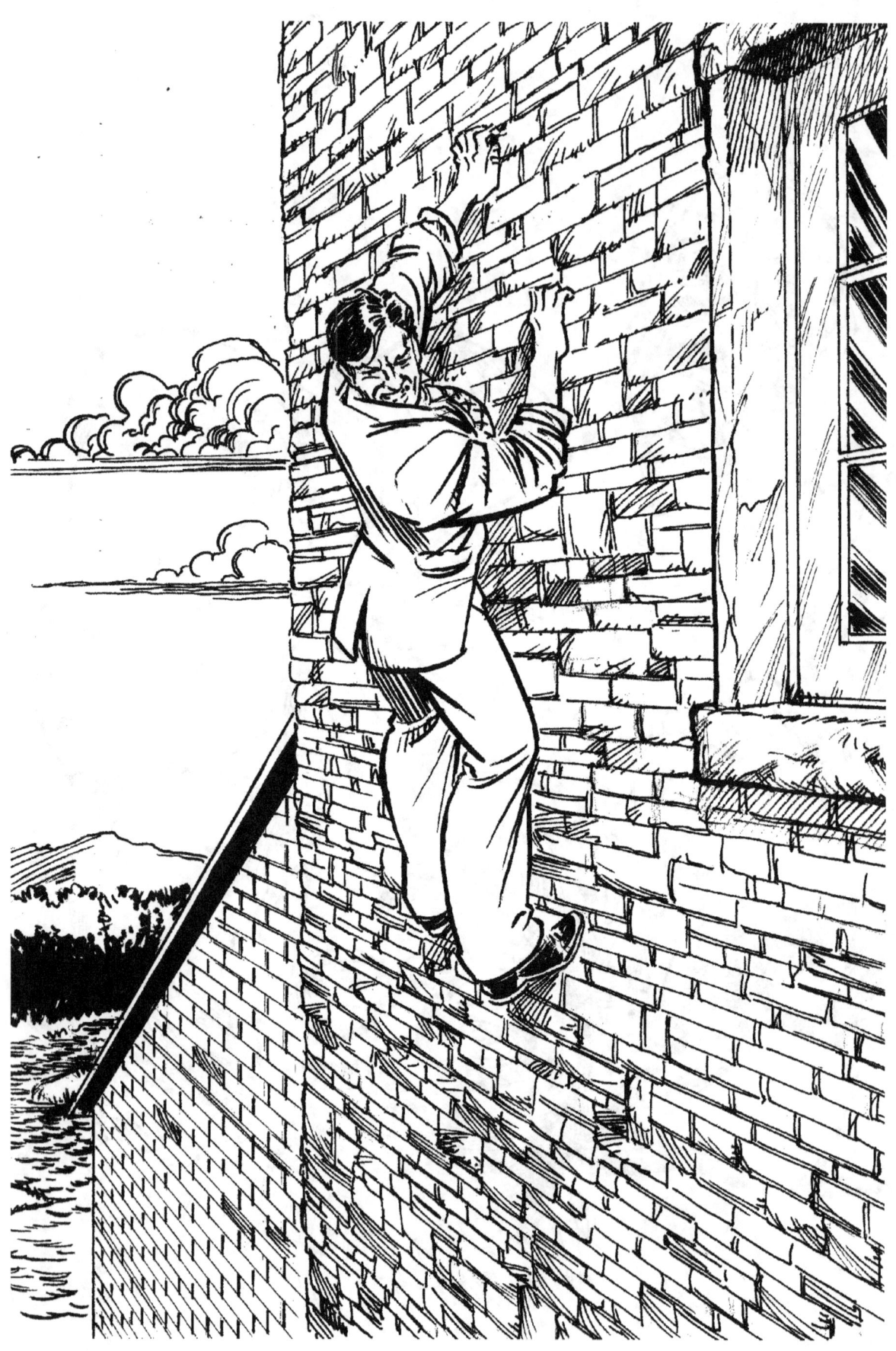

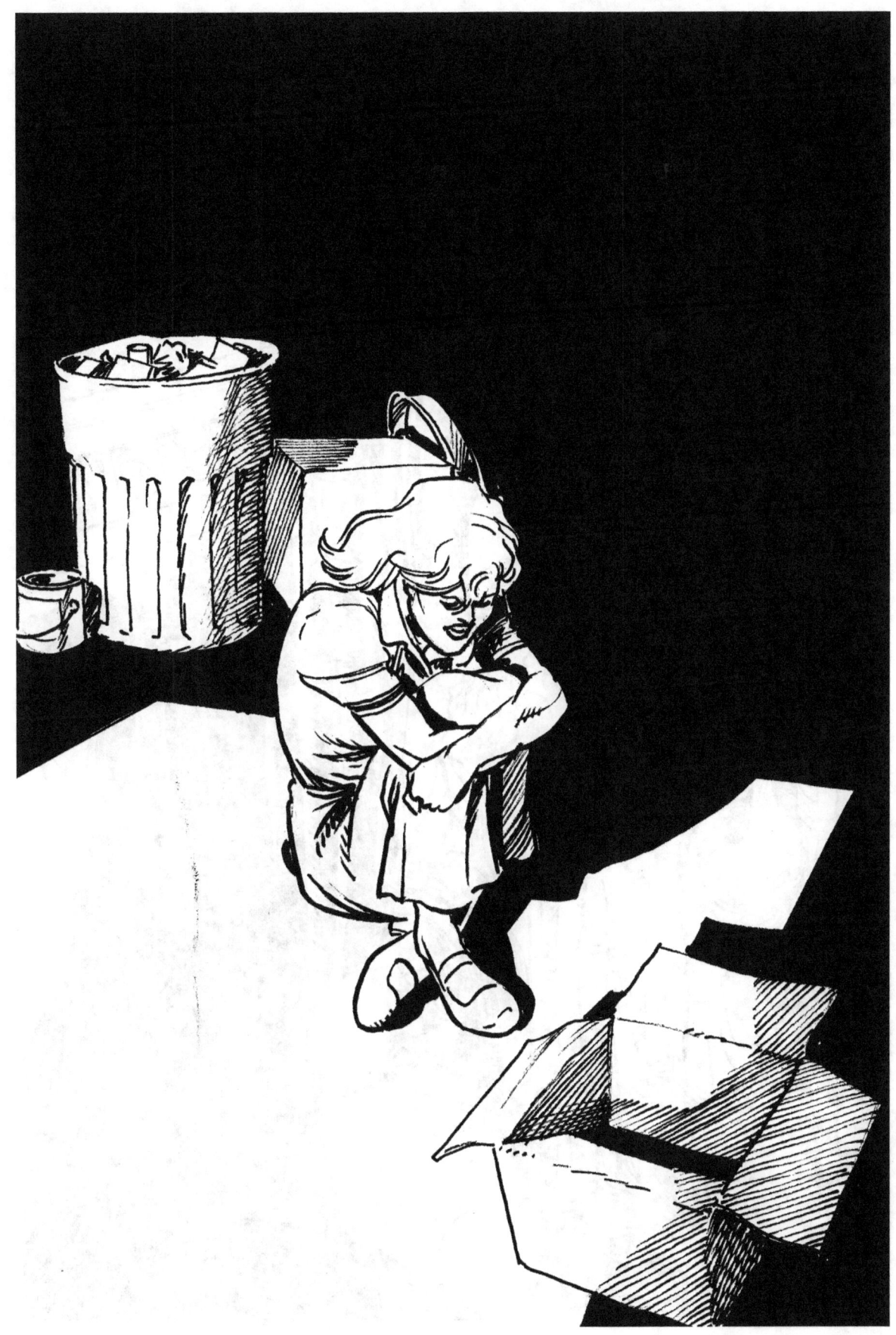

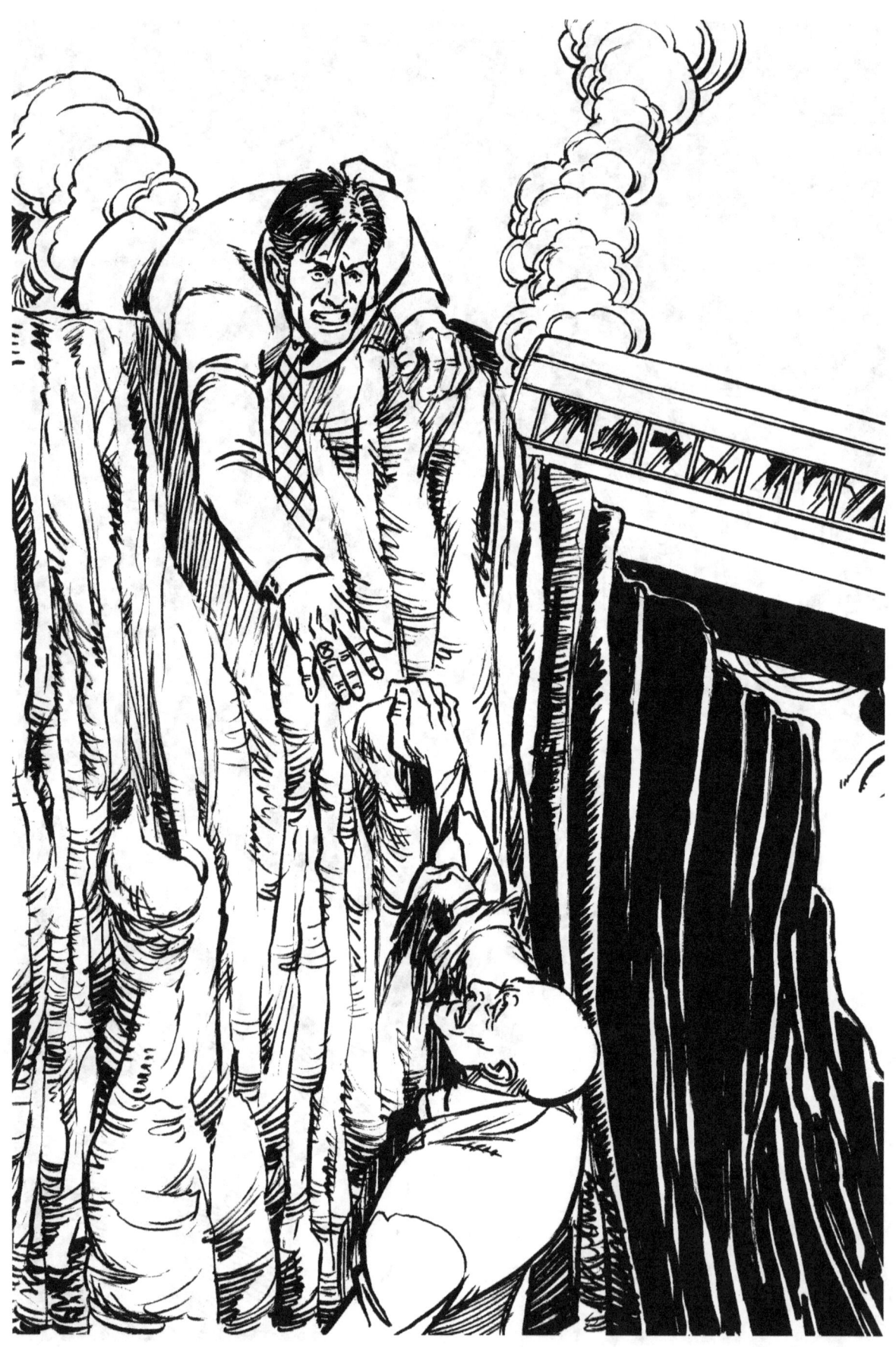

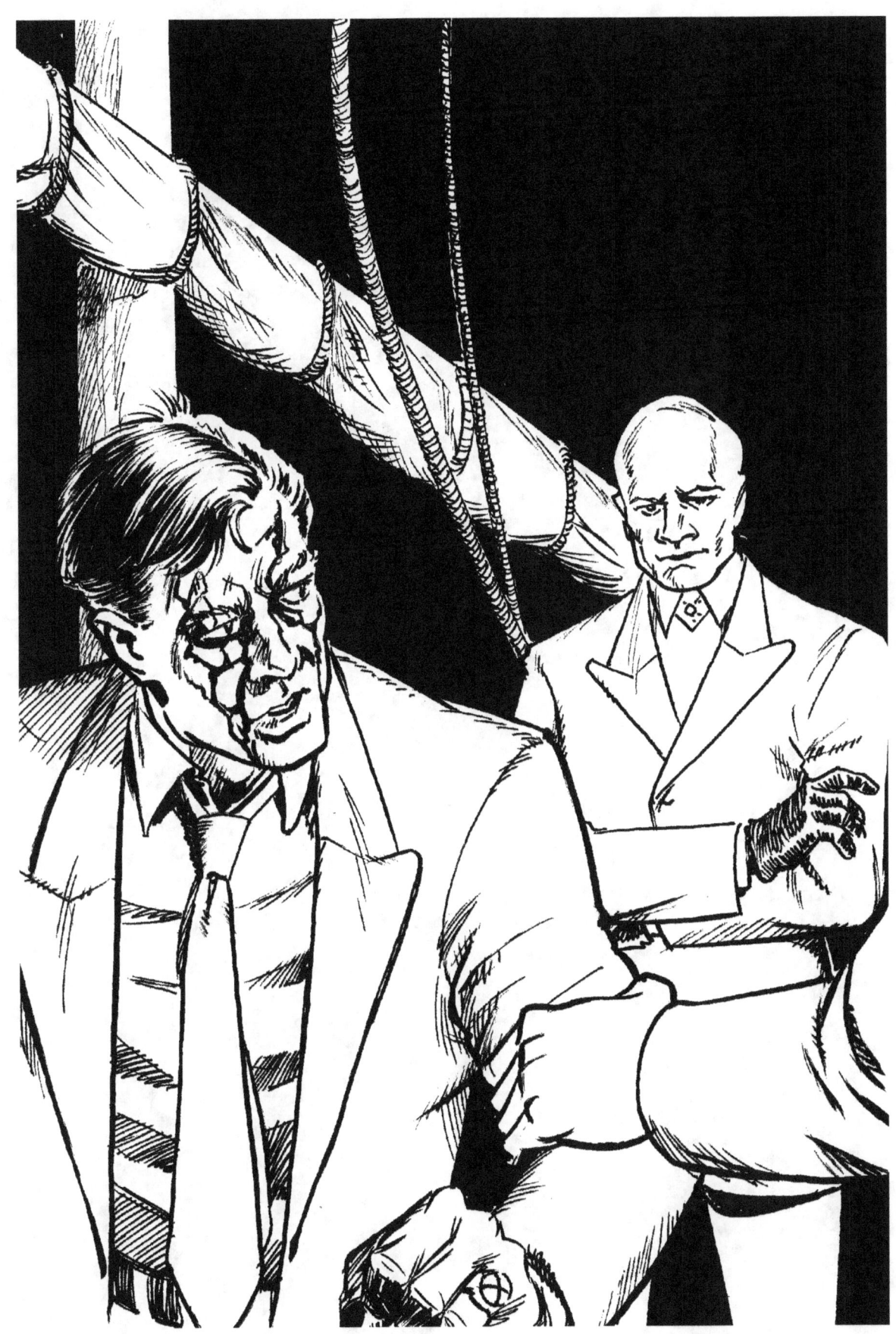

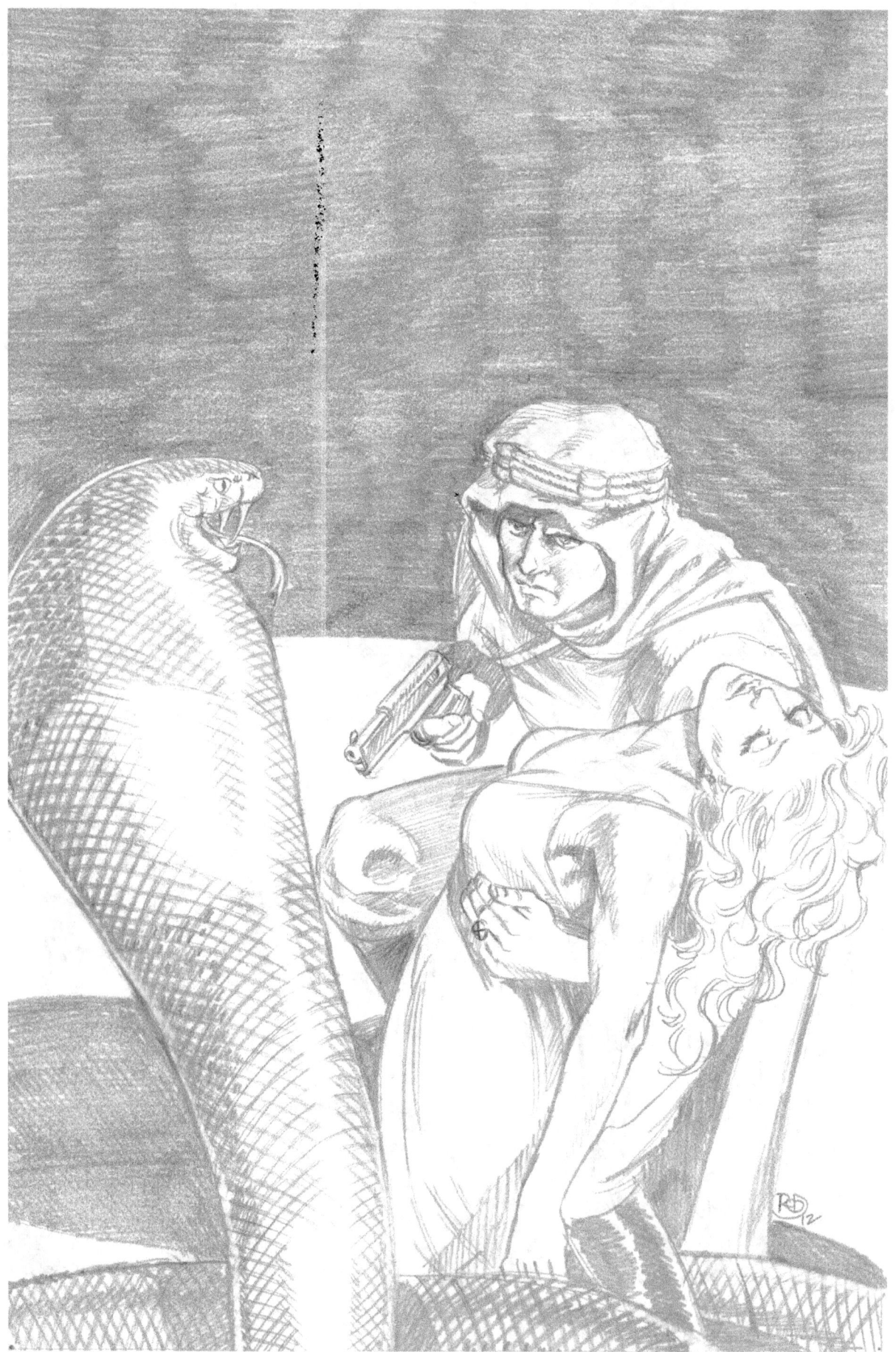

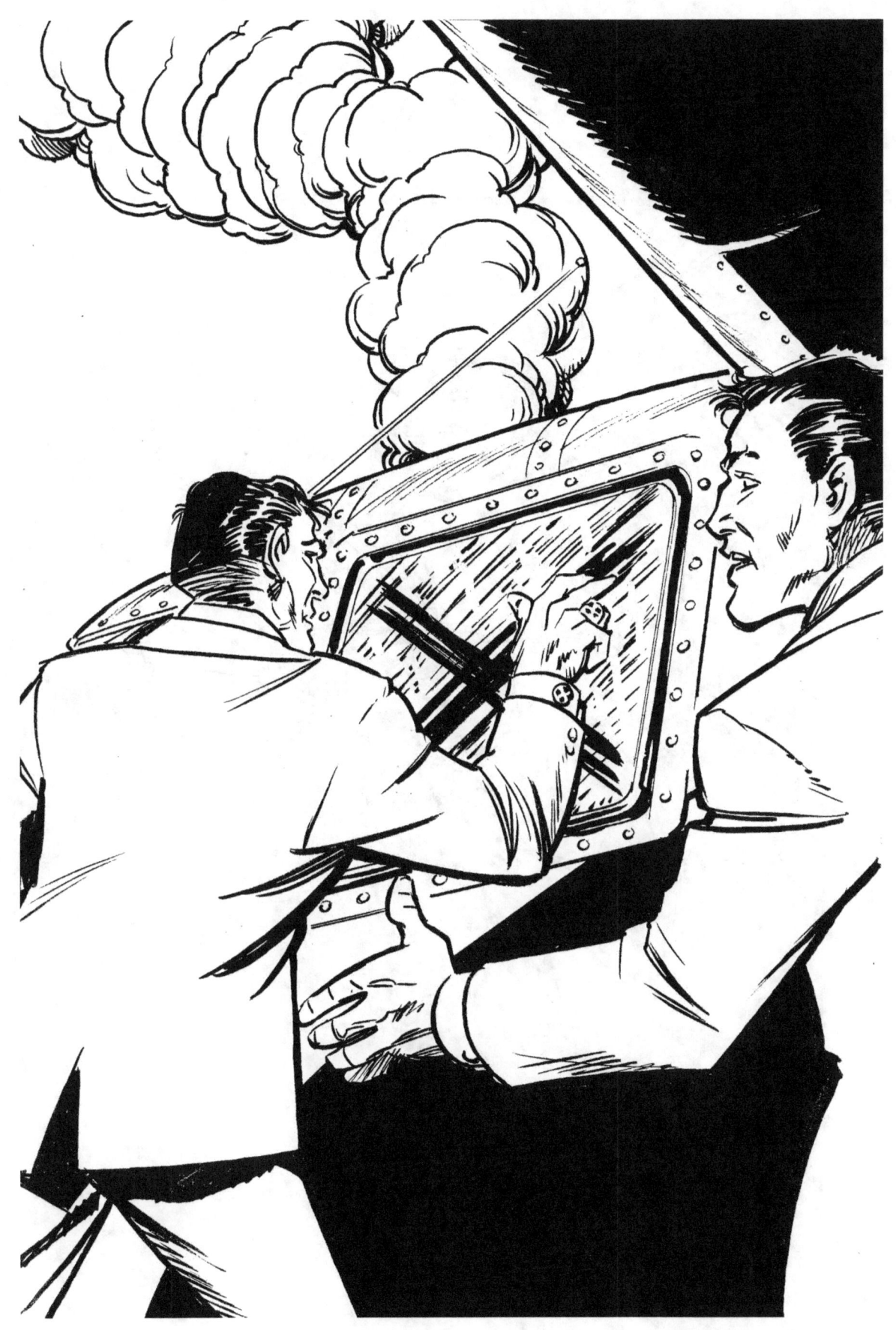

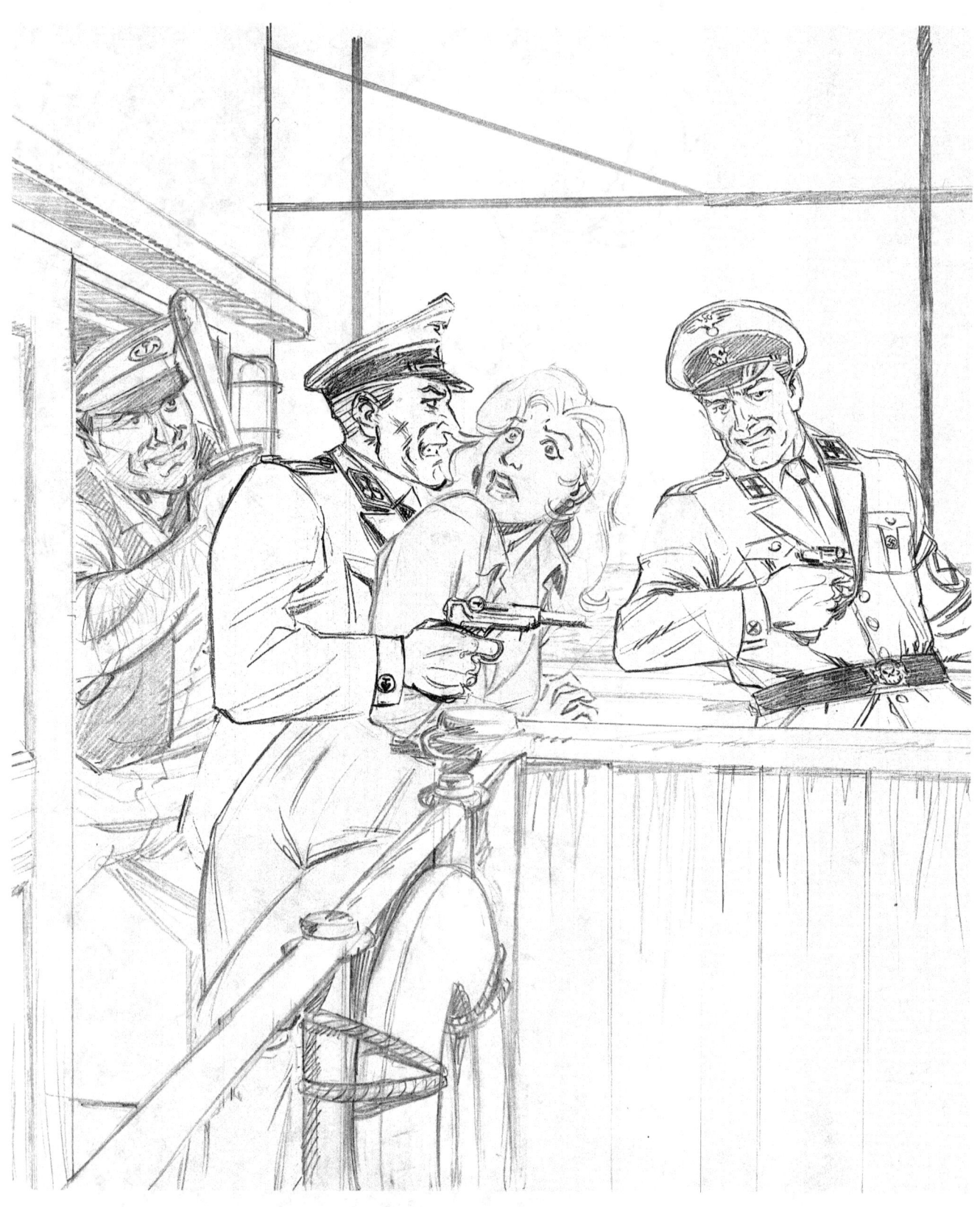

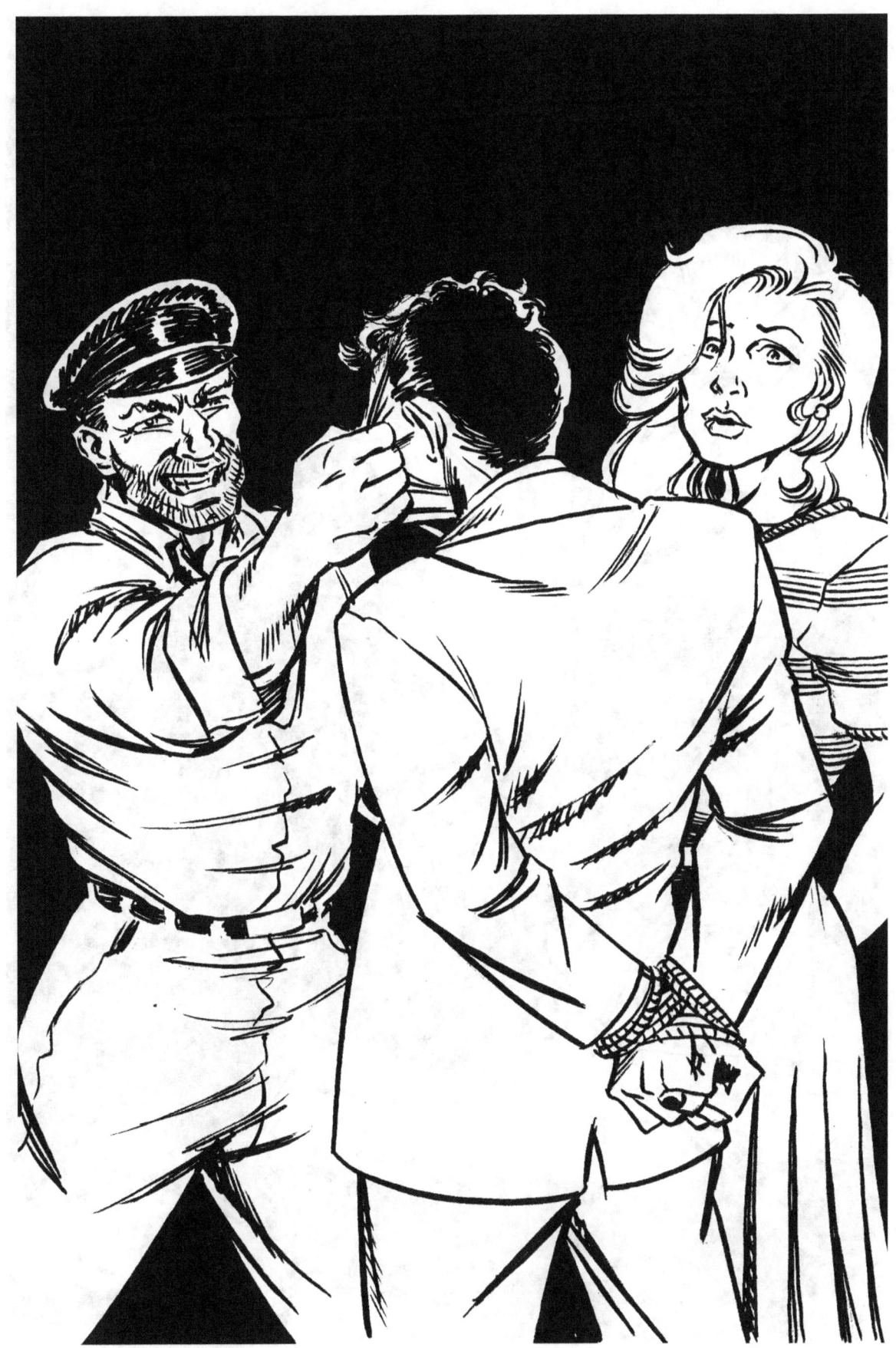

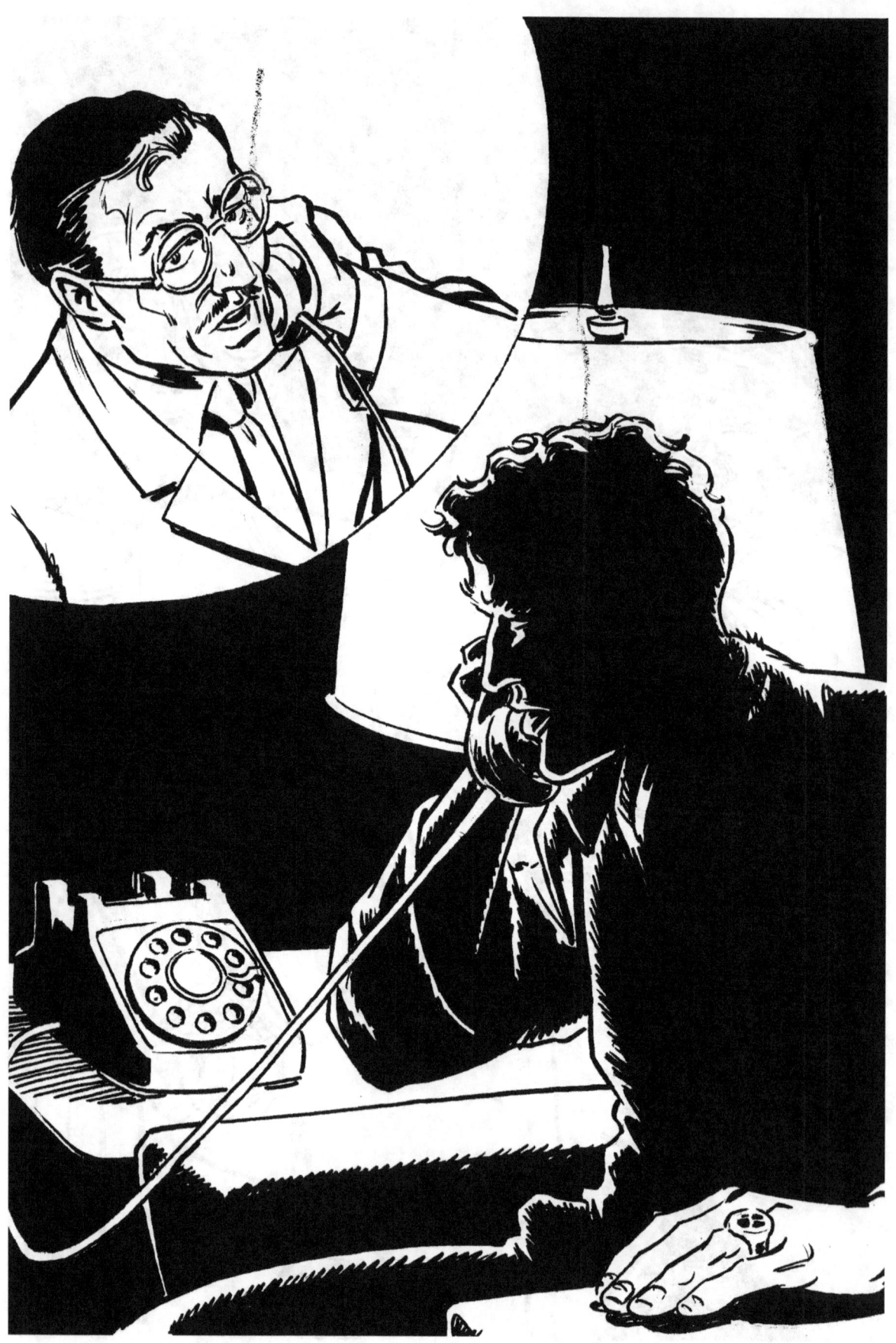

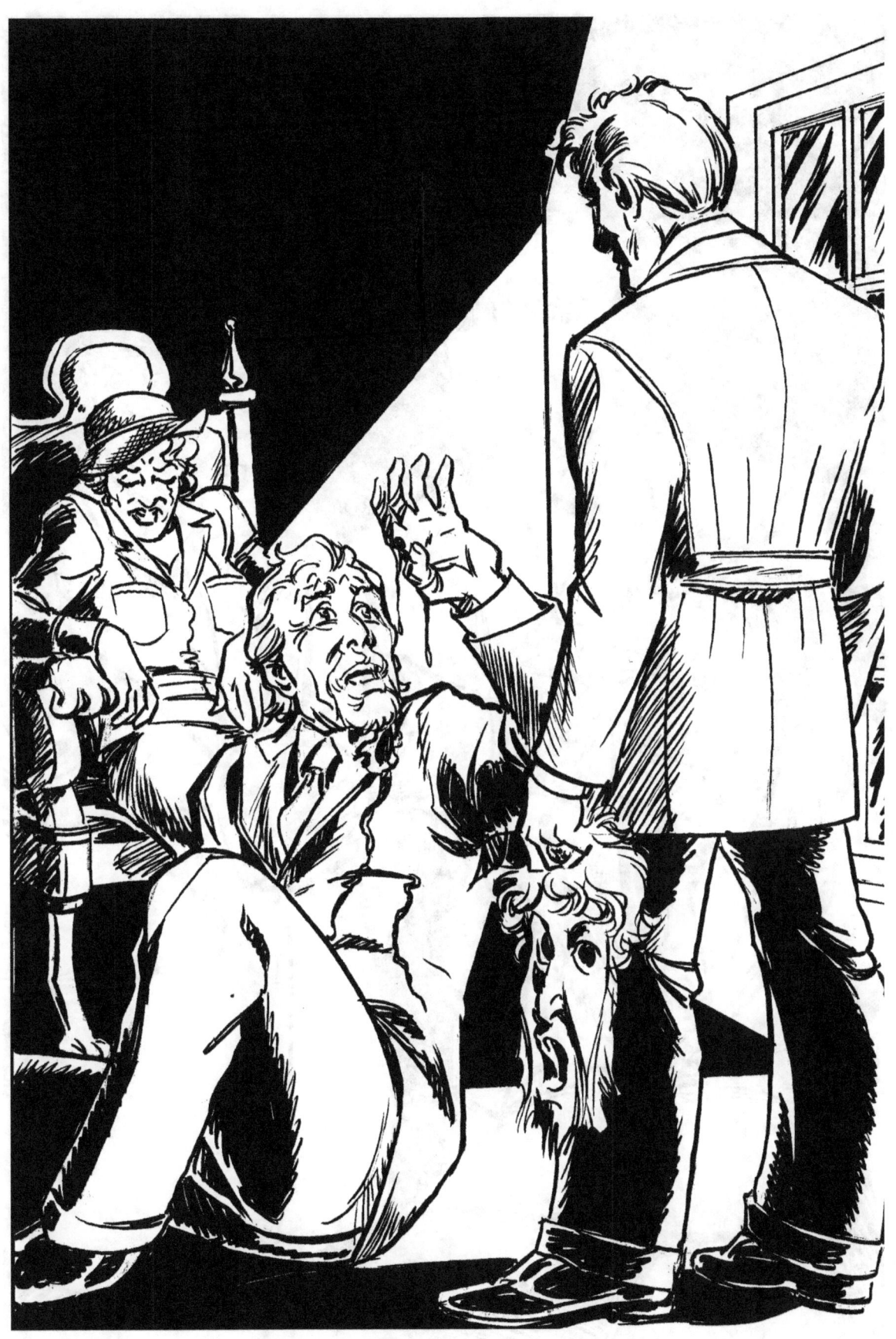

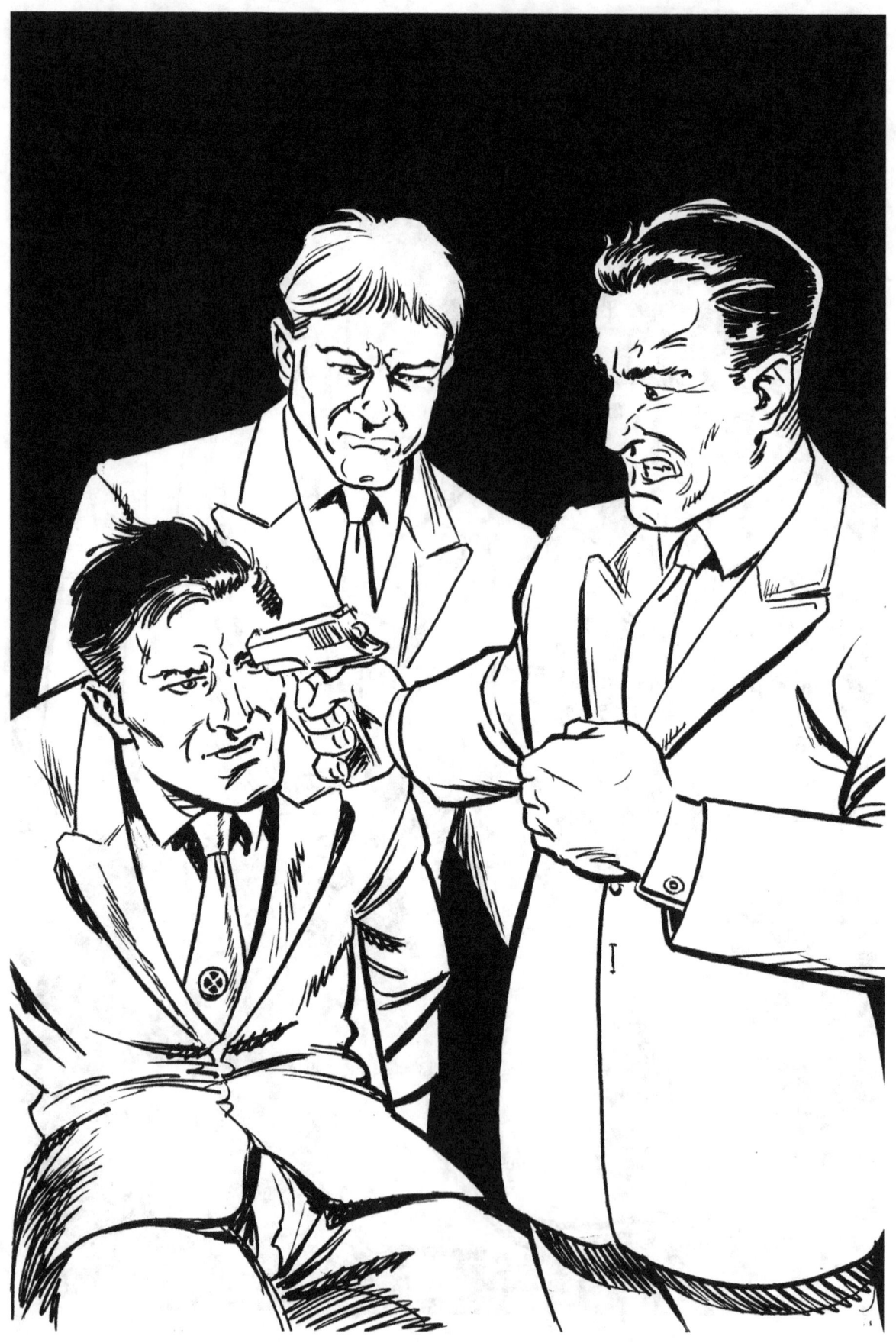

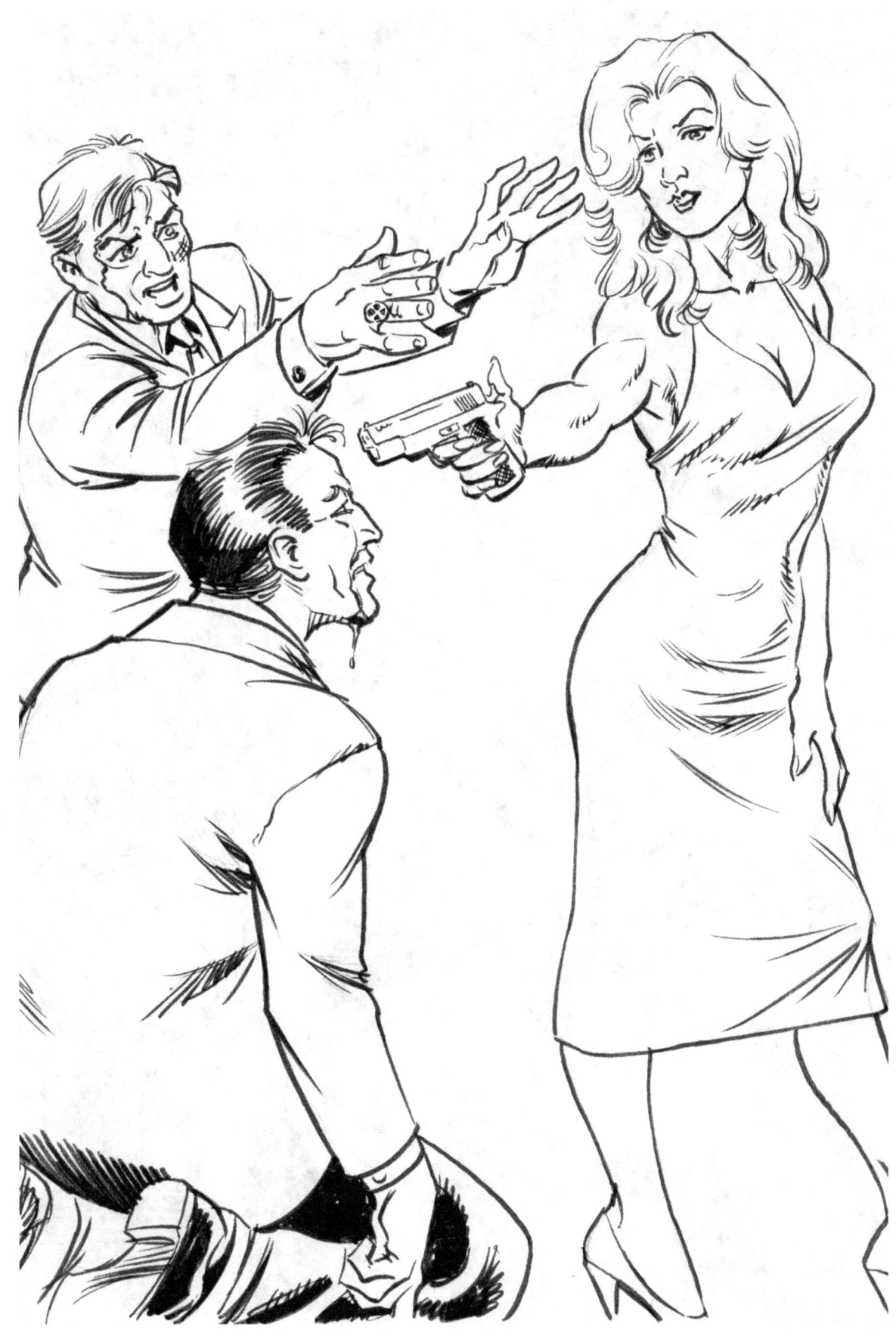

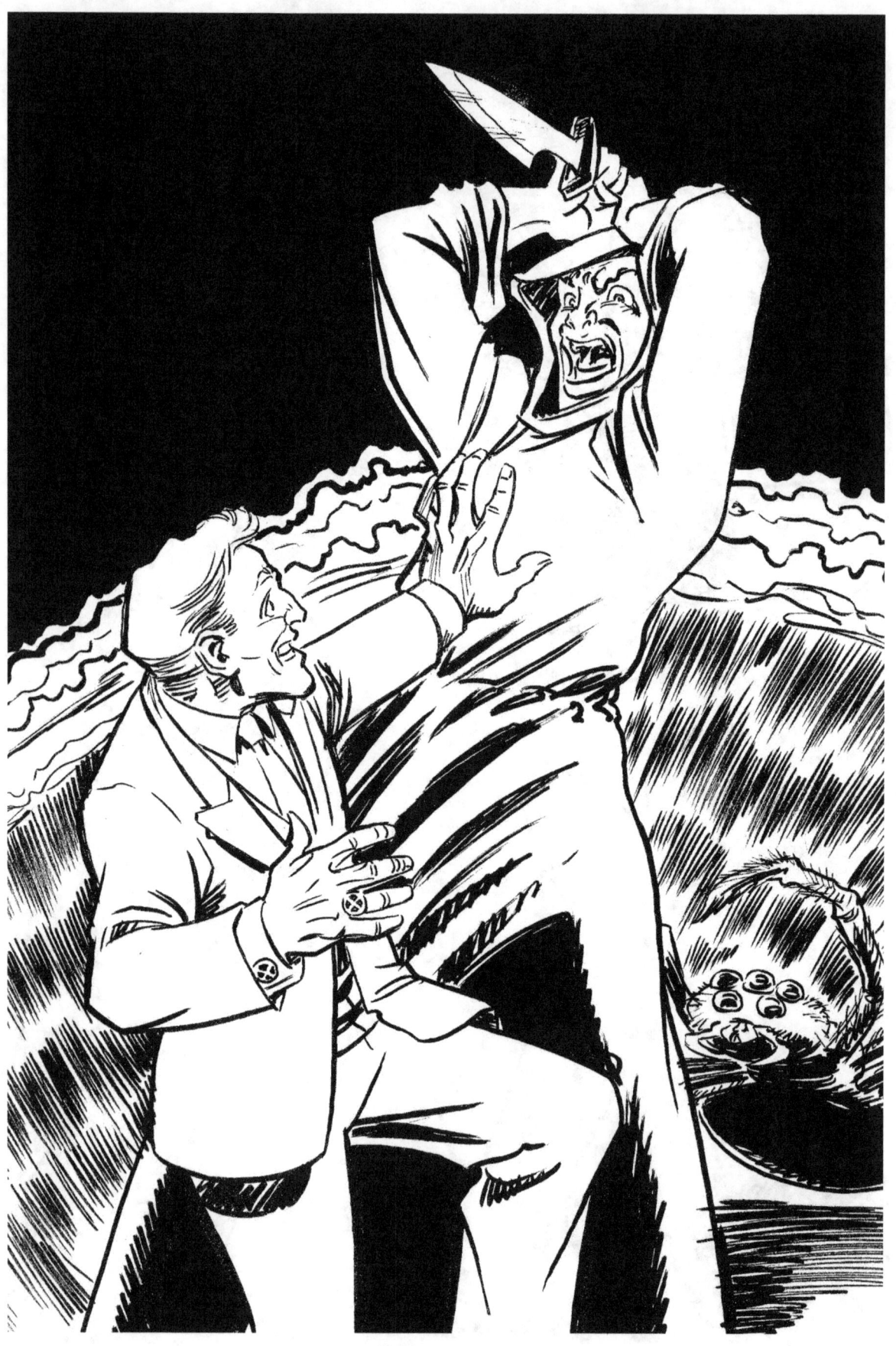

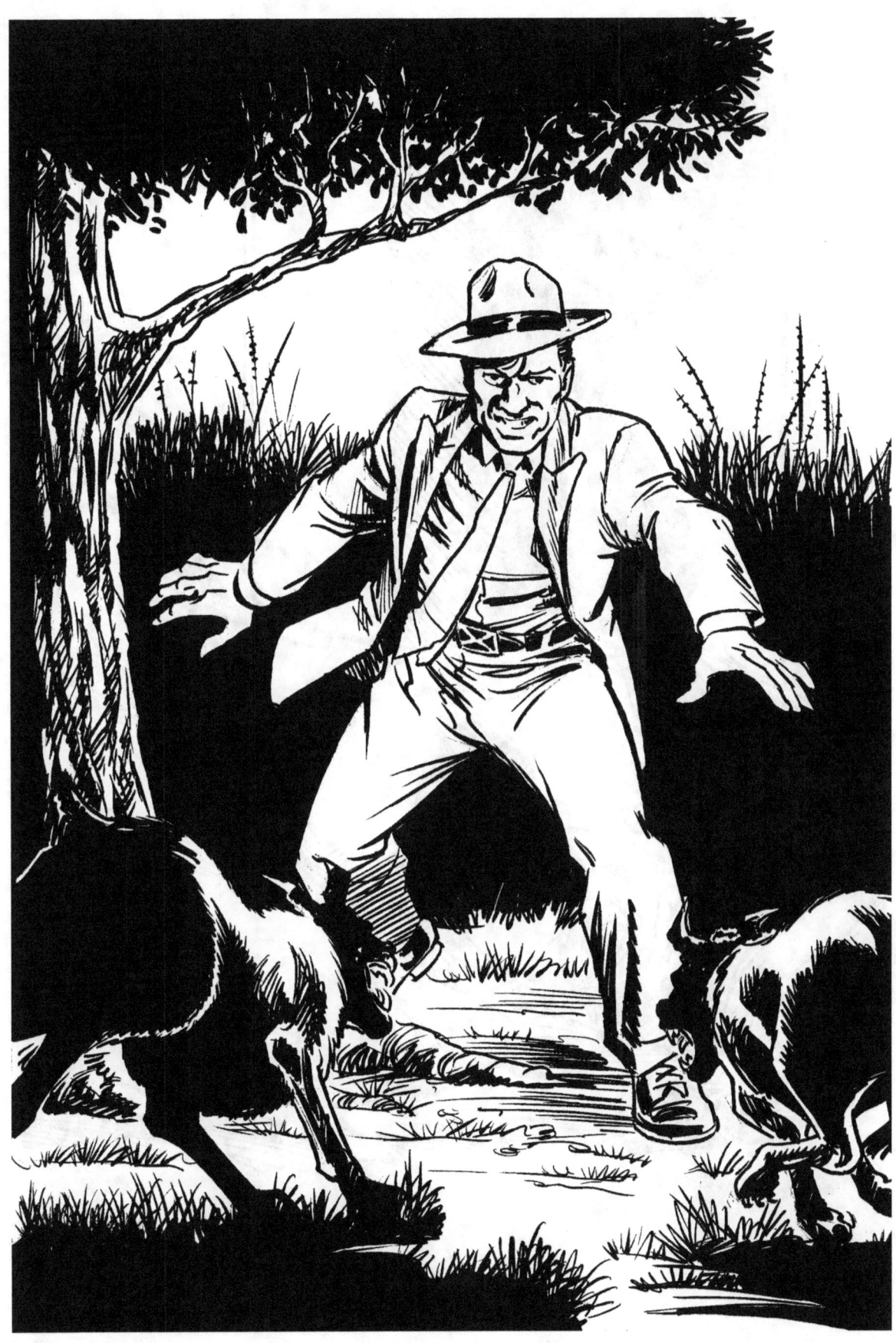

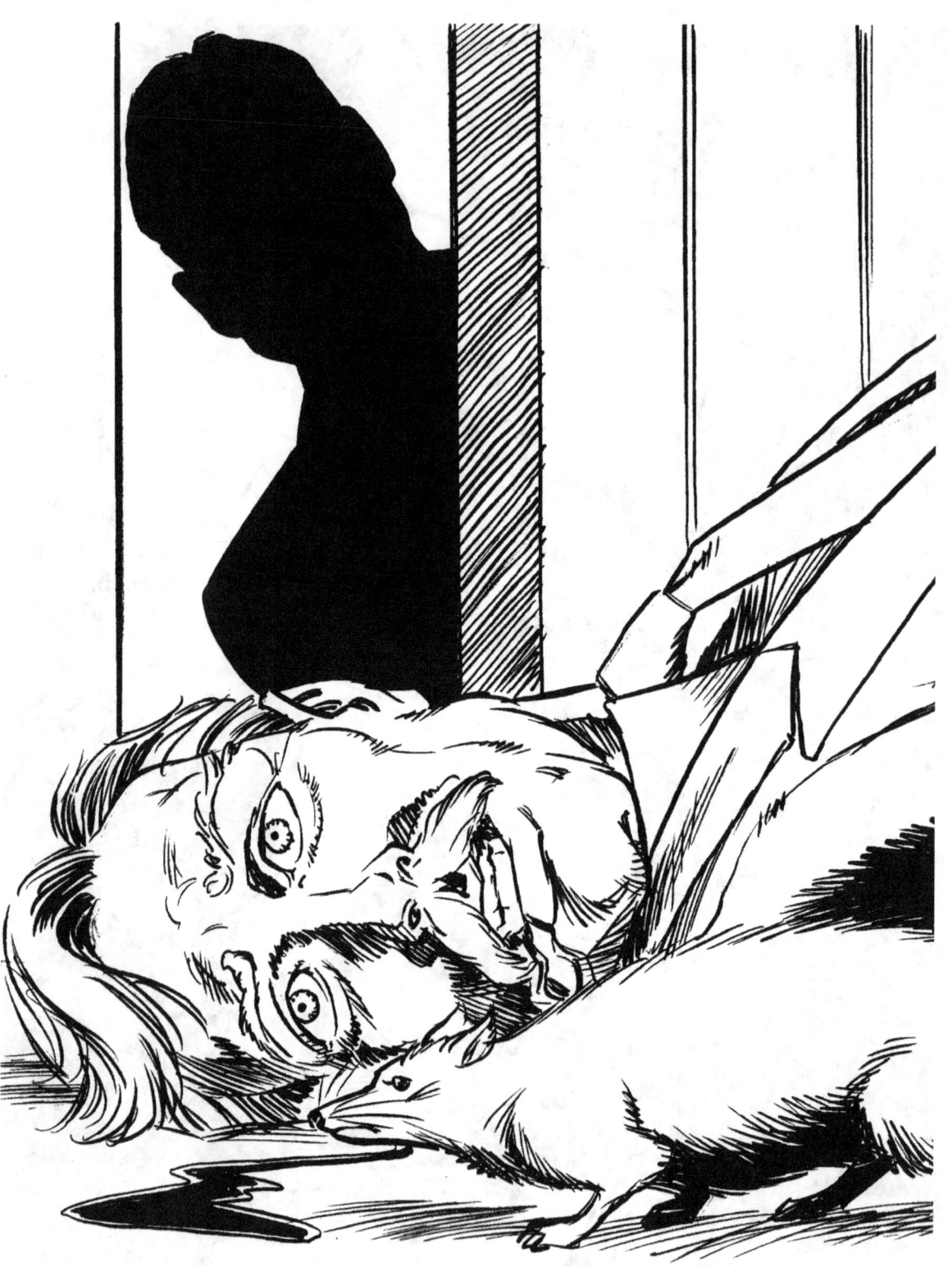

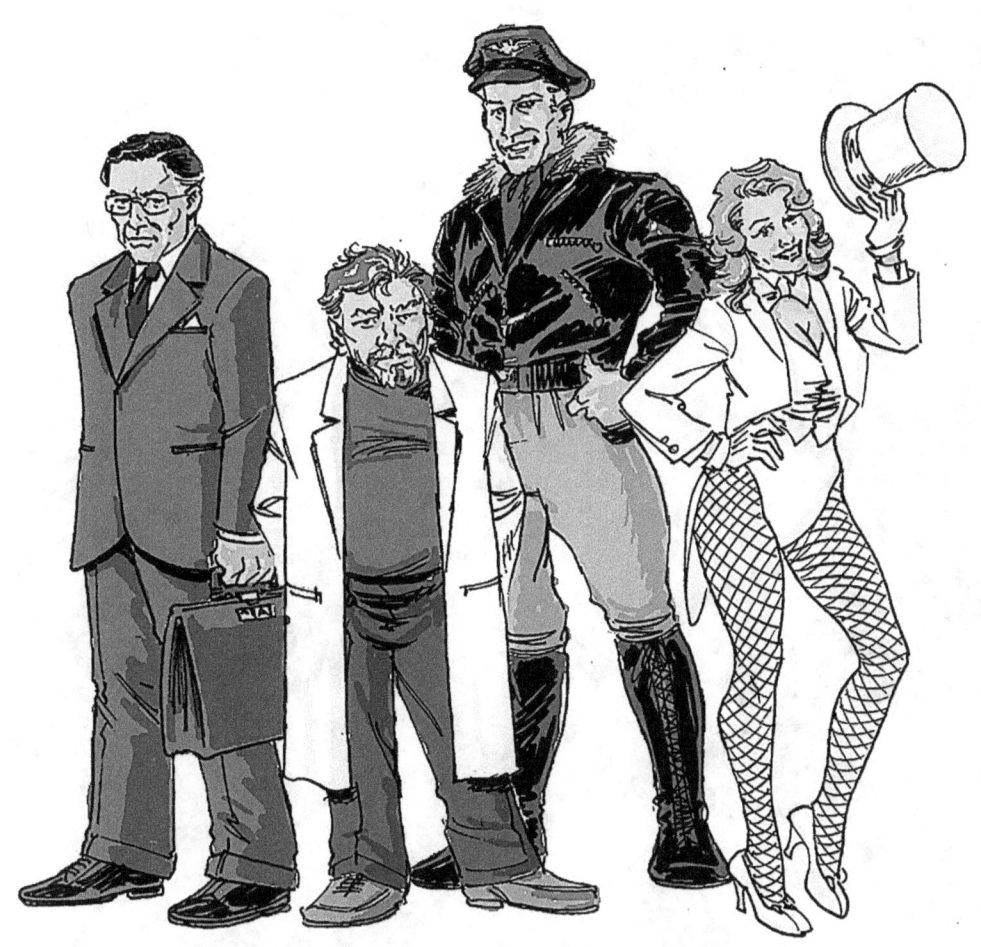

GHOST SQUAD

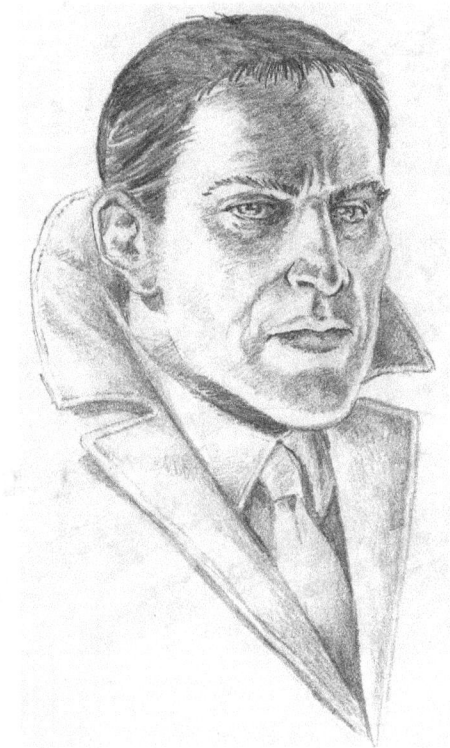

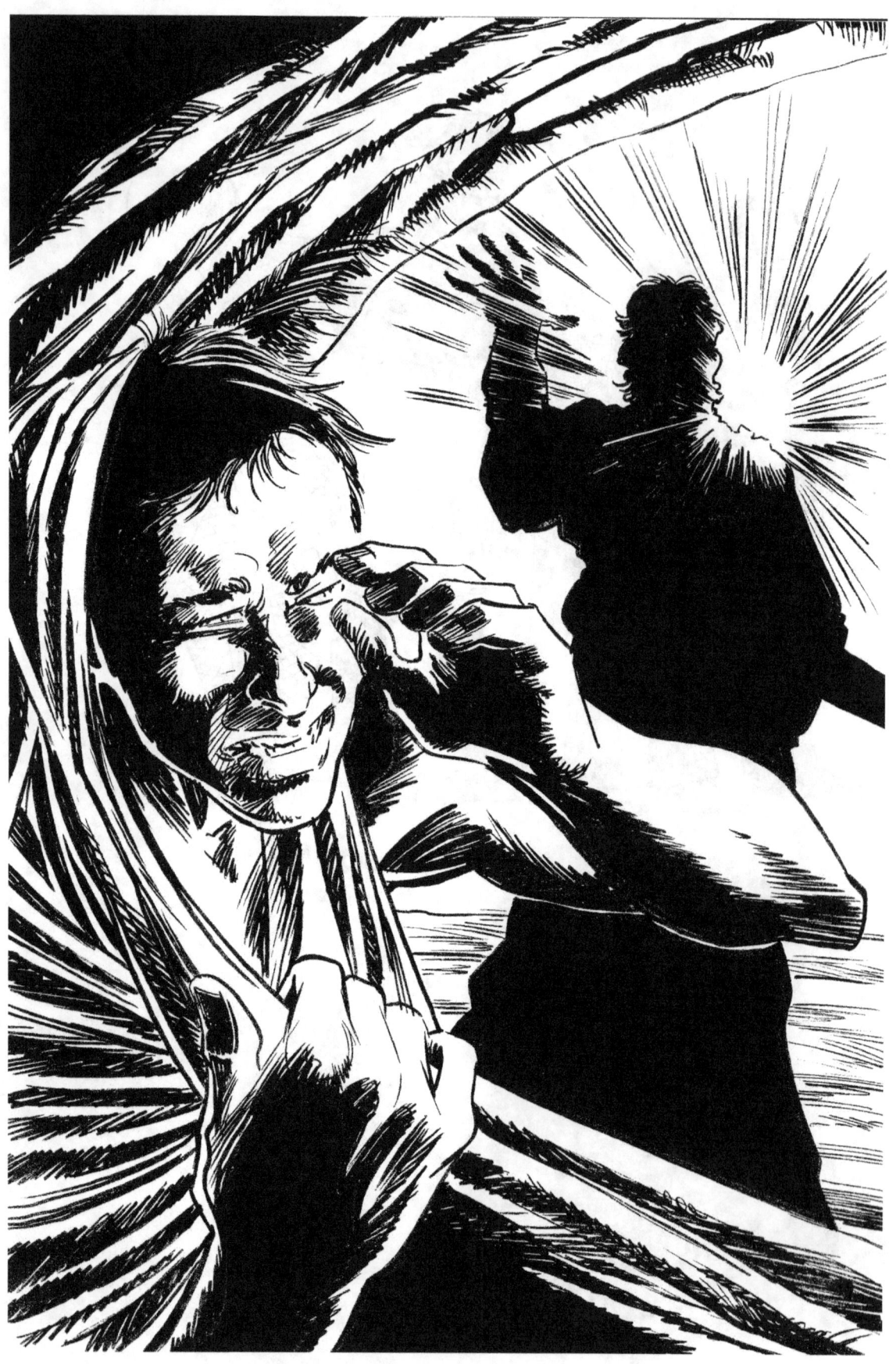

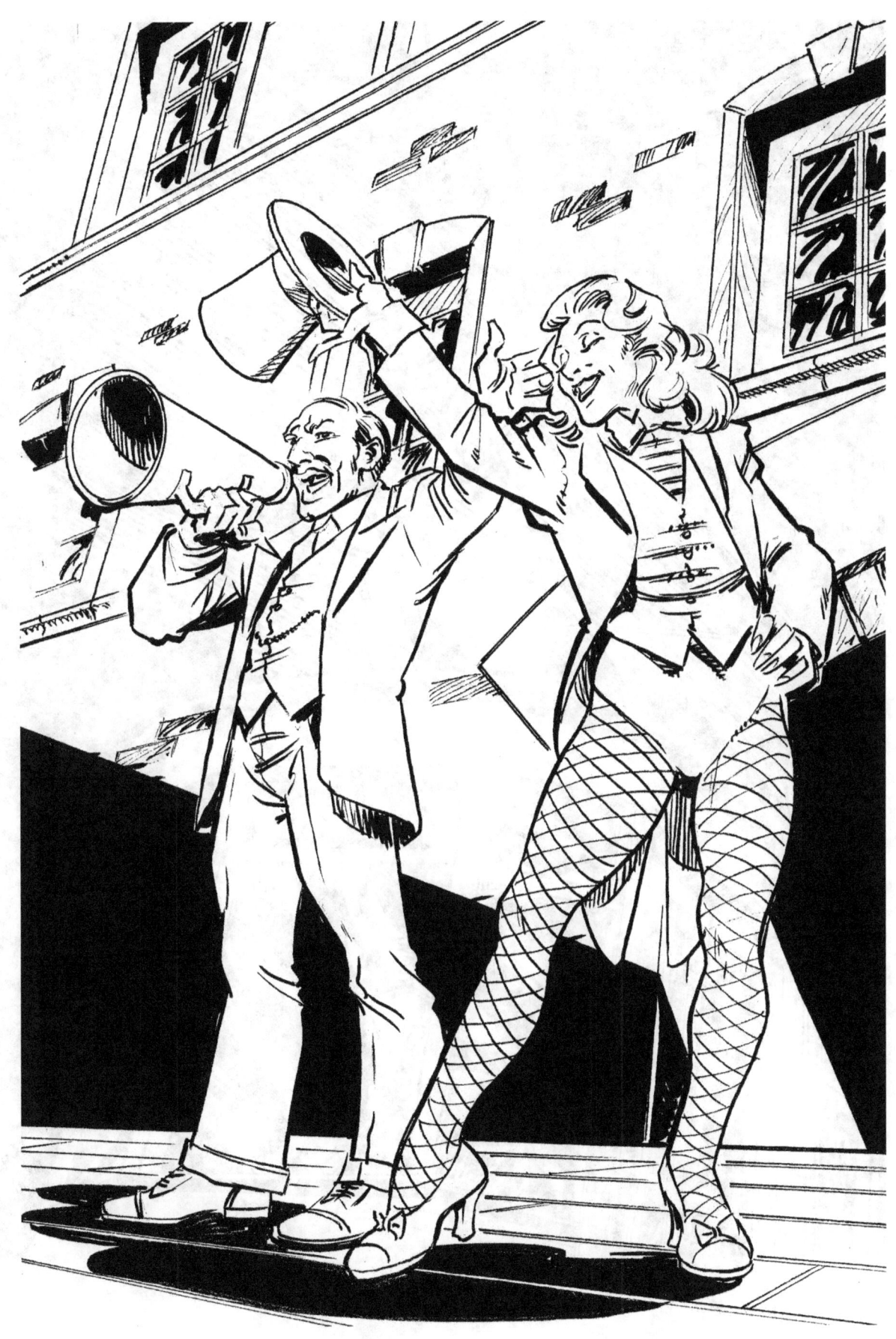

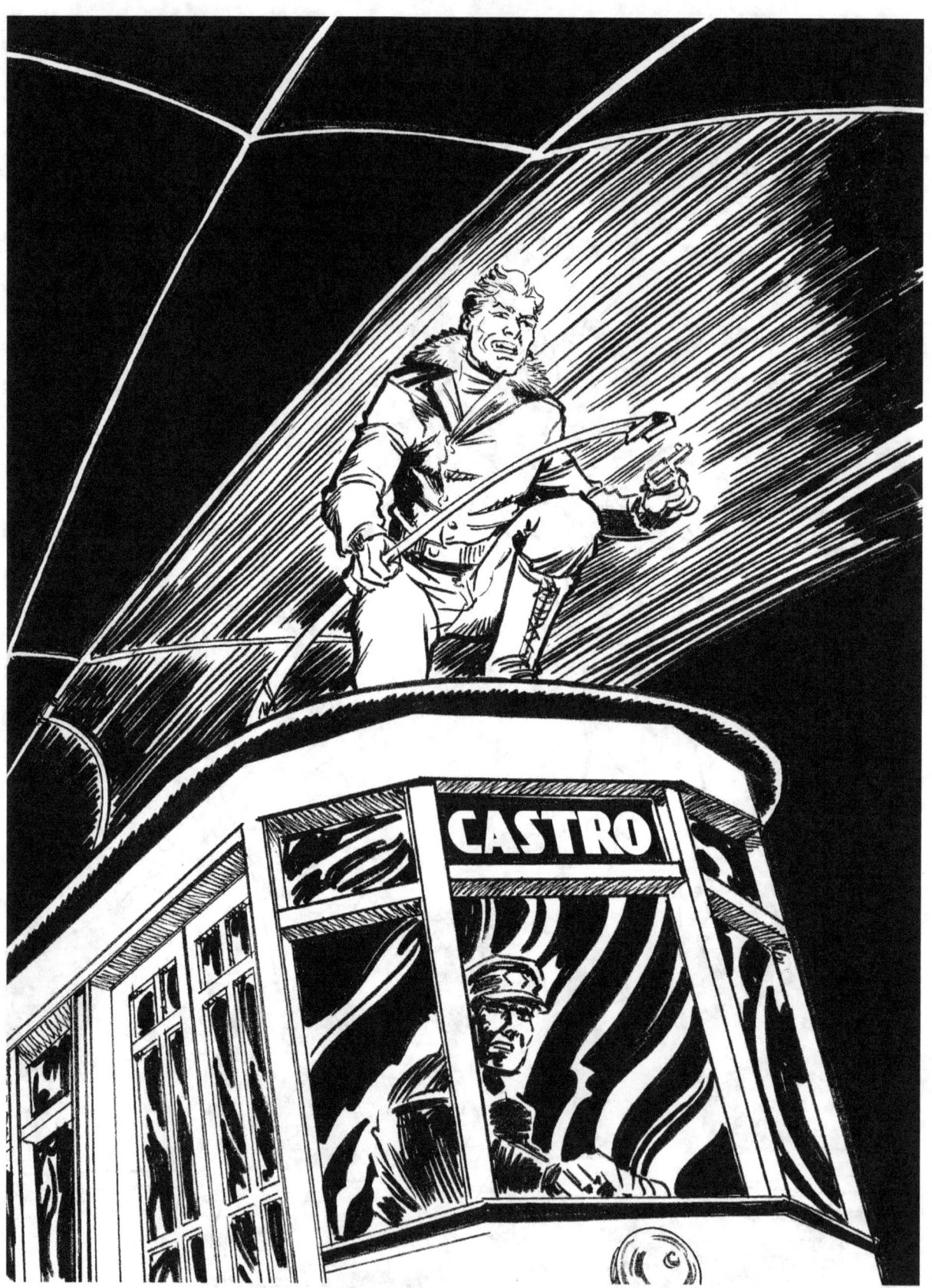

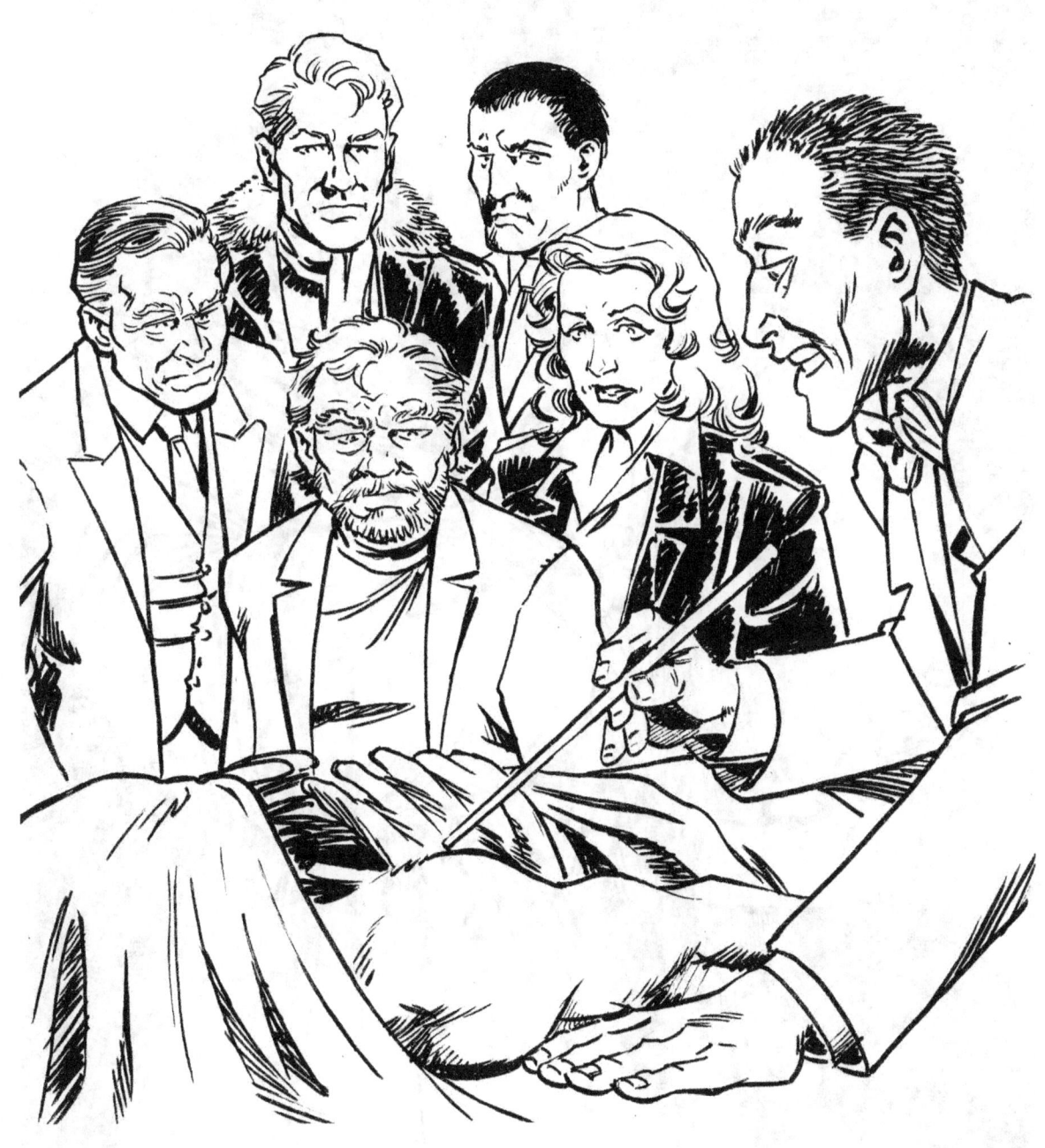

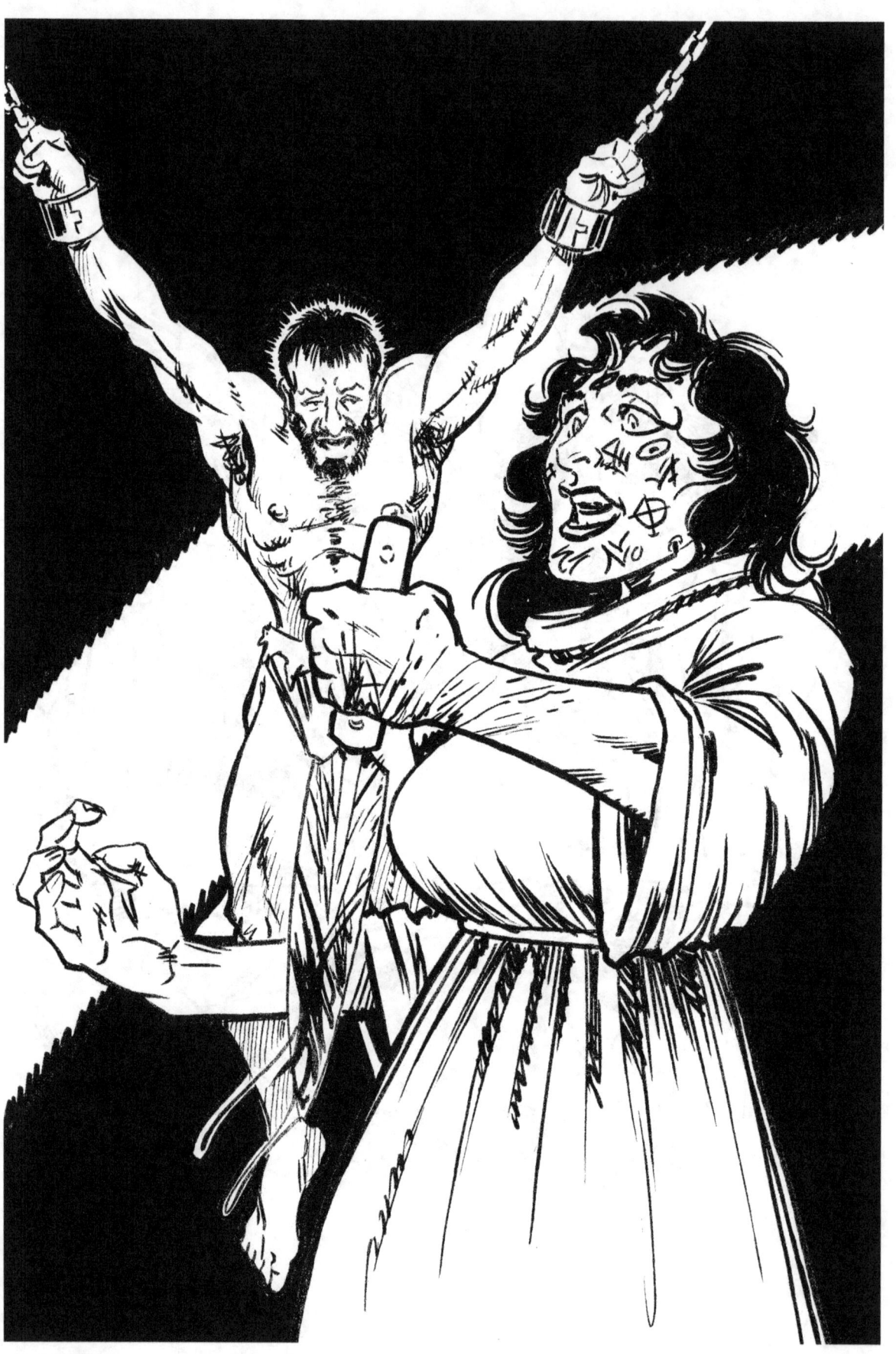

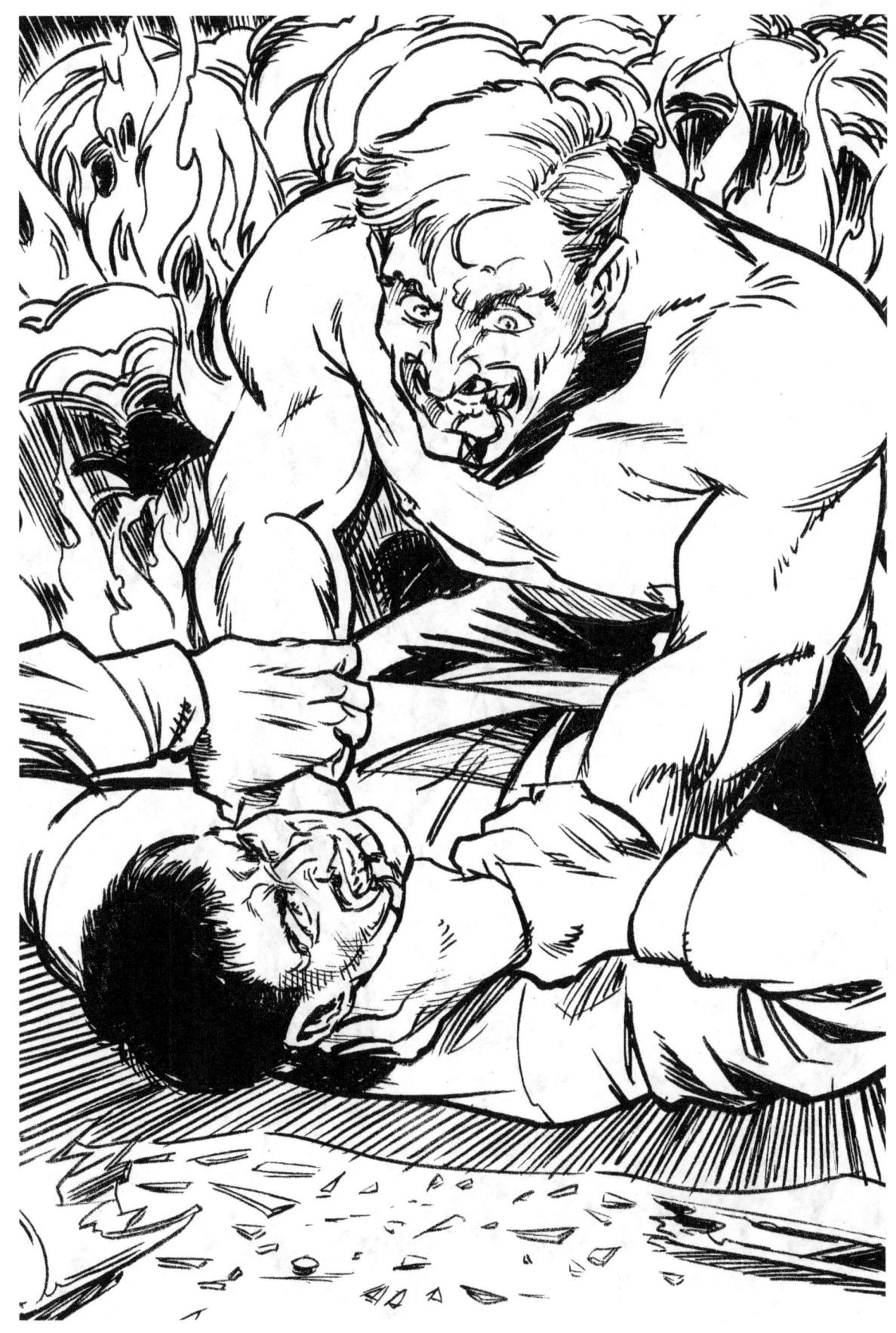

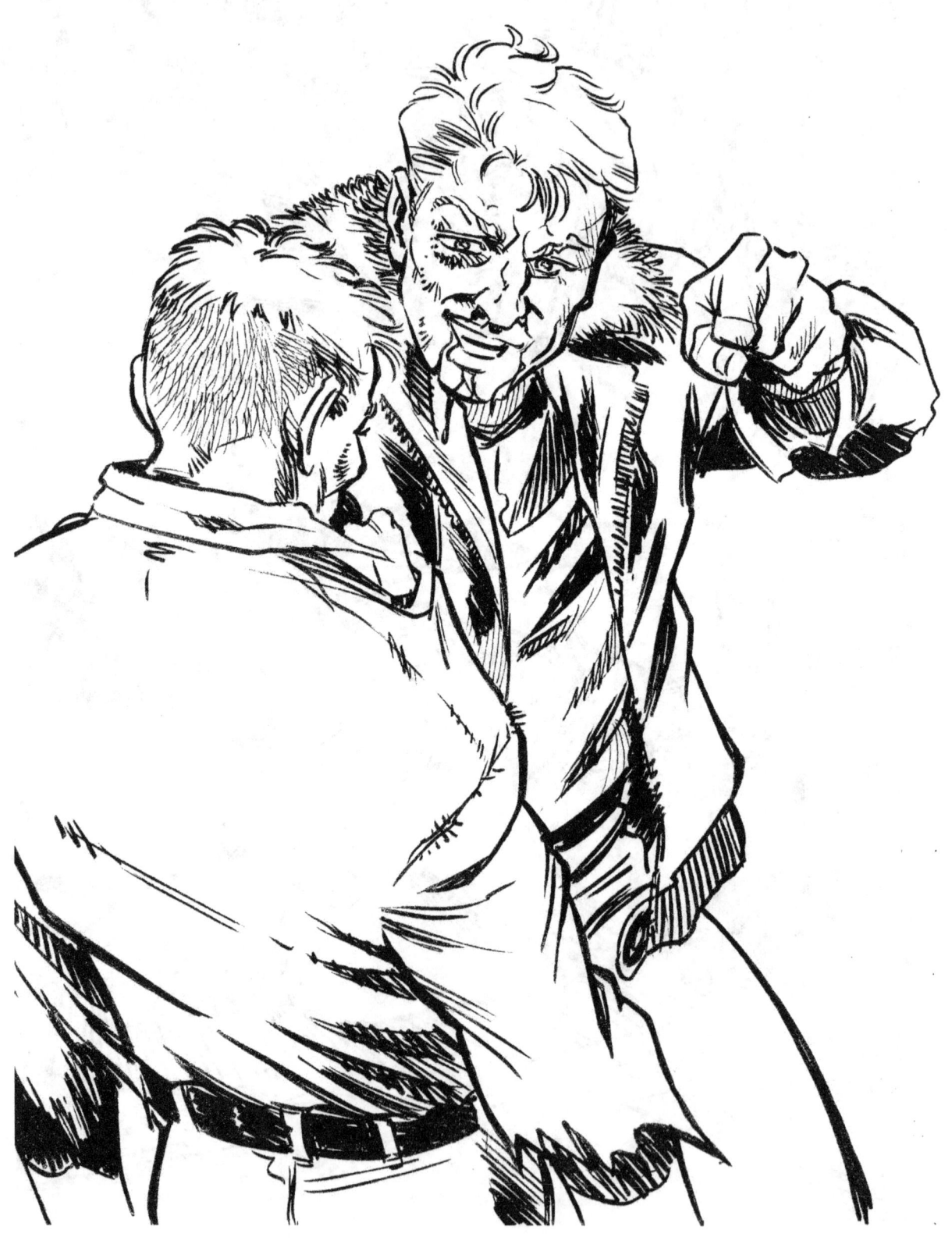

CHAPTER 4
THE RETURN OF
ROBIN HOOD

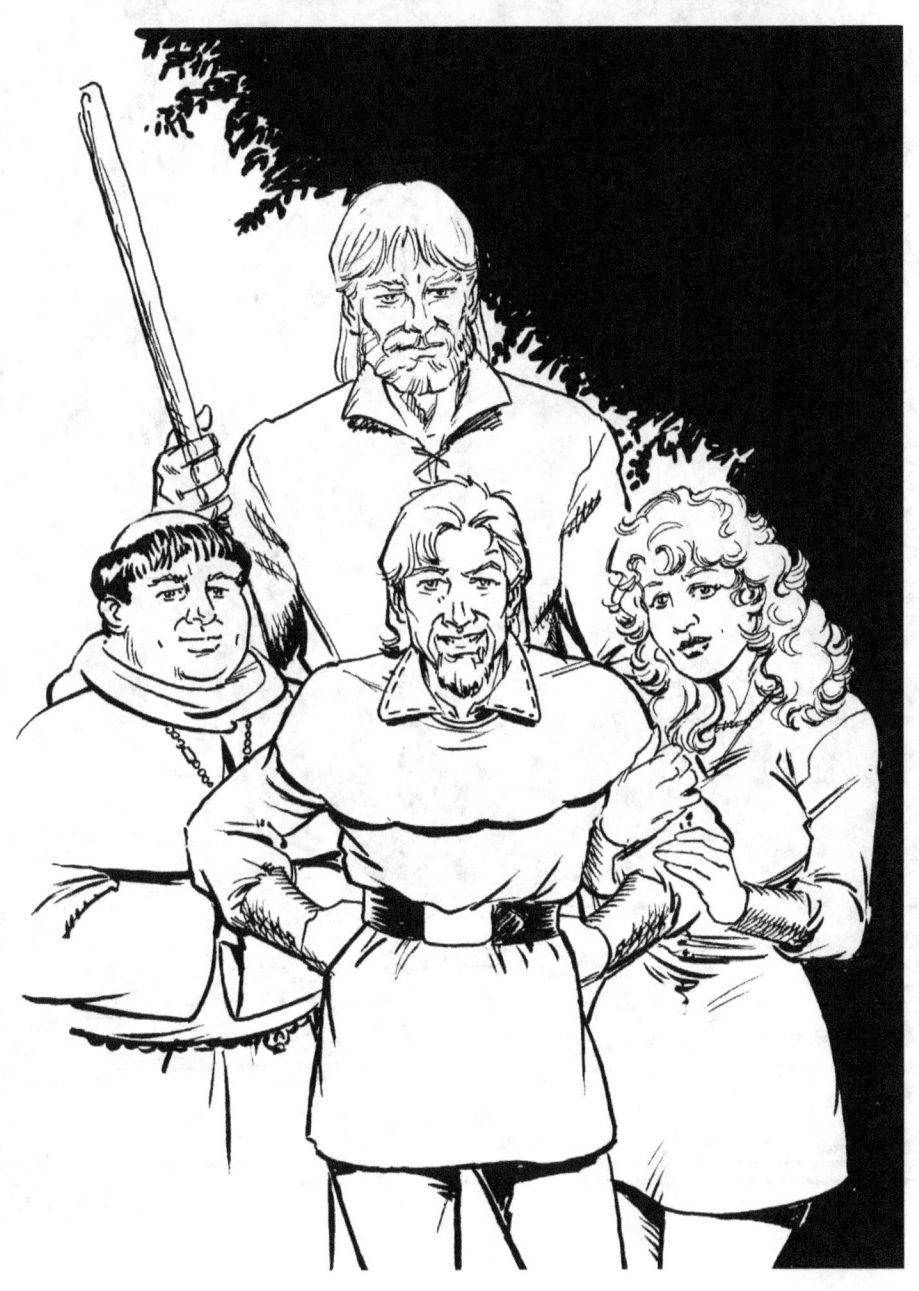

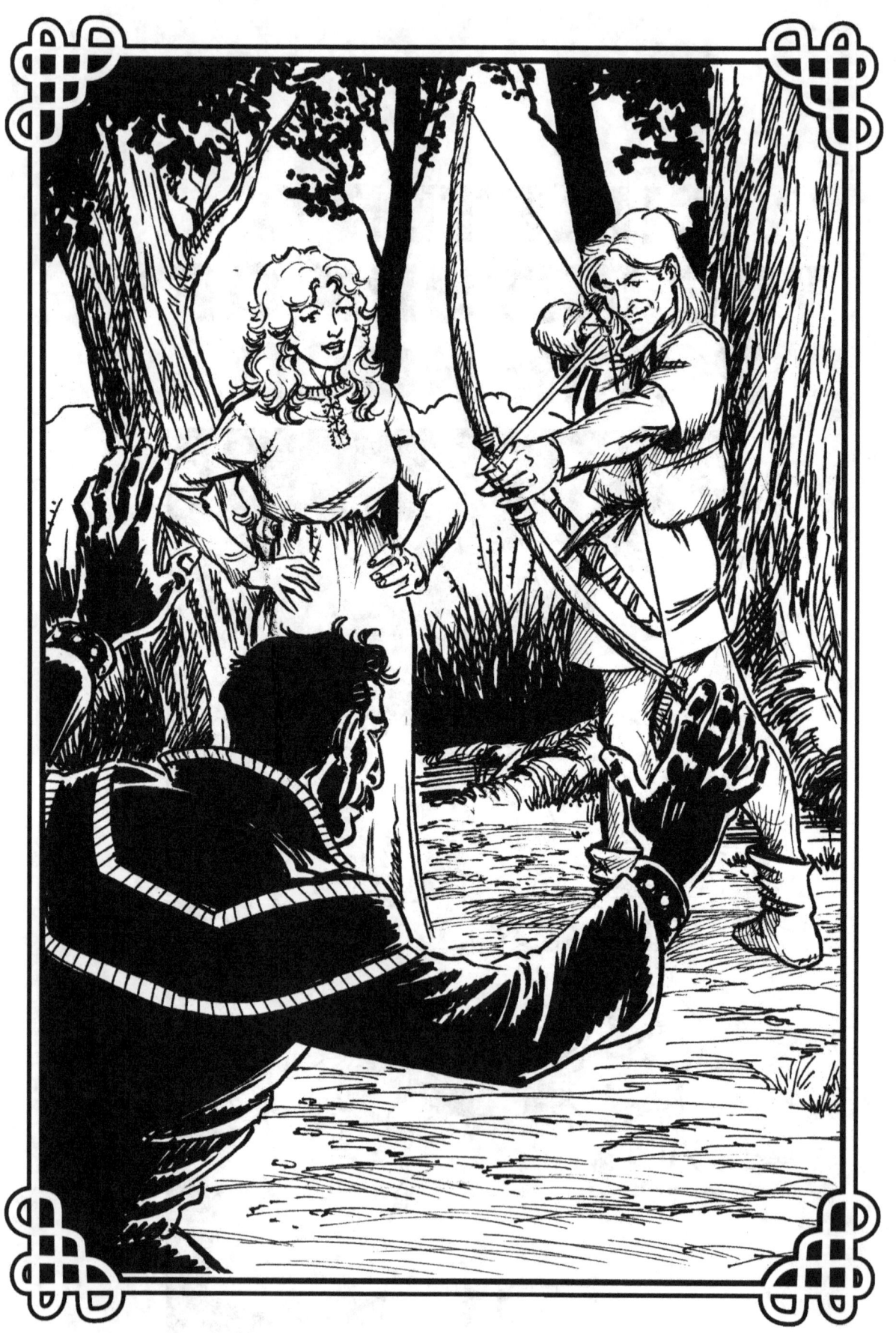

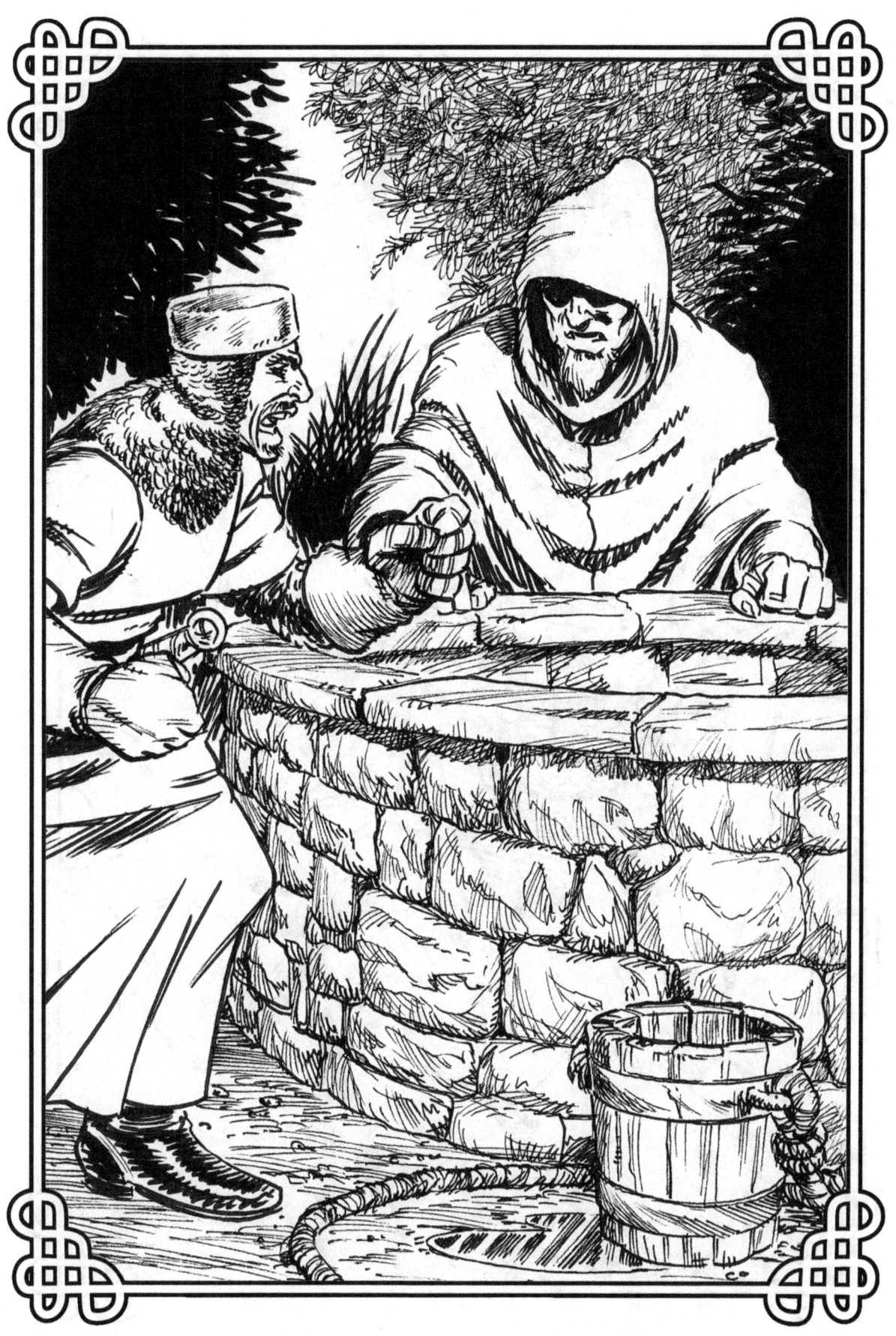

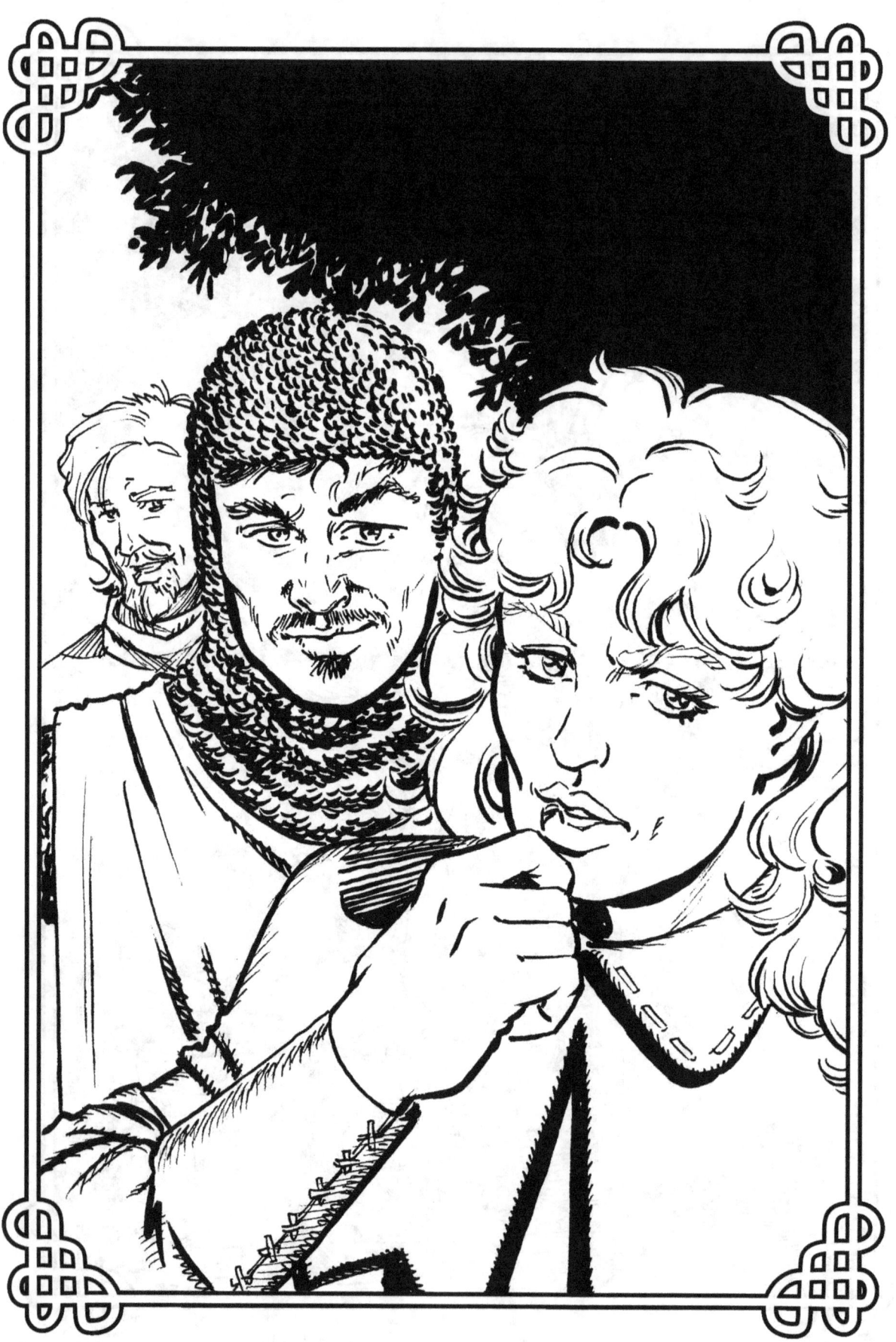

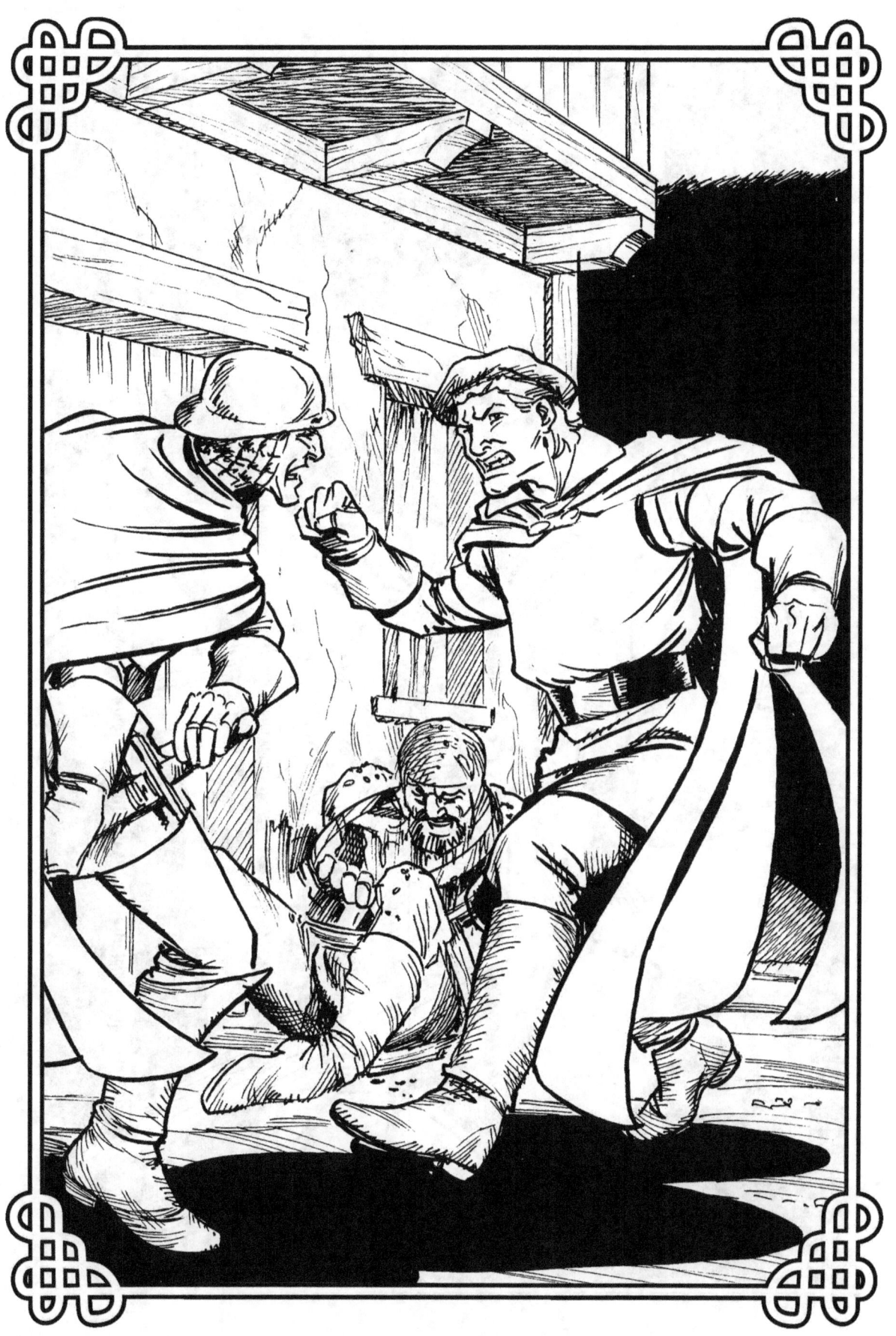

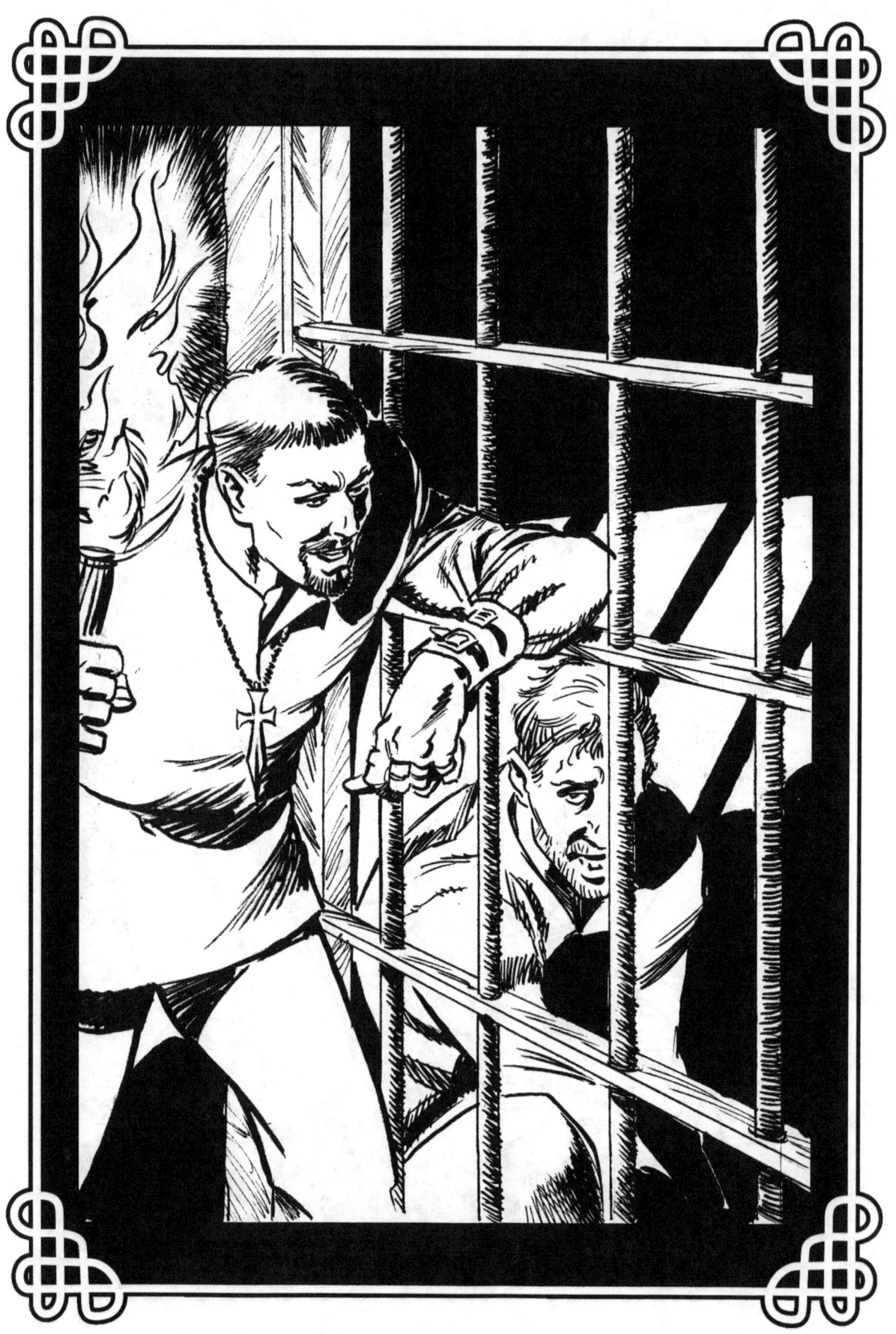

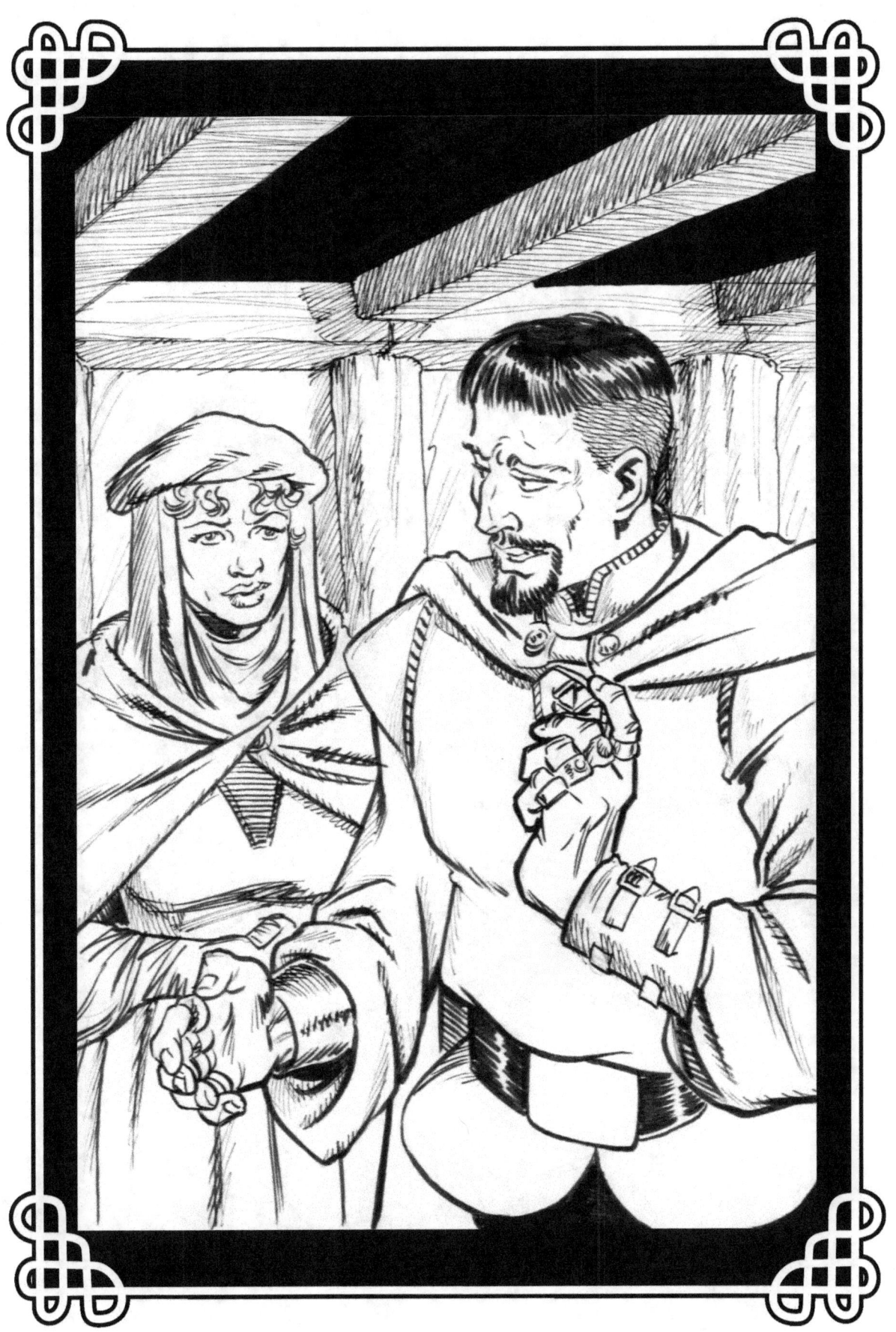

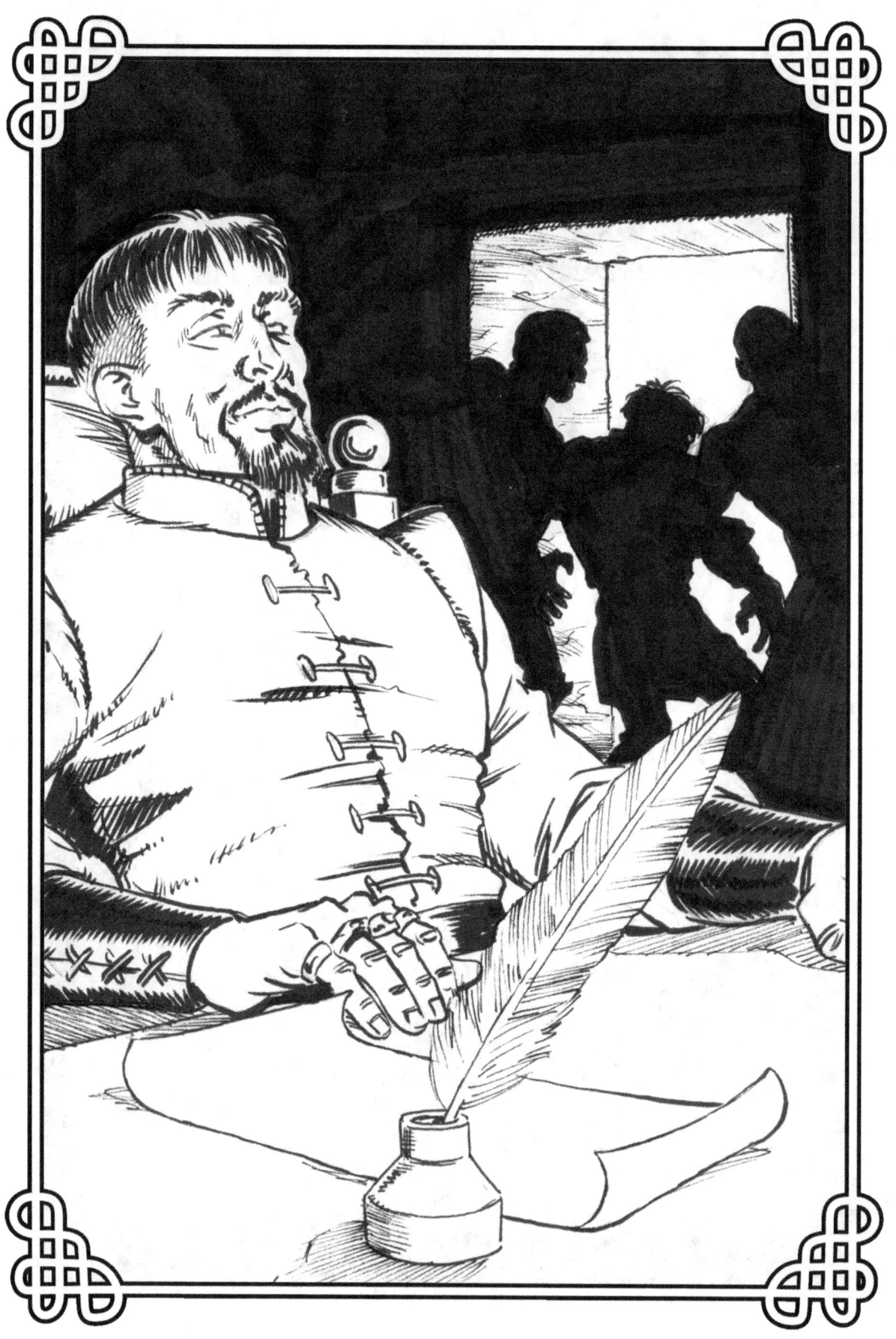

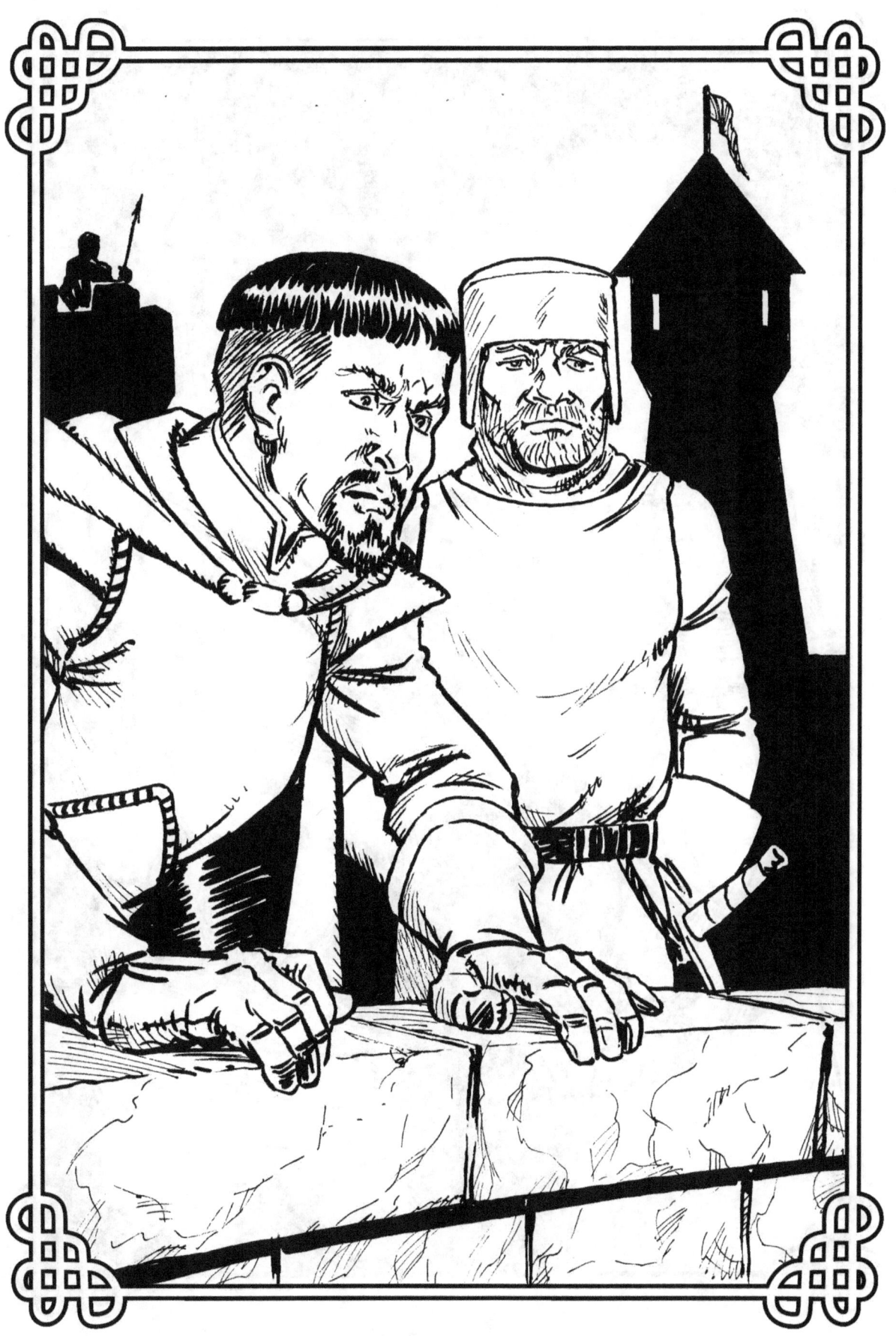

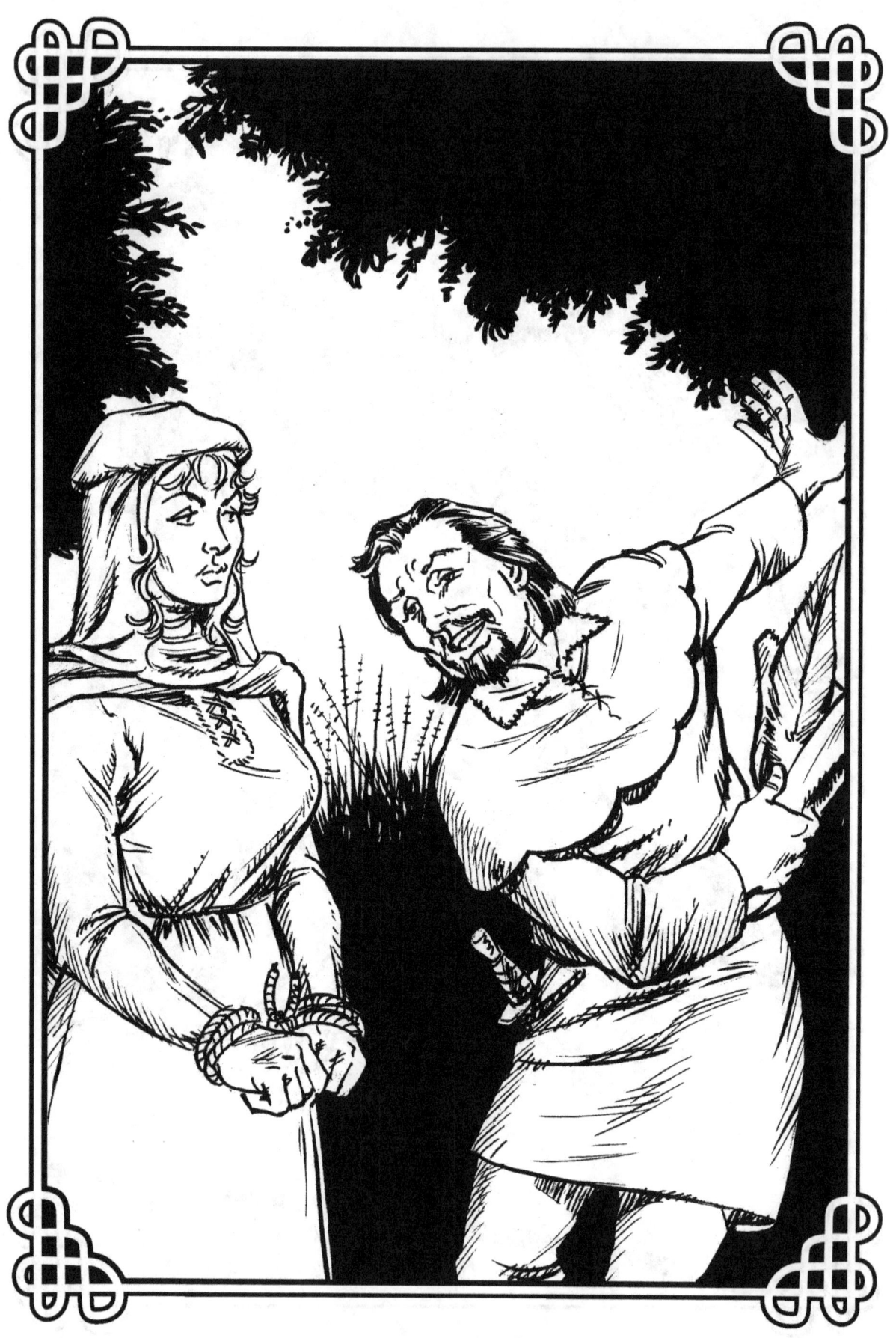

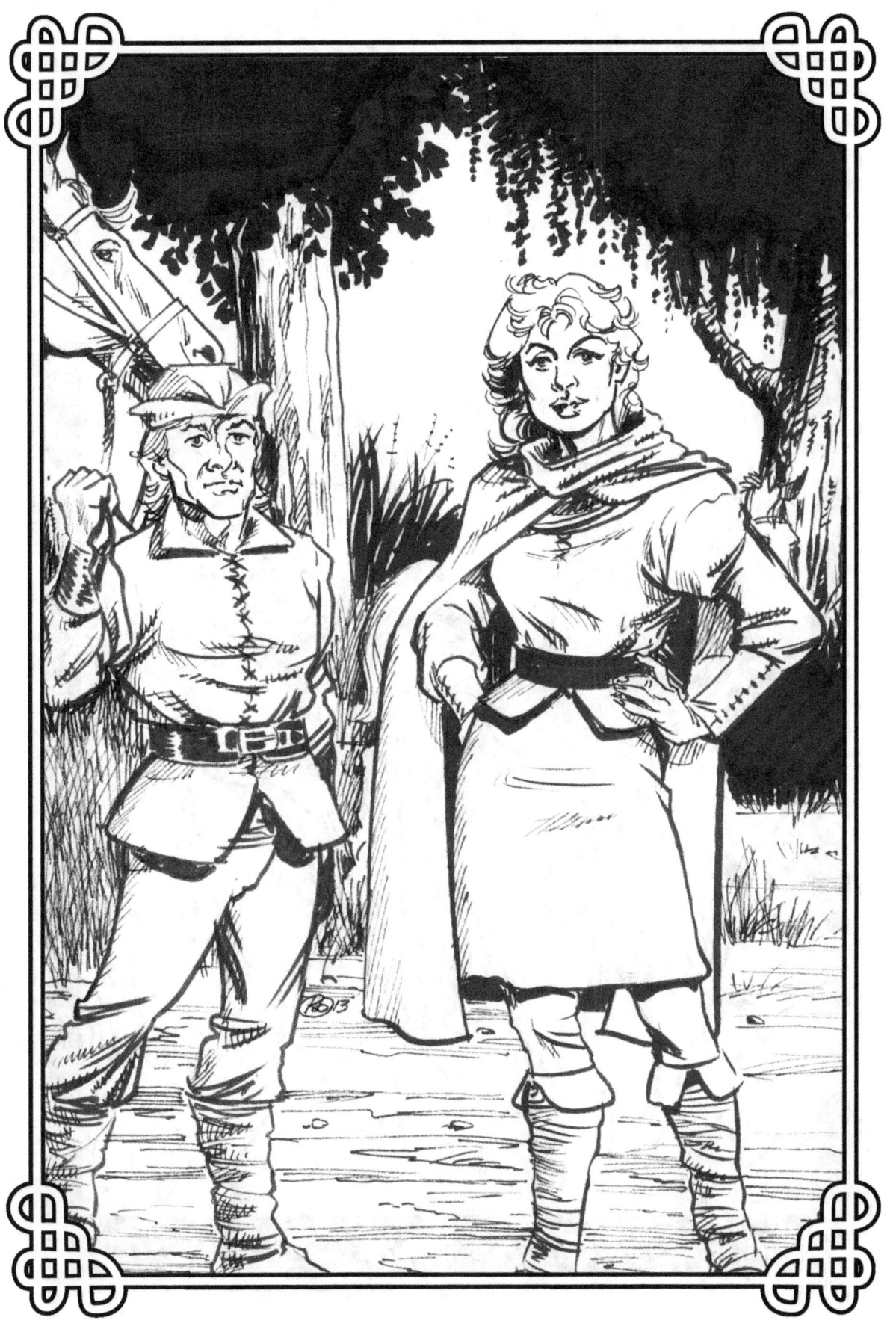

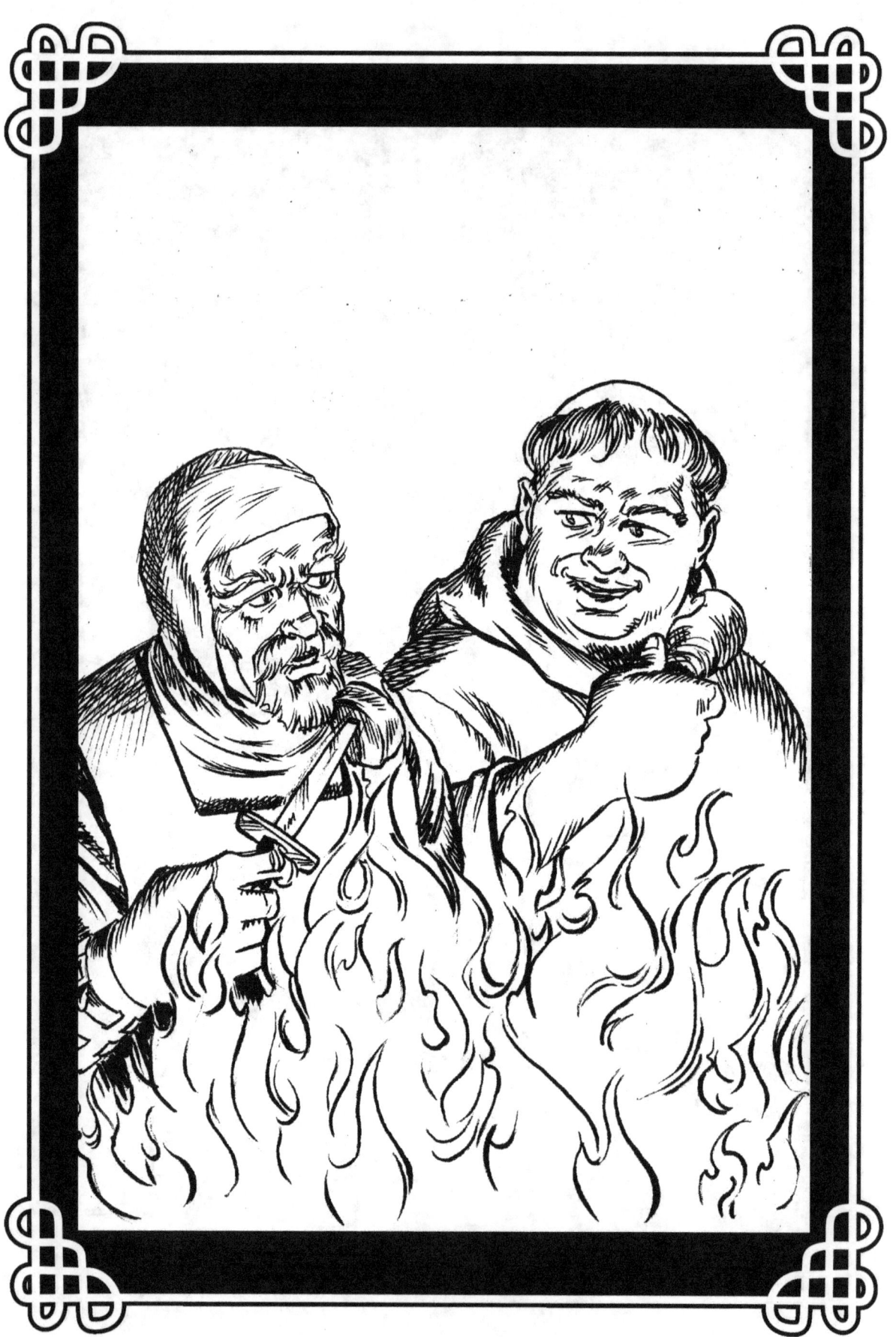

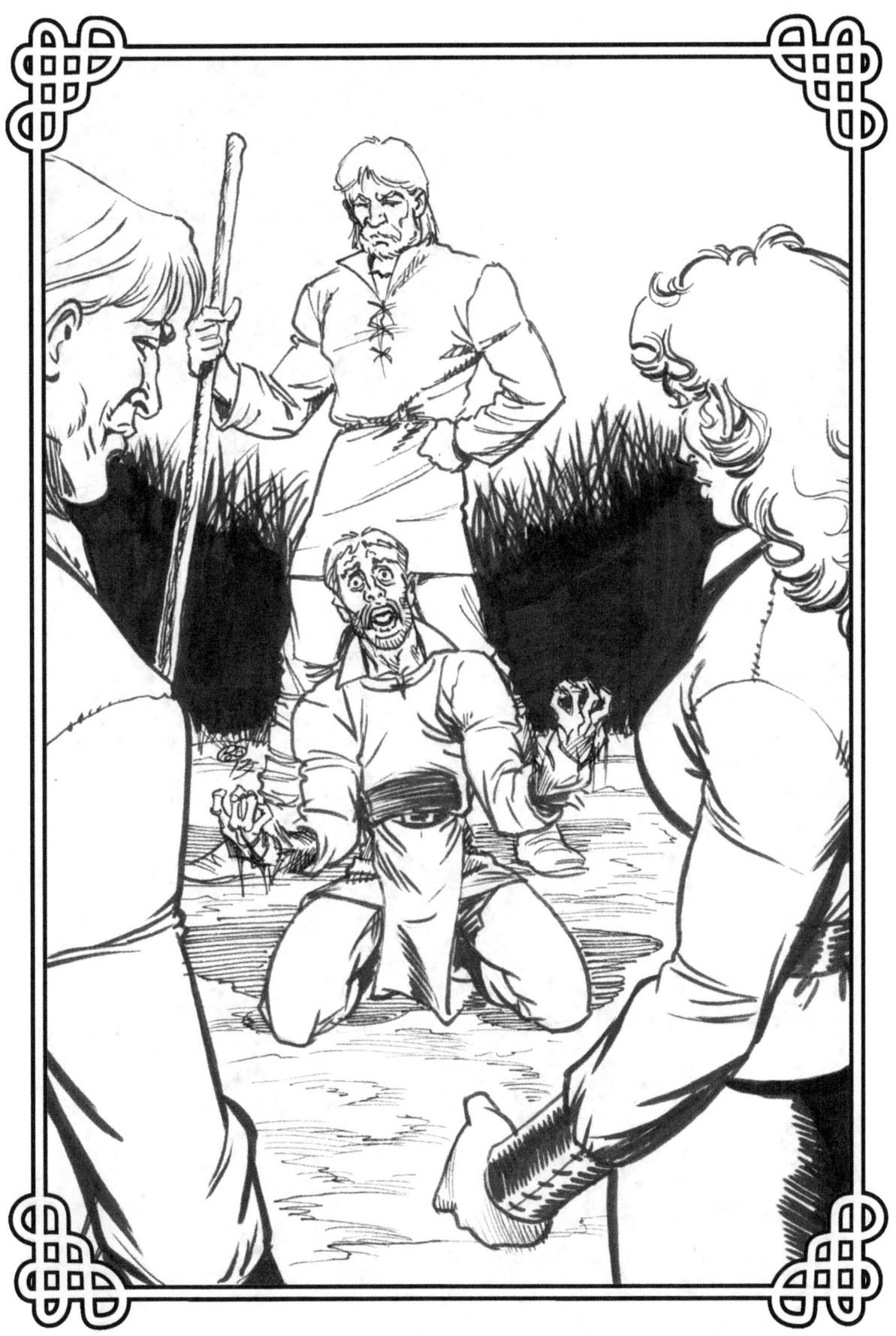

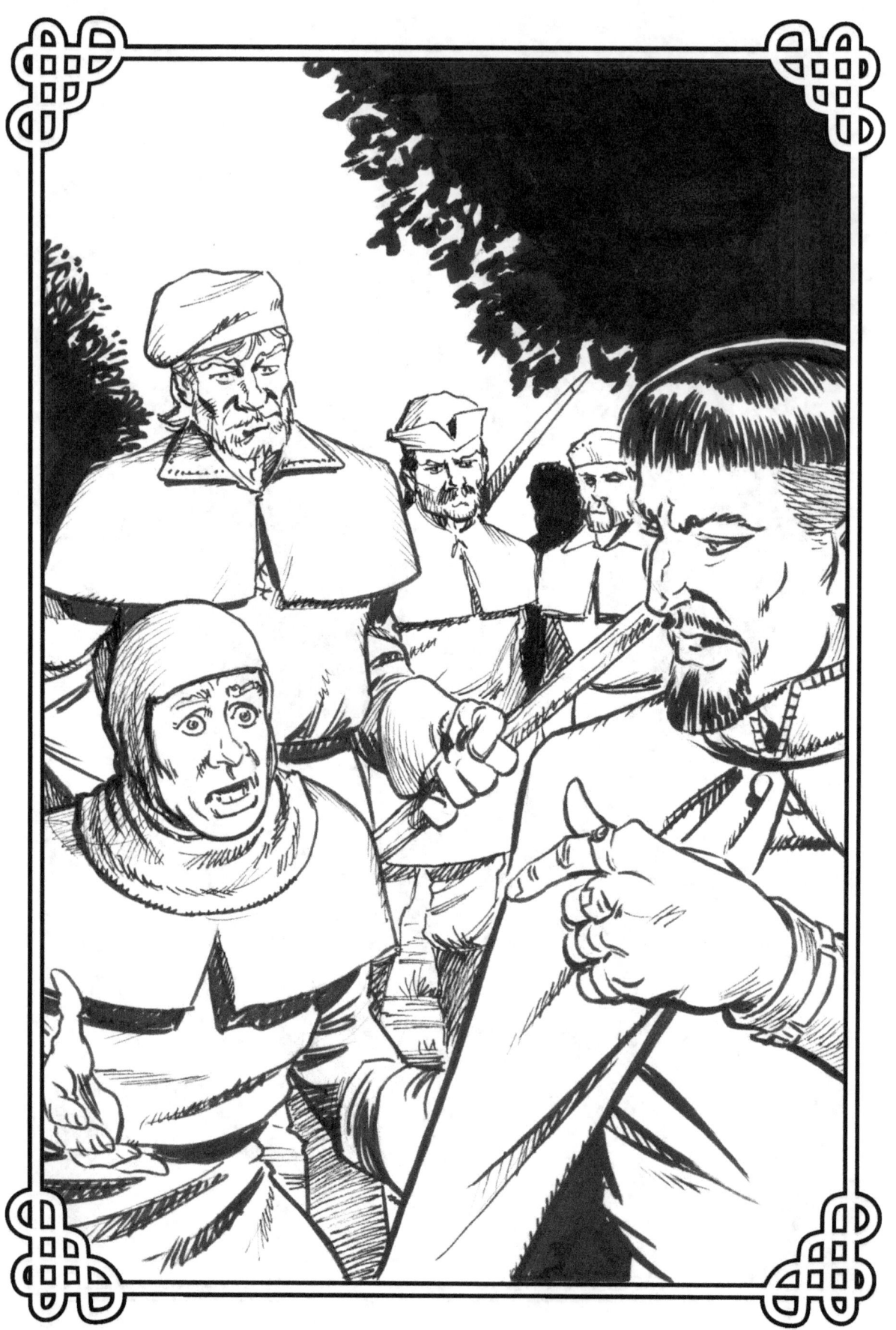

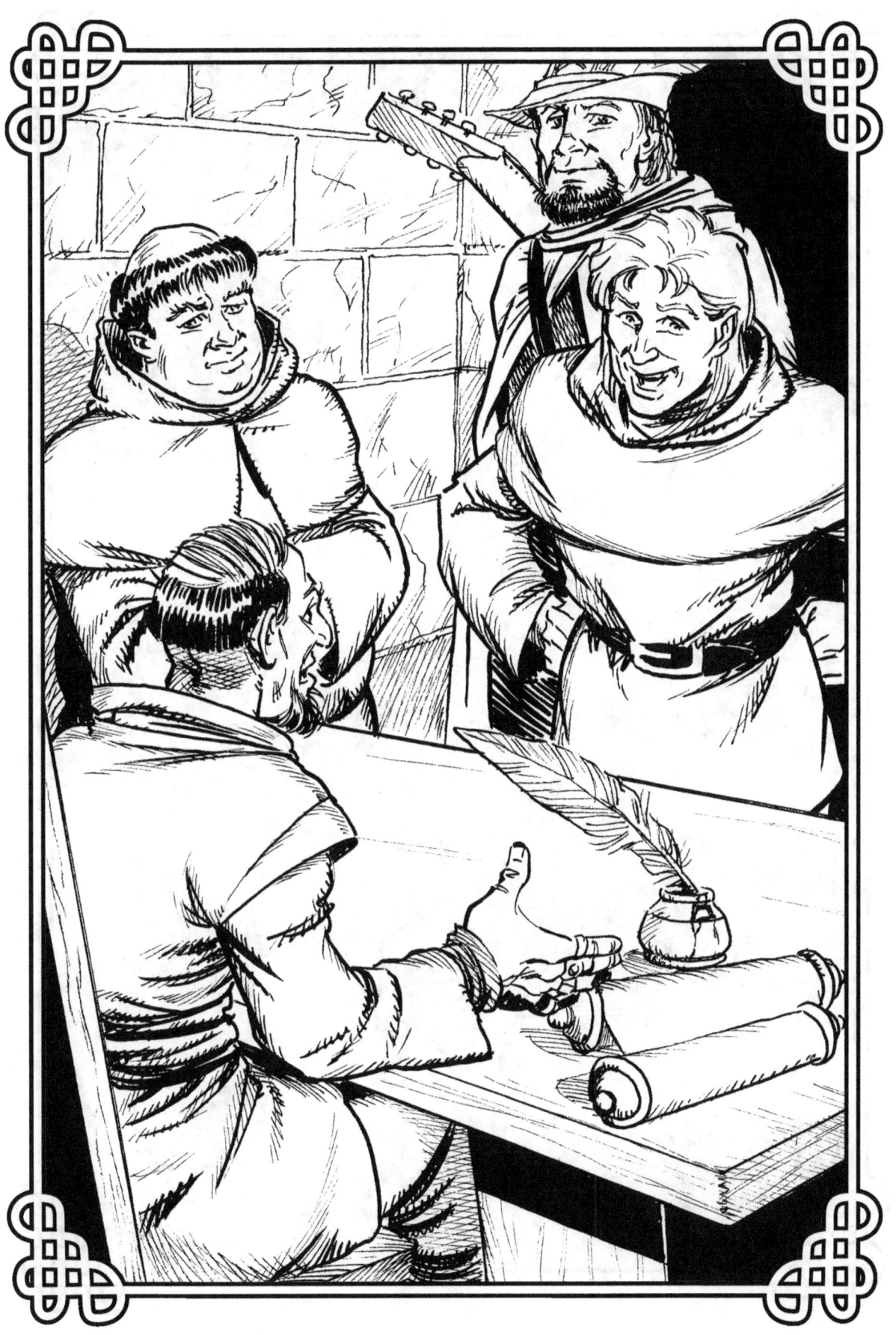

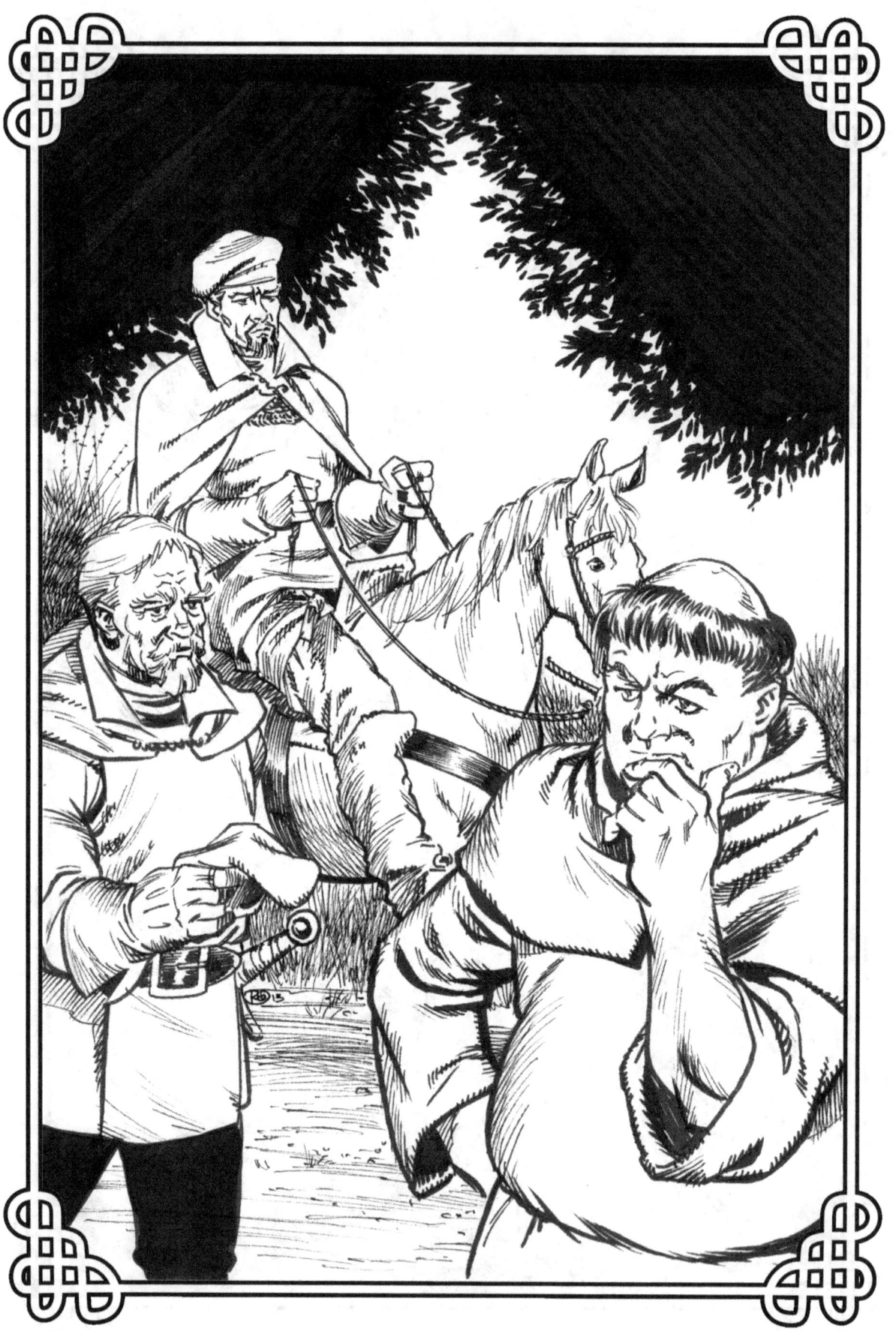

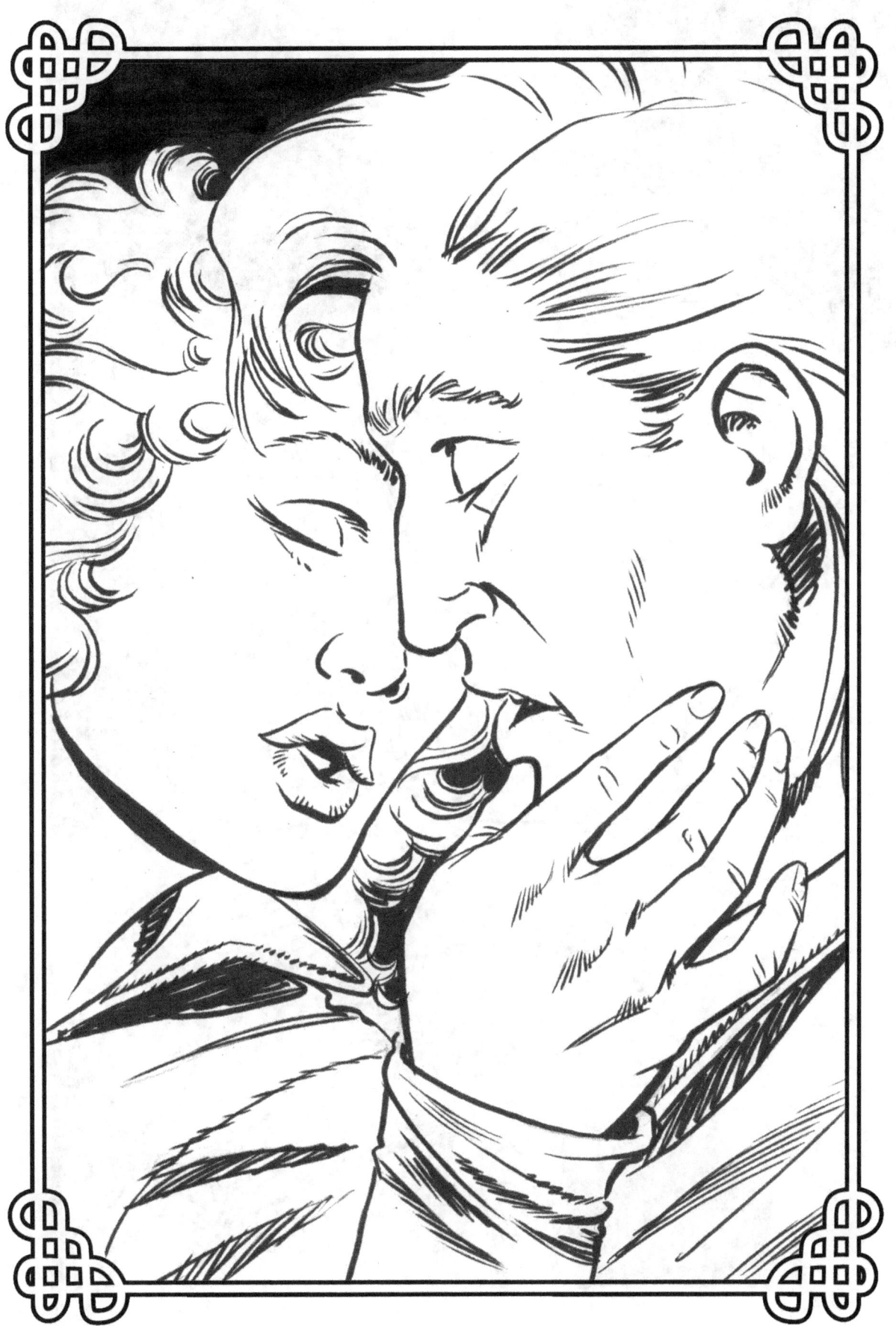

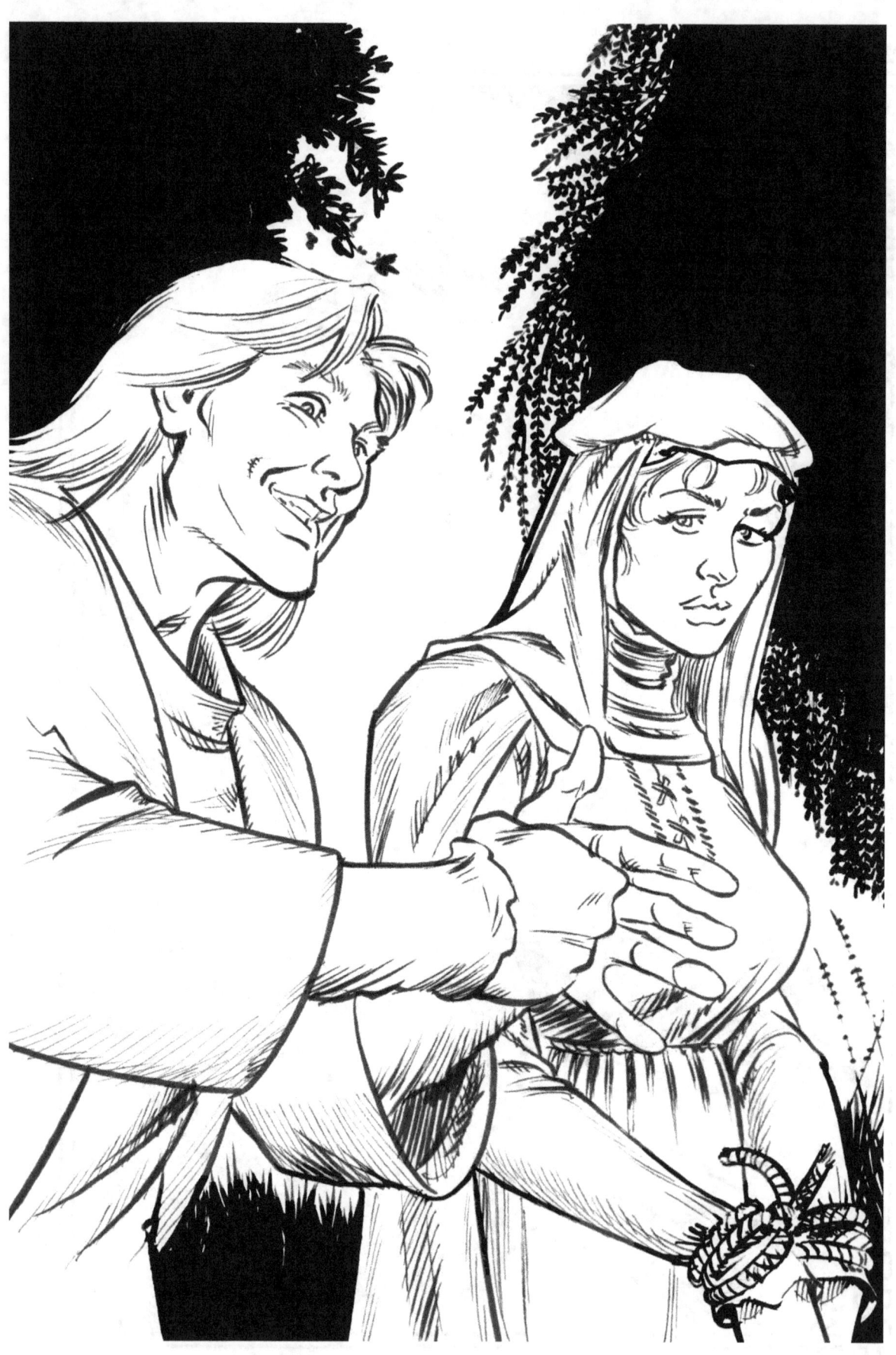

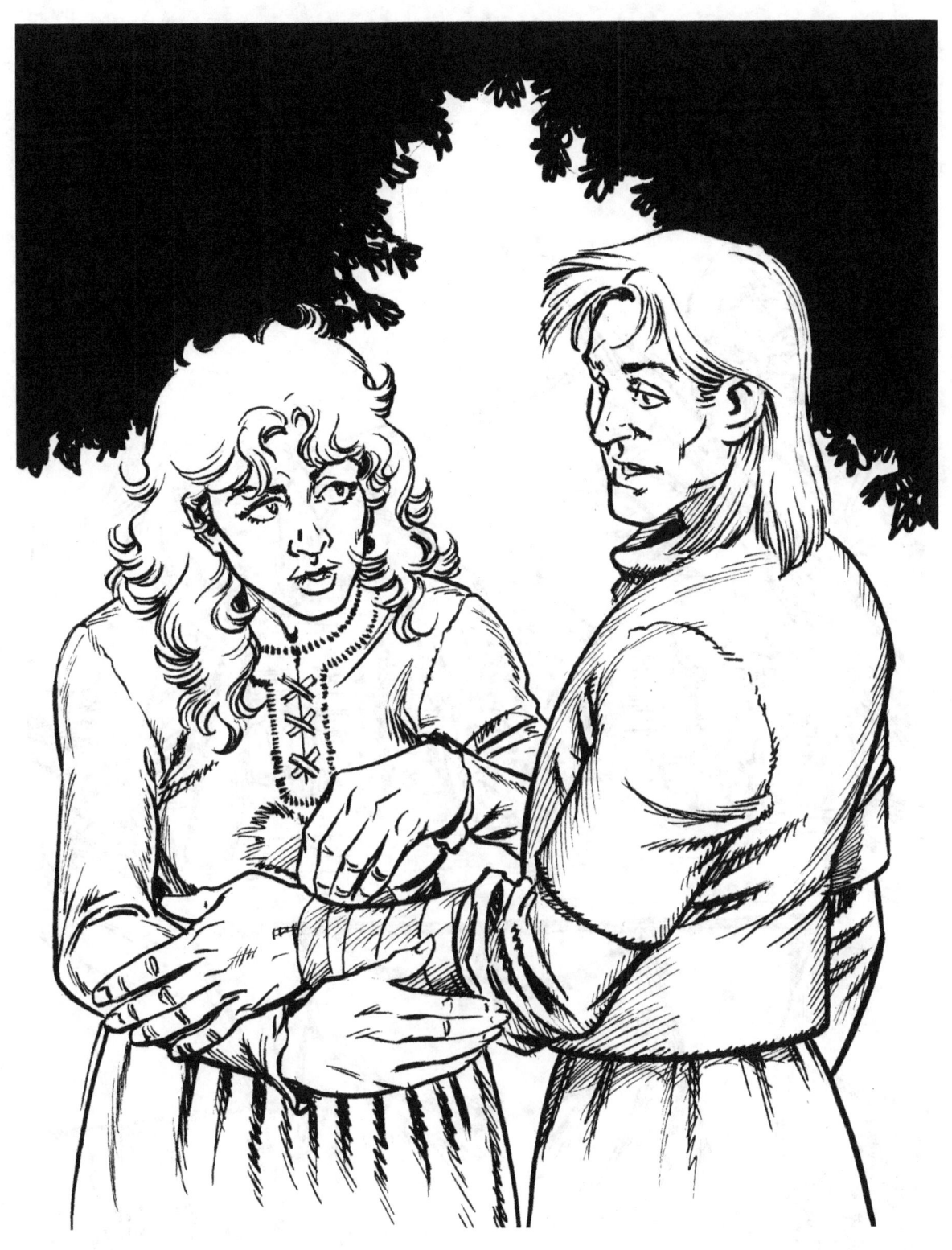

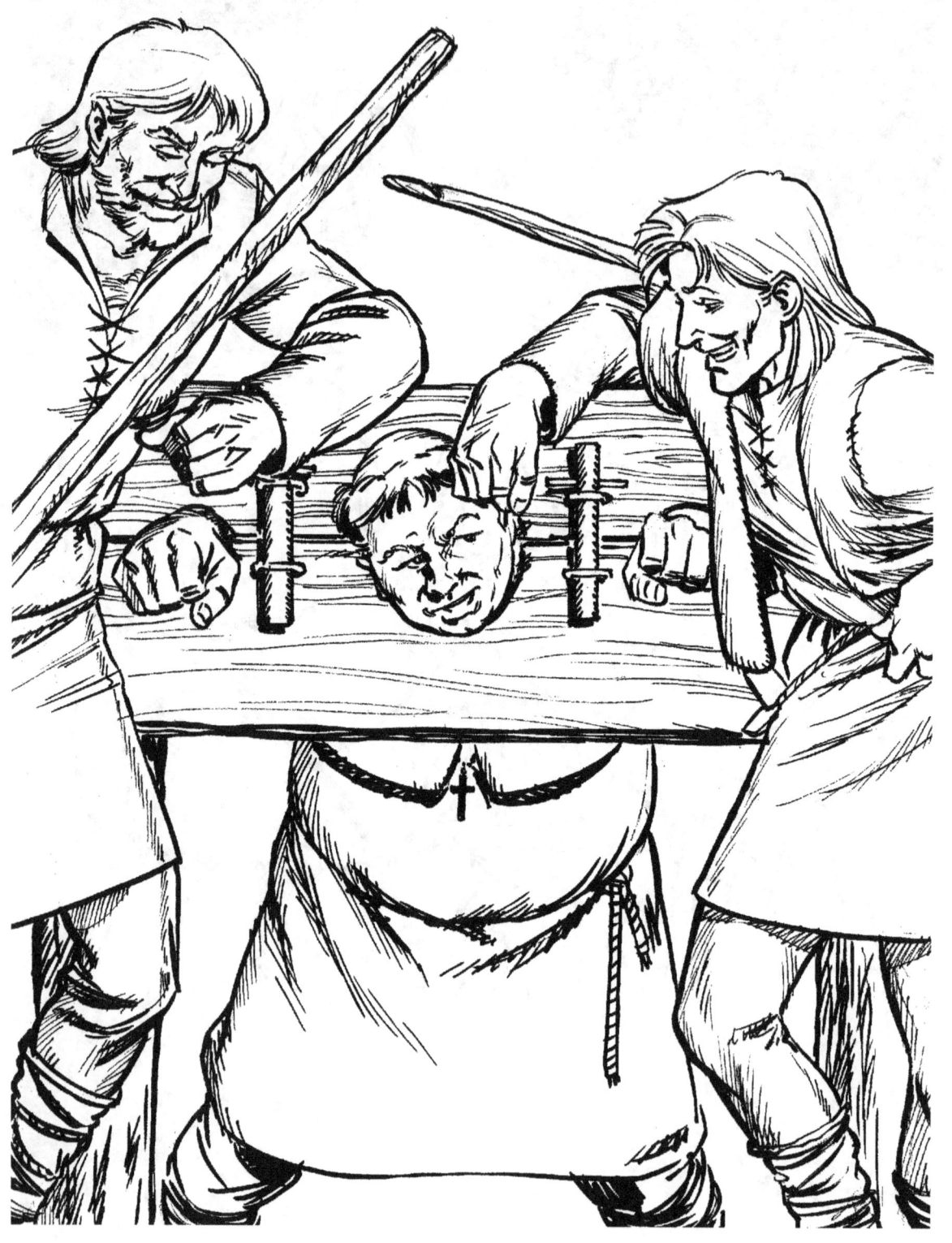

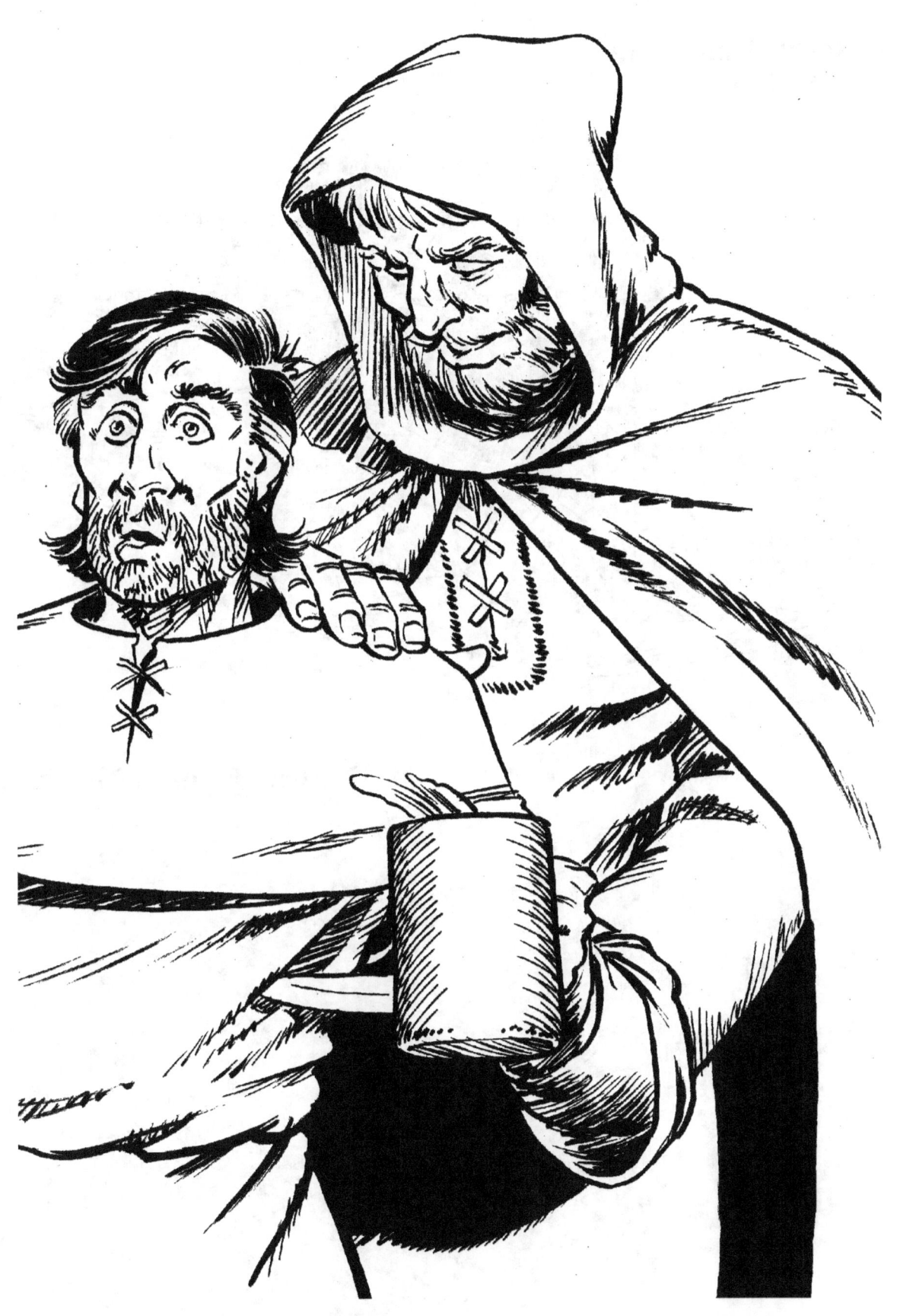

Nottingham Castle
A.D. 1194

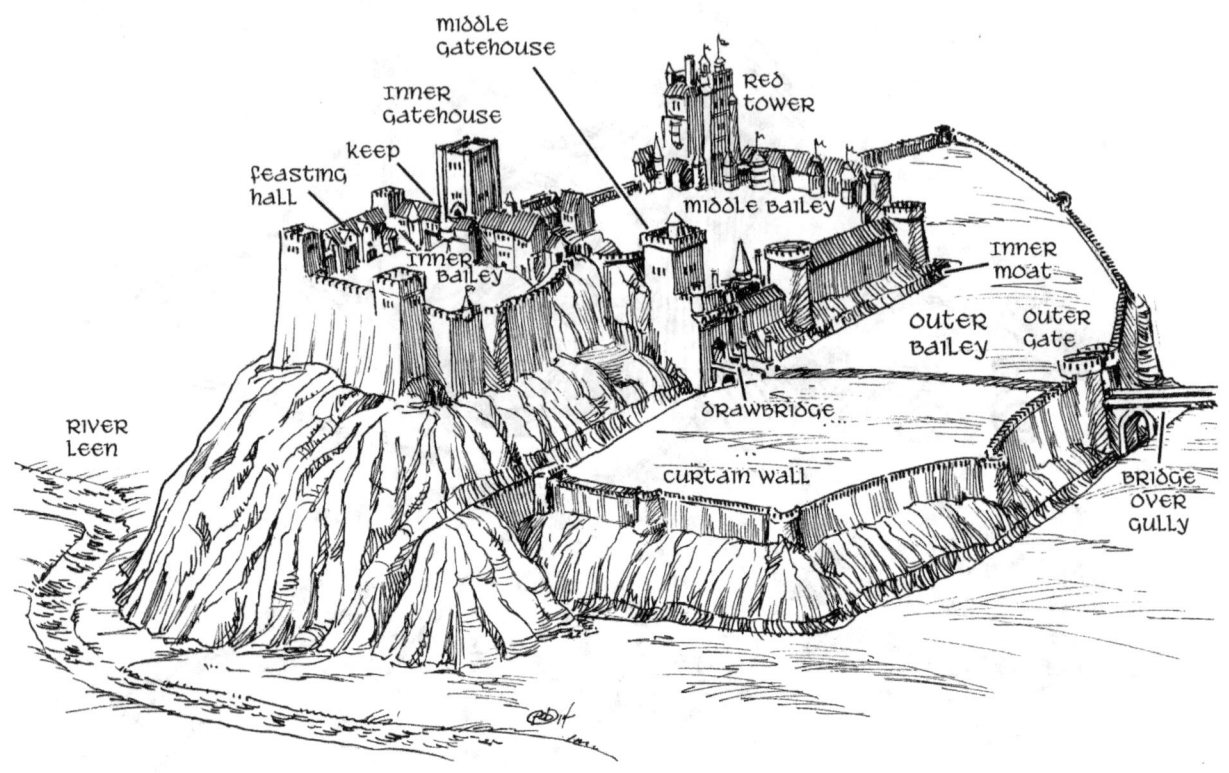

middle
gatehouse

inner
gatehouse

keep

feasting
hall

RED
TOWER

MIDDLE BAILEY

INNER
BAILEY

inner
moat

outer
BAILEY

outer
gate

RIVER
LeeN

DRAWBRIDGE

CURTAIN WALL

BRIDGE
OVER
GULLY

Robin Hood's London

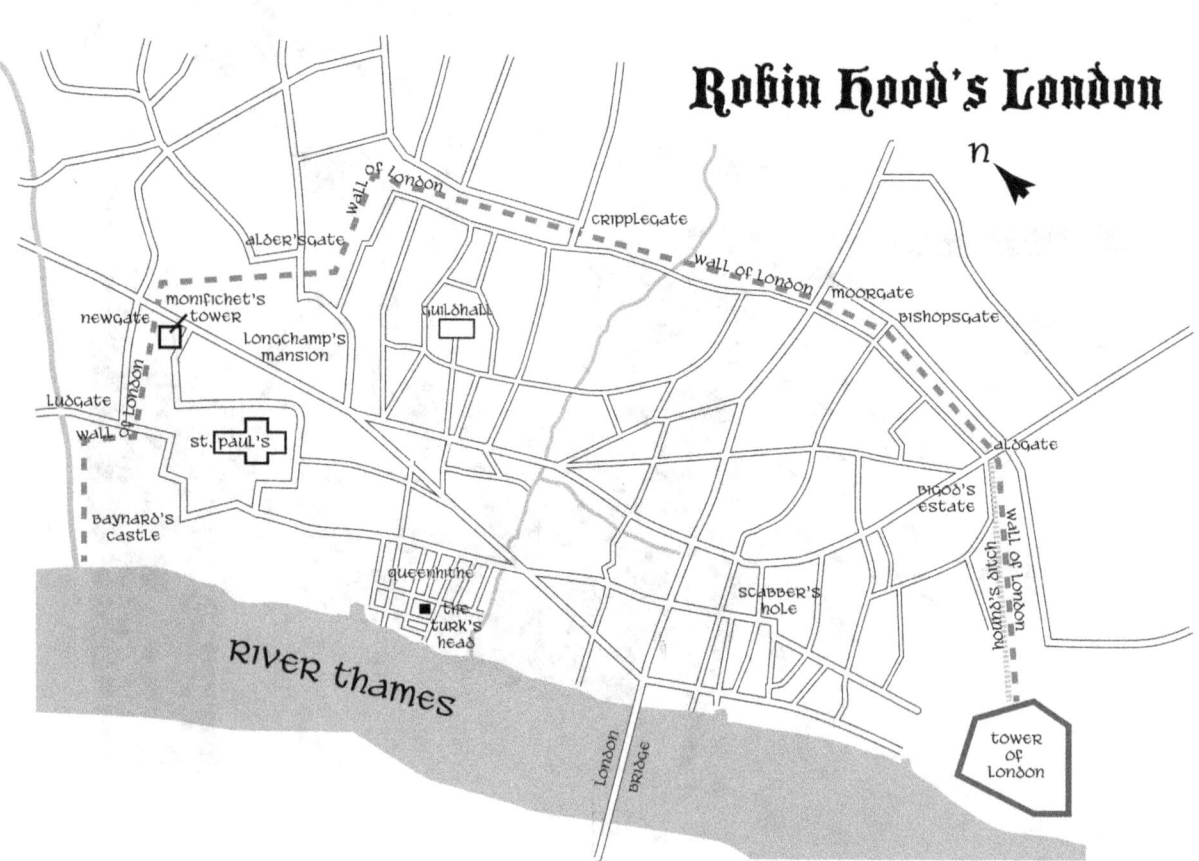

n

Wall of London

CRIPPLEGATE

alder'sgate

Wall of London

MOORGATE

monfichet's
tower

GUILDHALL

BISHOPSGATE

newgate

Longchamp's
mansion

ludgate

Wall of London

st. paul's

aldgate

BHood's
estate

Baynard's
castle

houndsditch

wall of London

Queenhithe

the
turk's
head

SCABBER's
hole

RIVER thames

London
Bridge

tower
of
London

140

CHAPTER 5
THE GREAT DETECTIVE

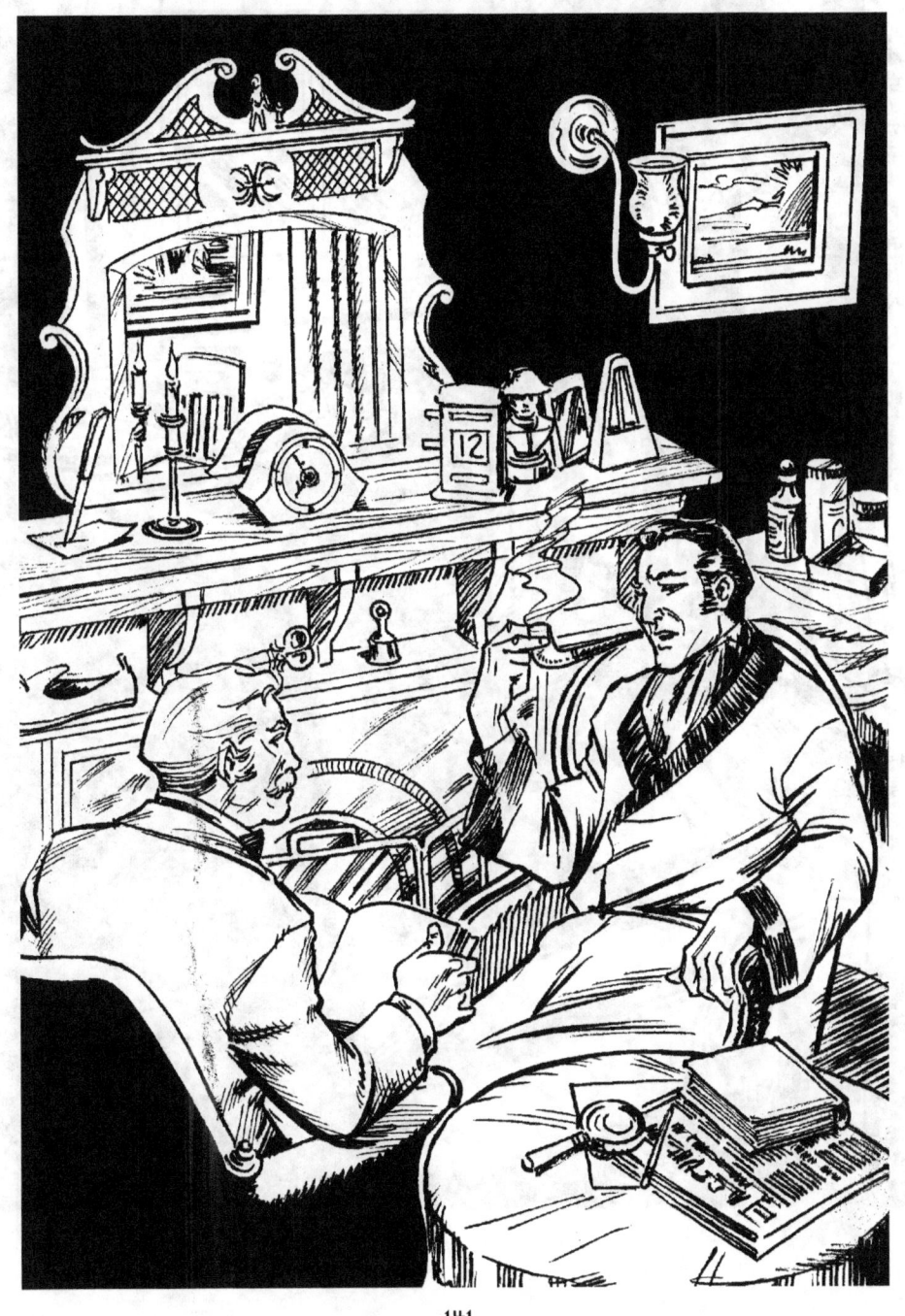

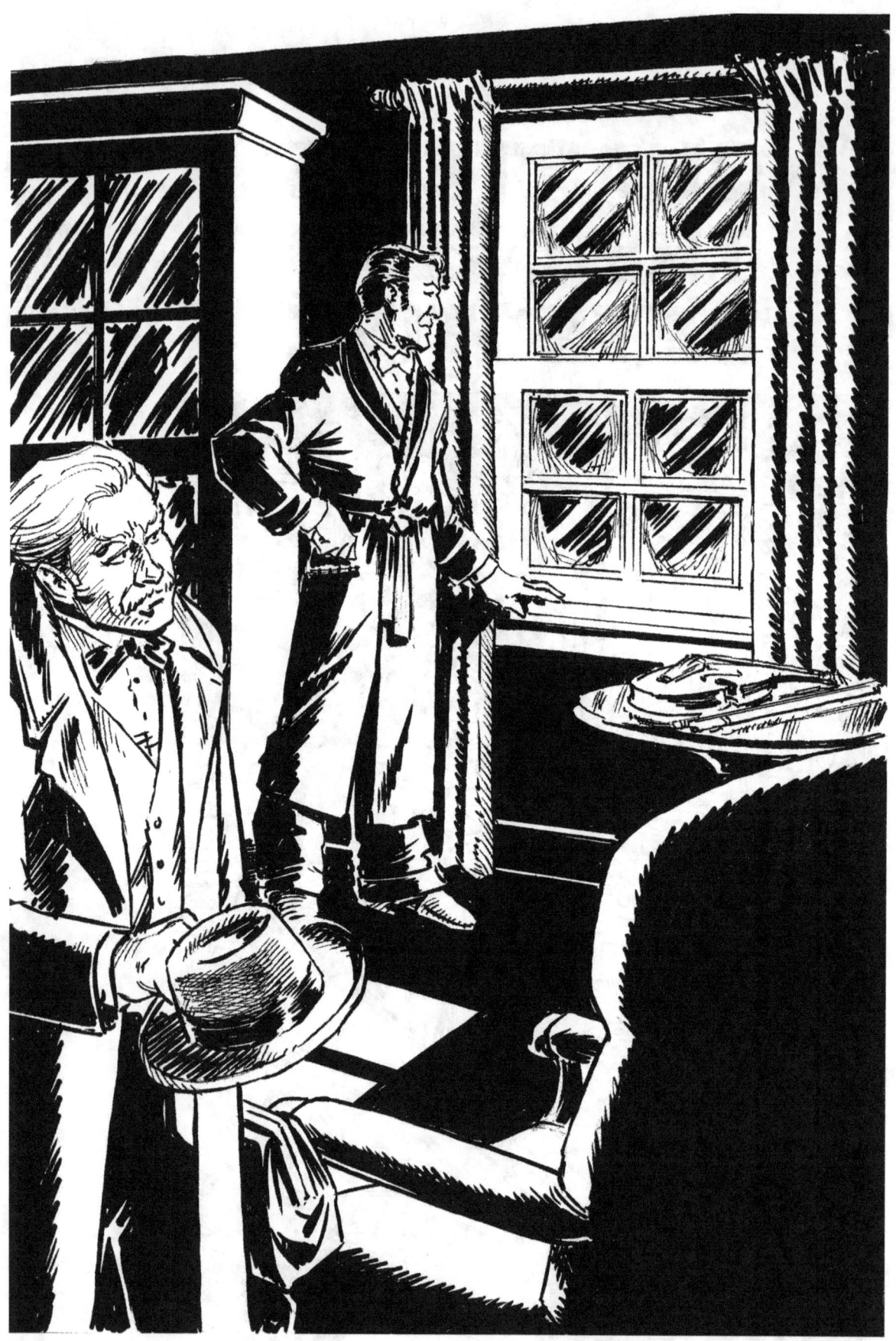

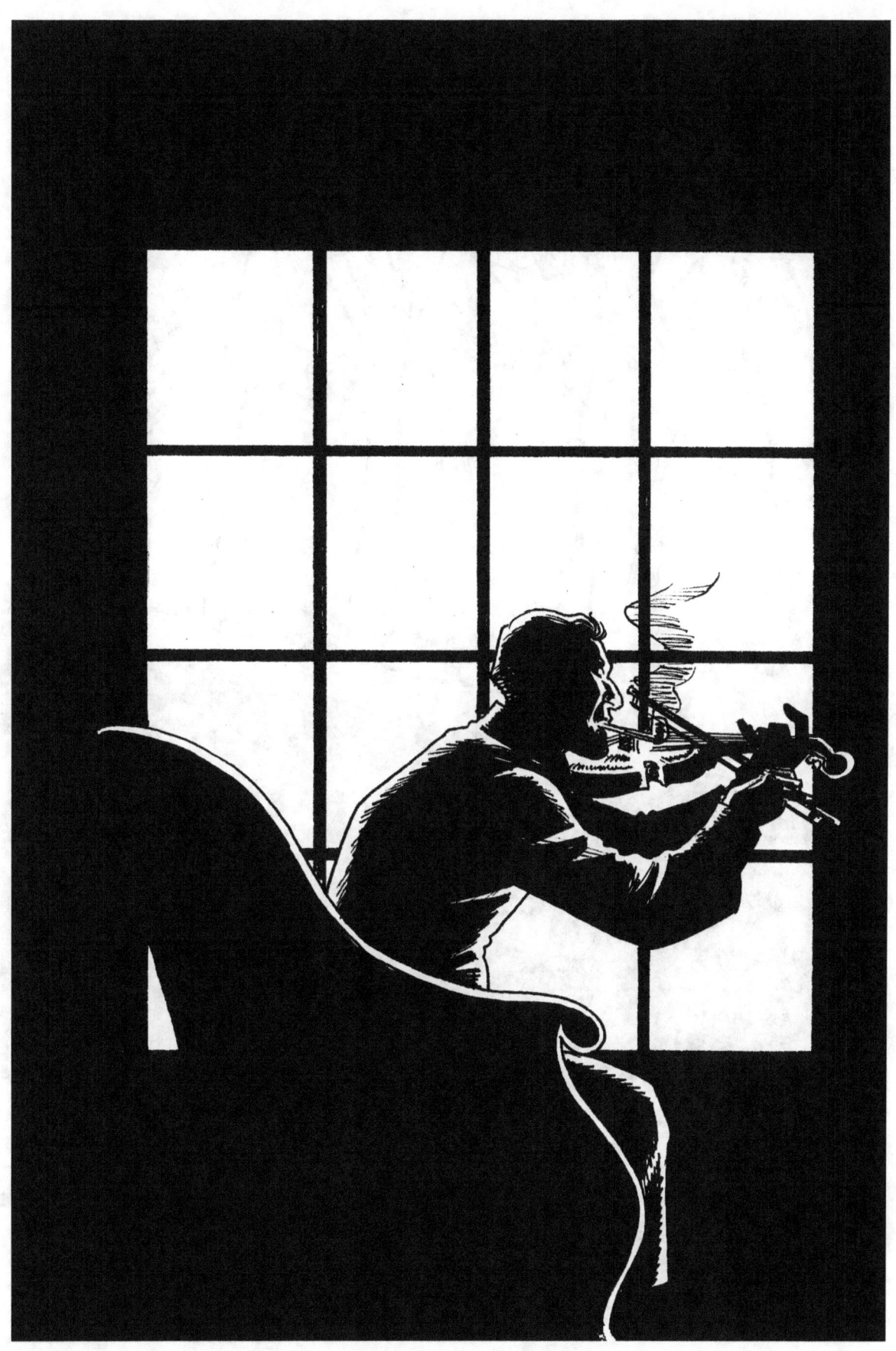

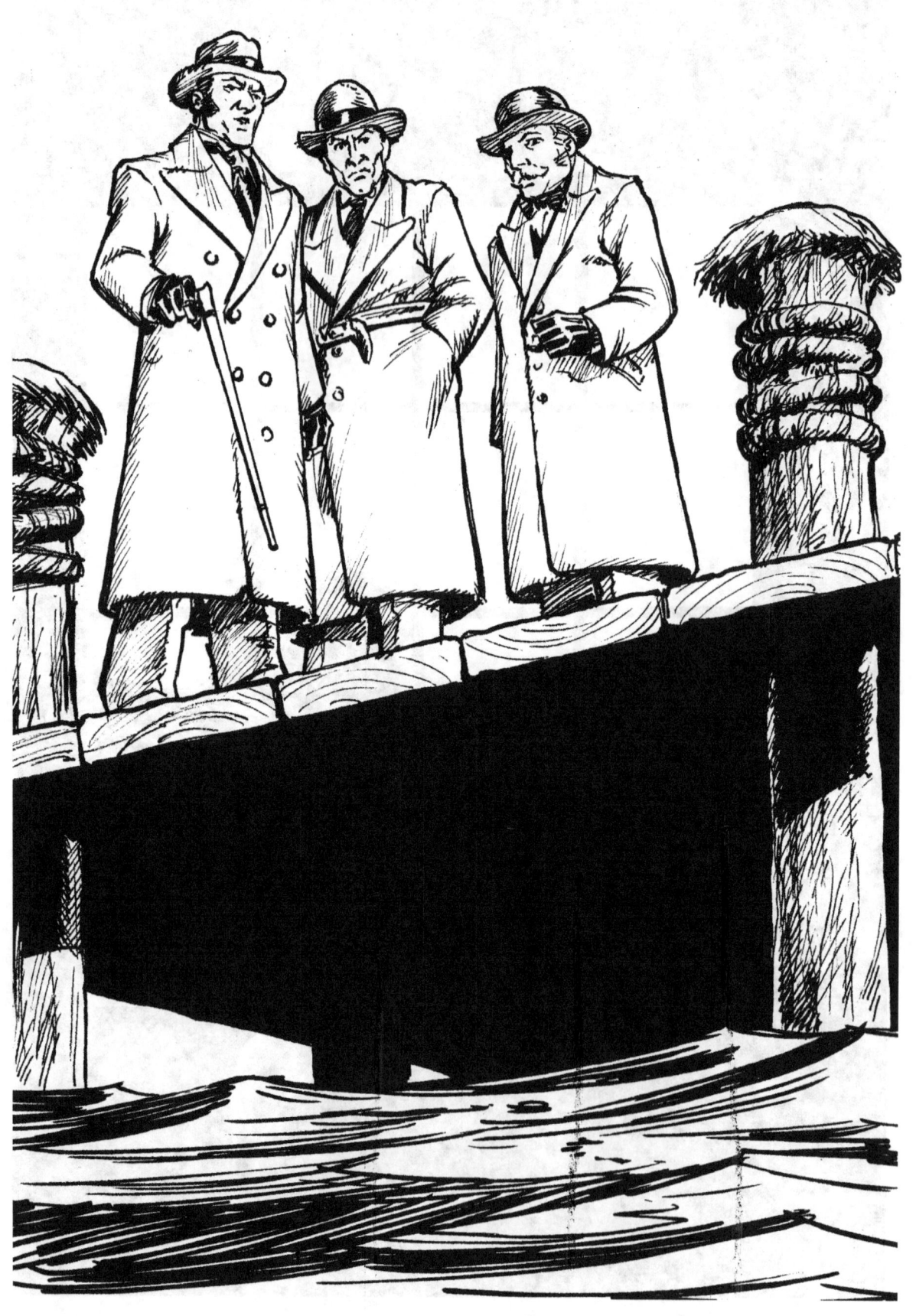

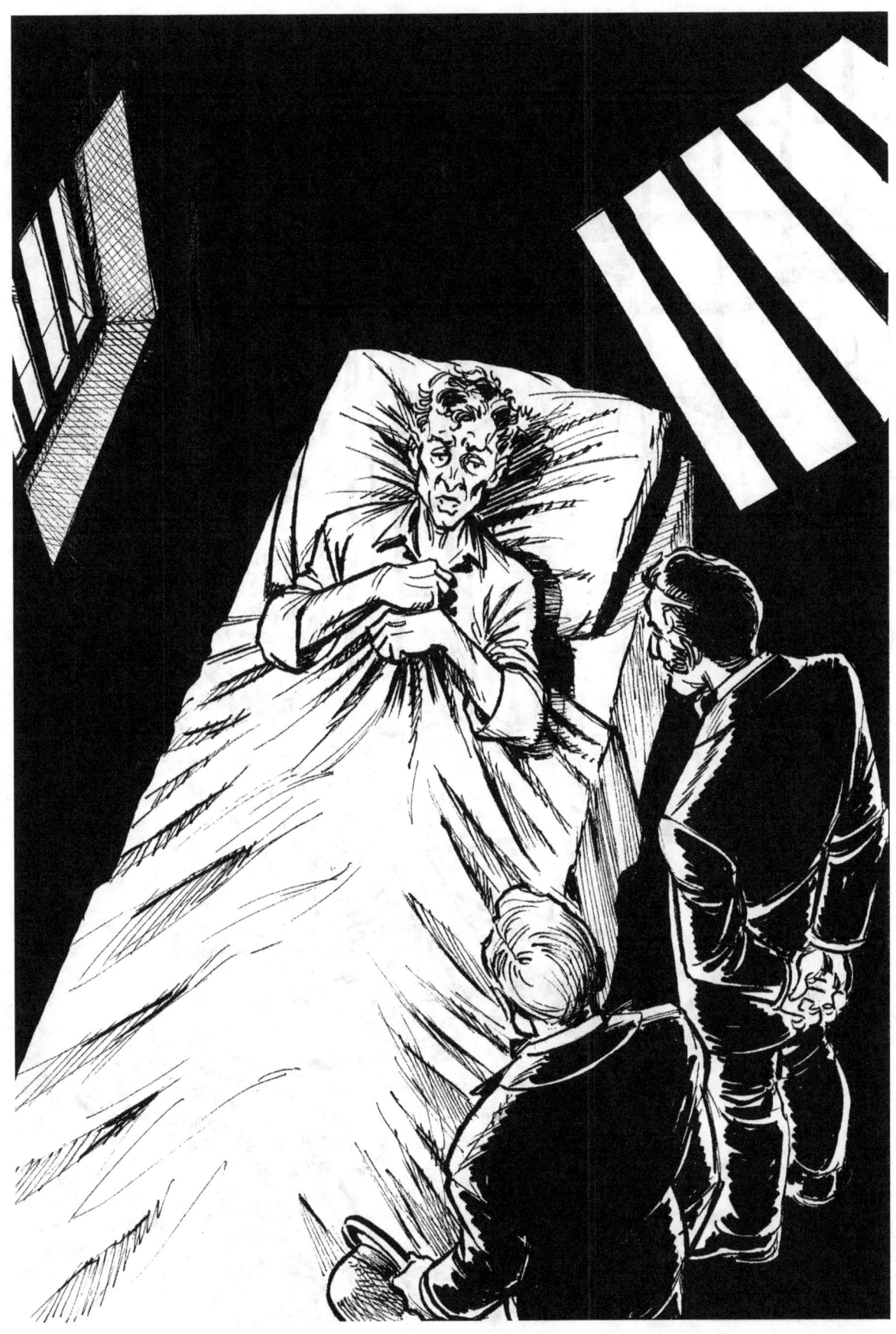

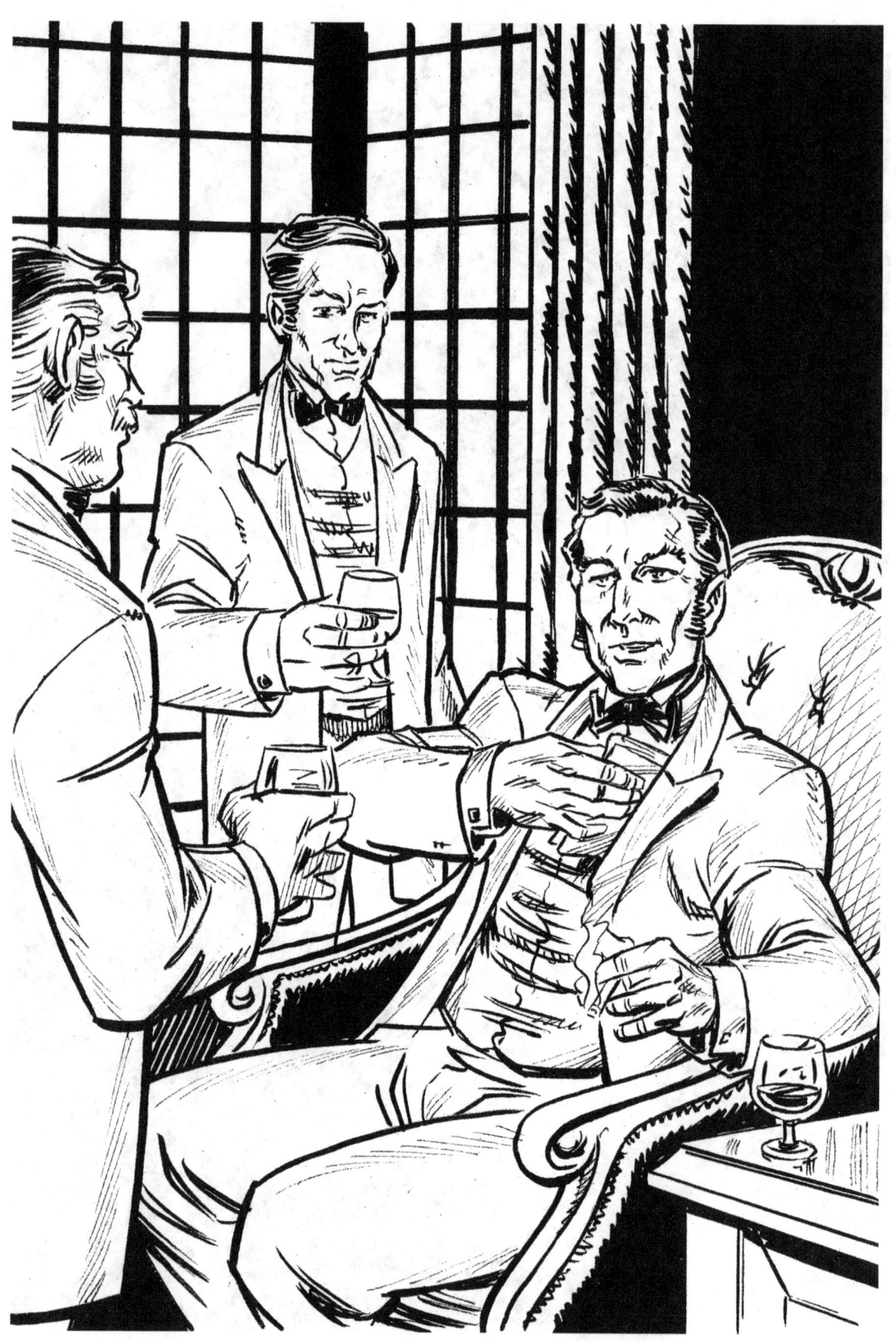

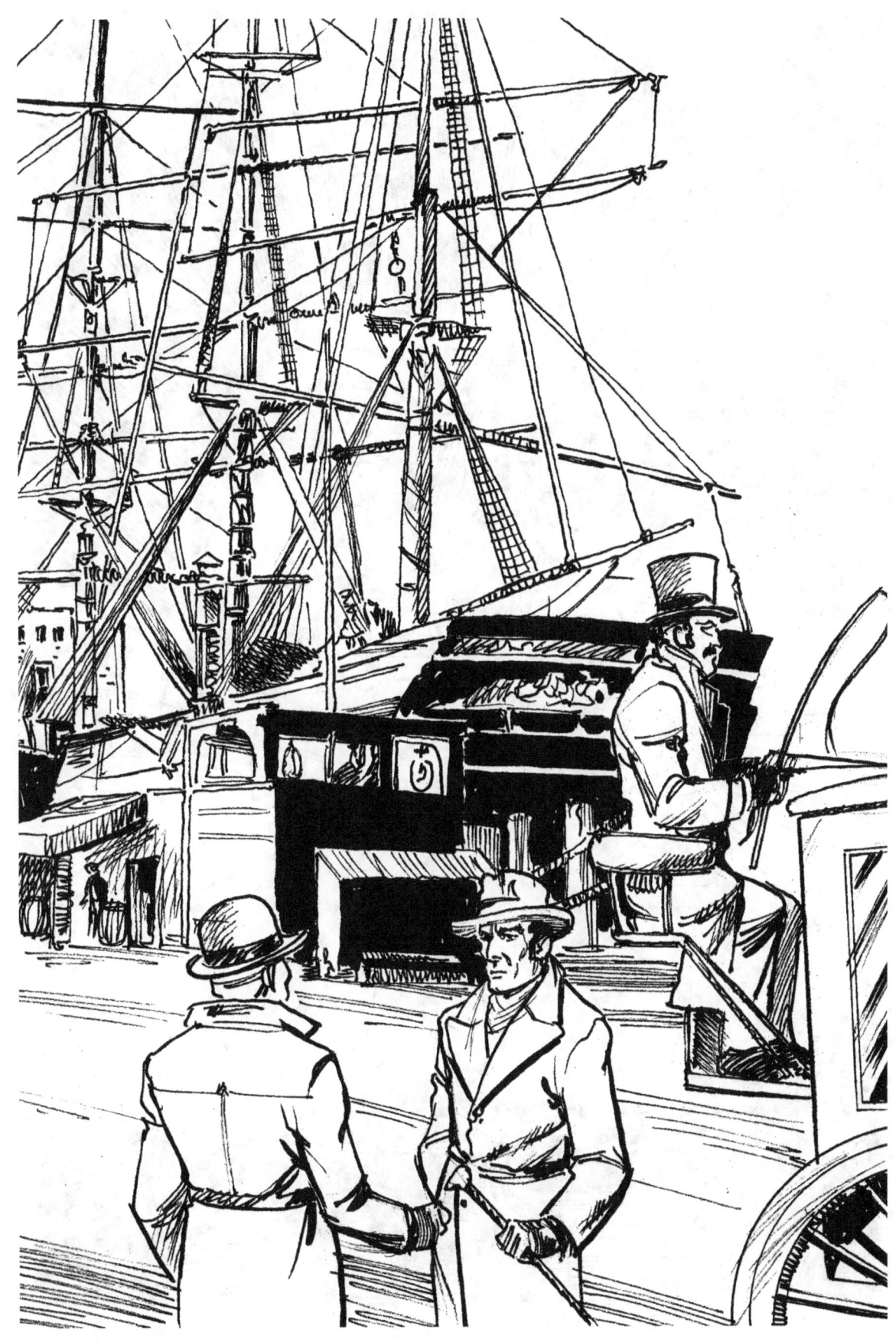

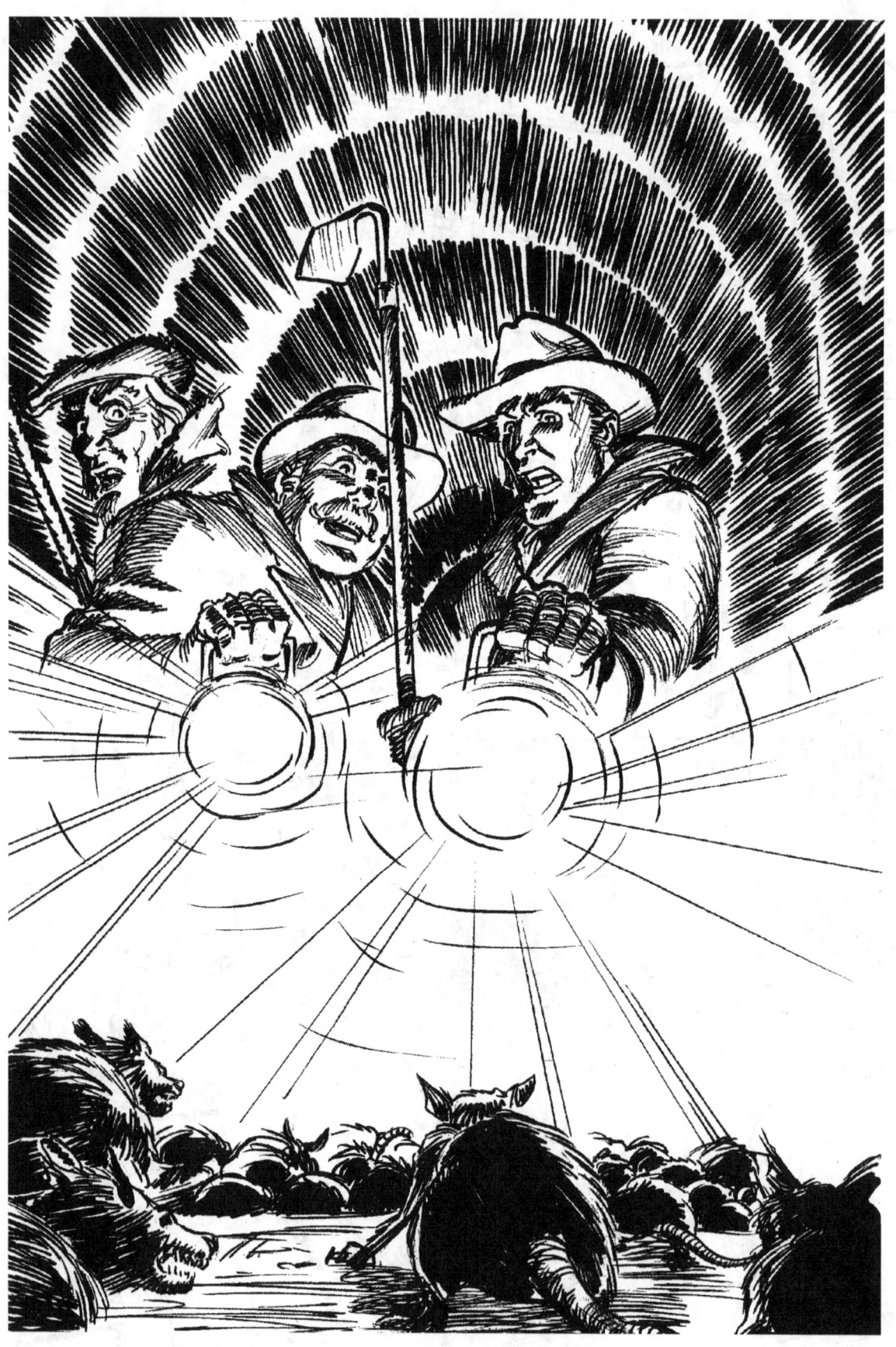

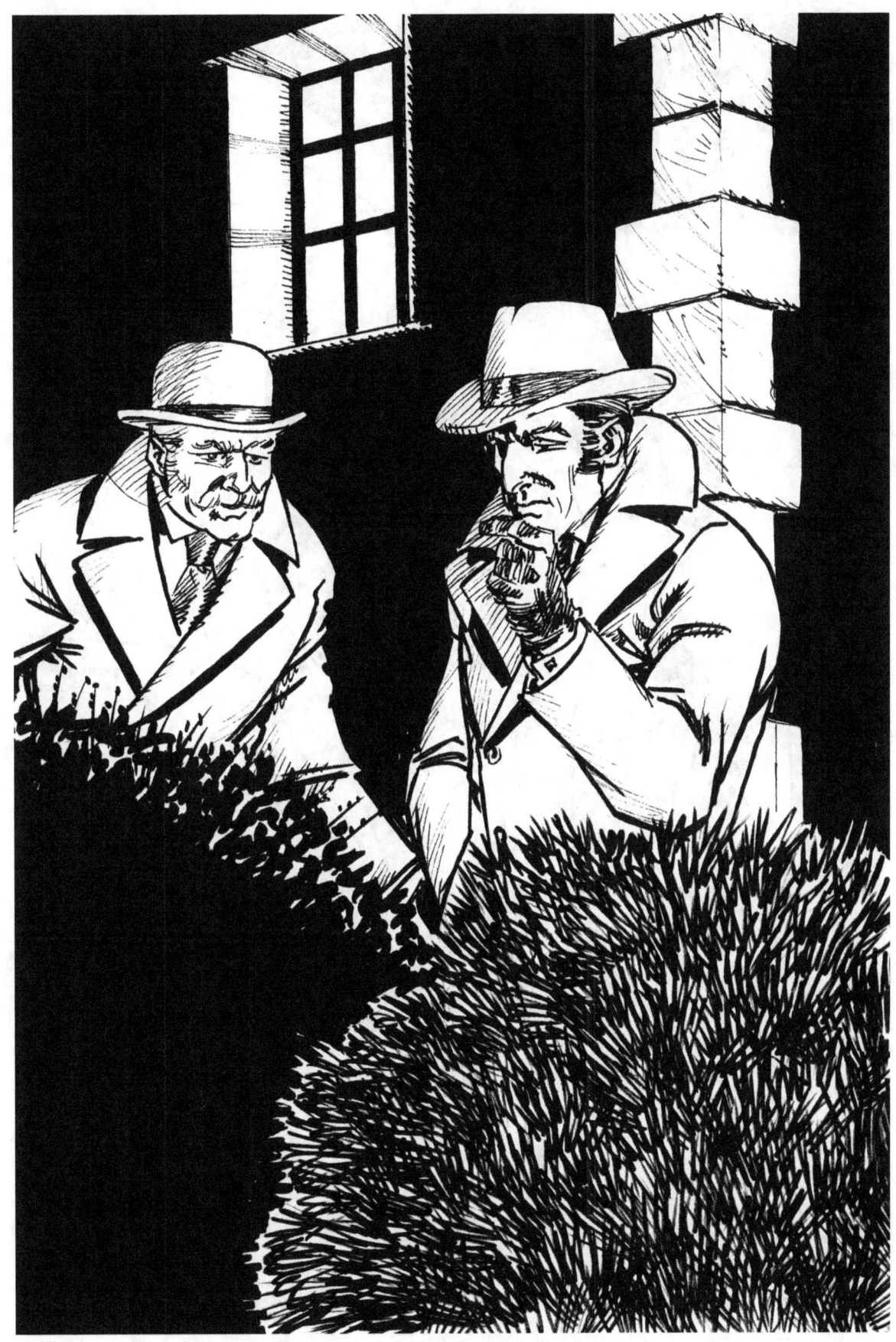

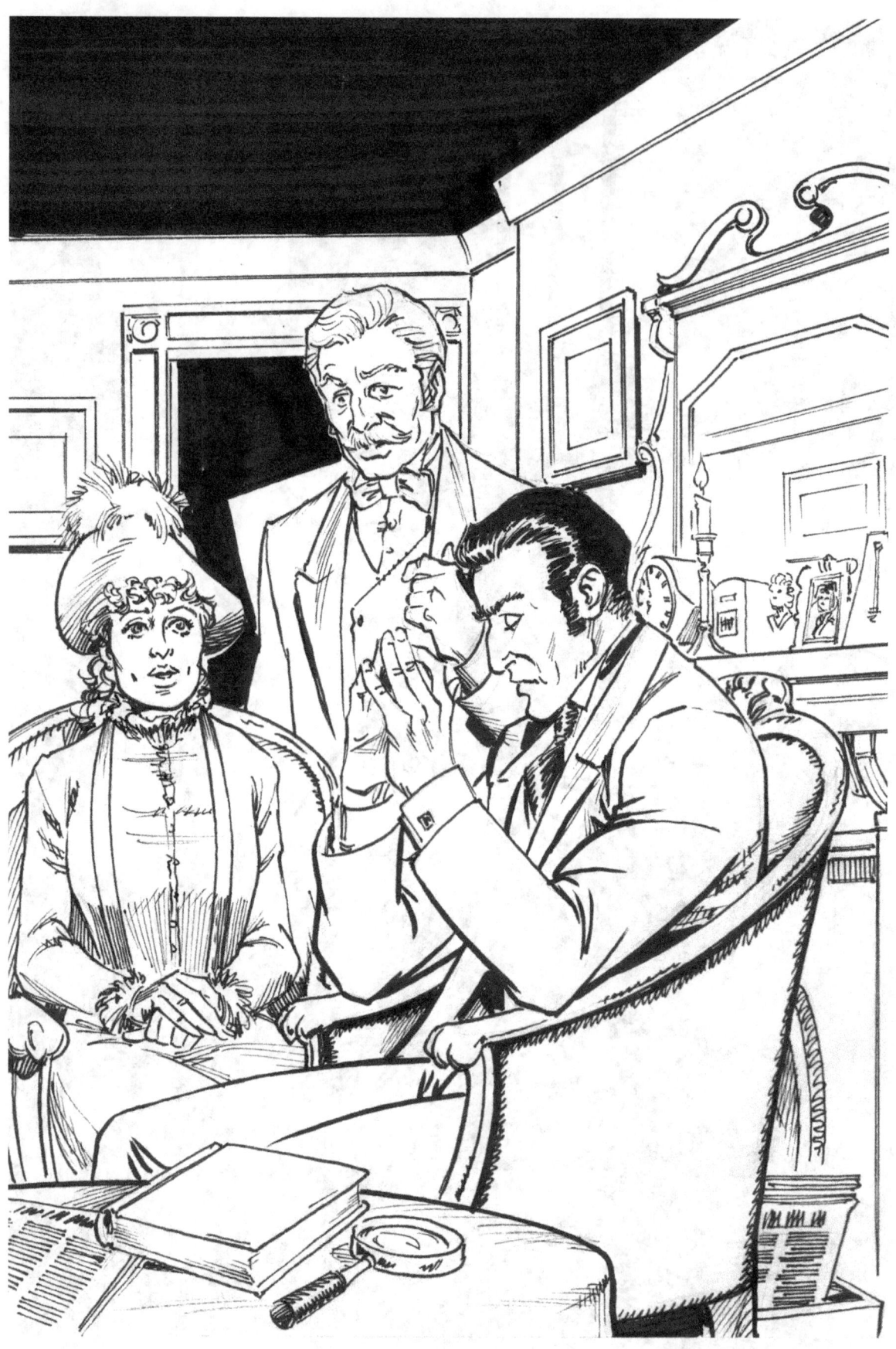

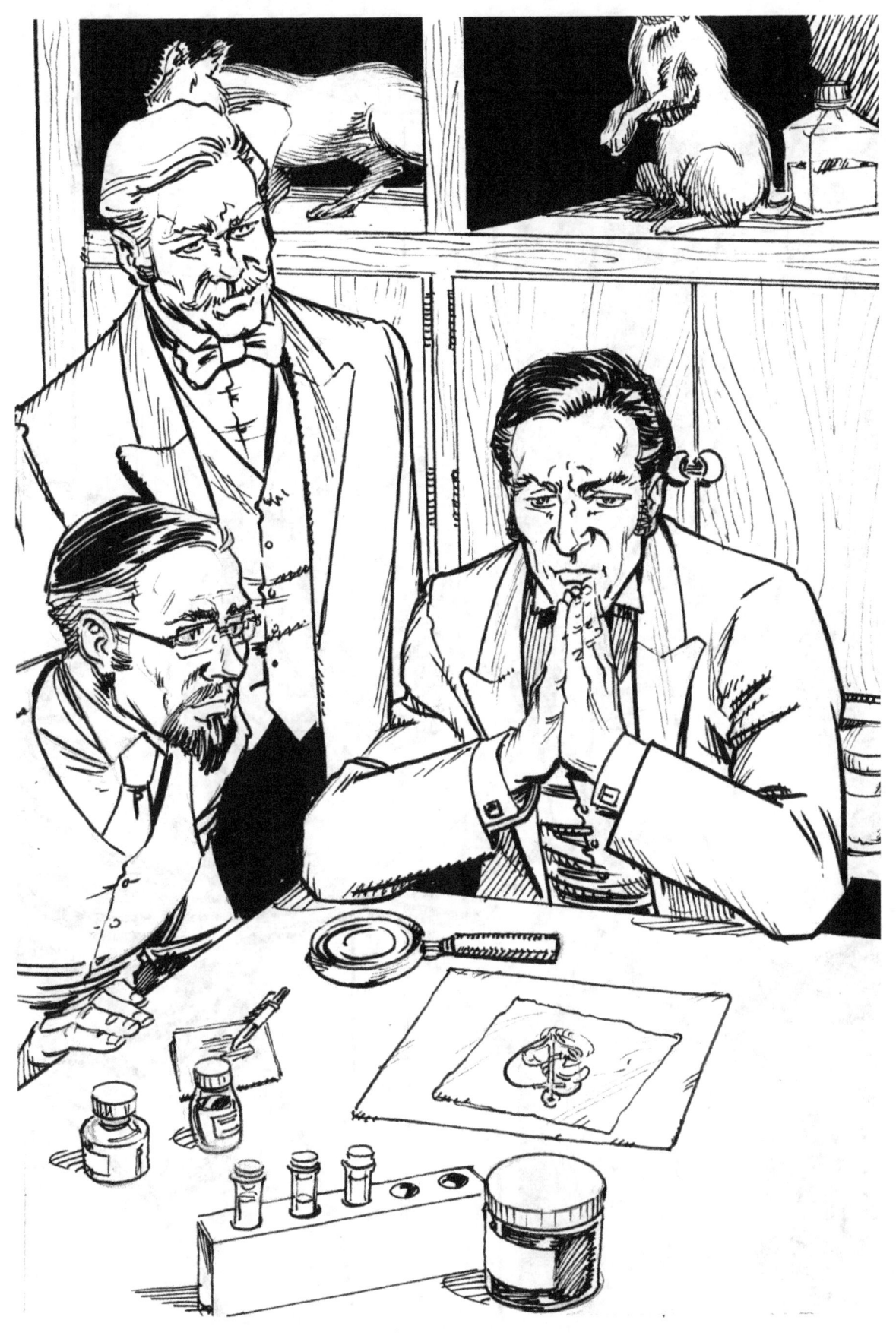

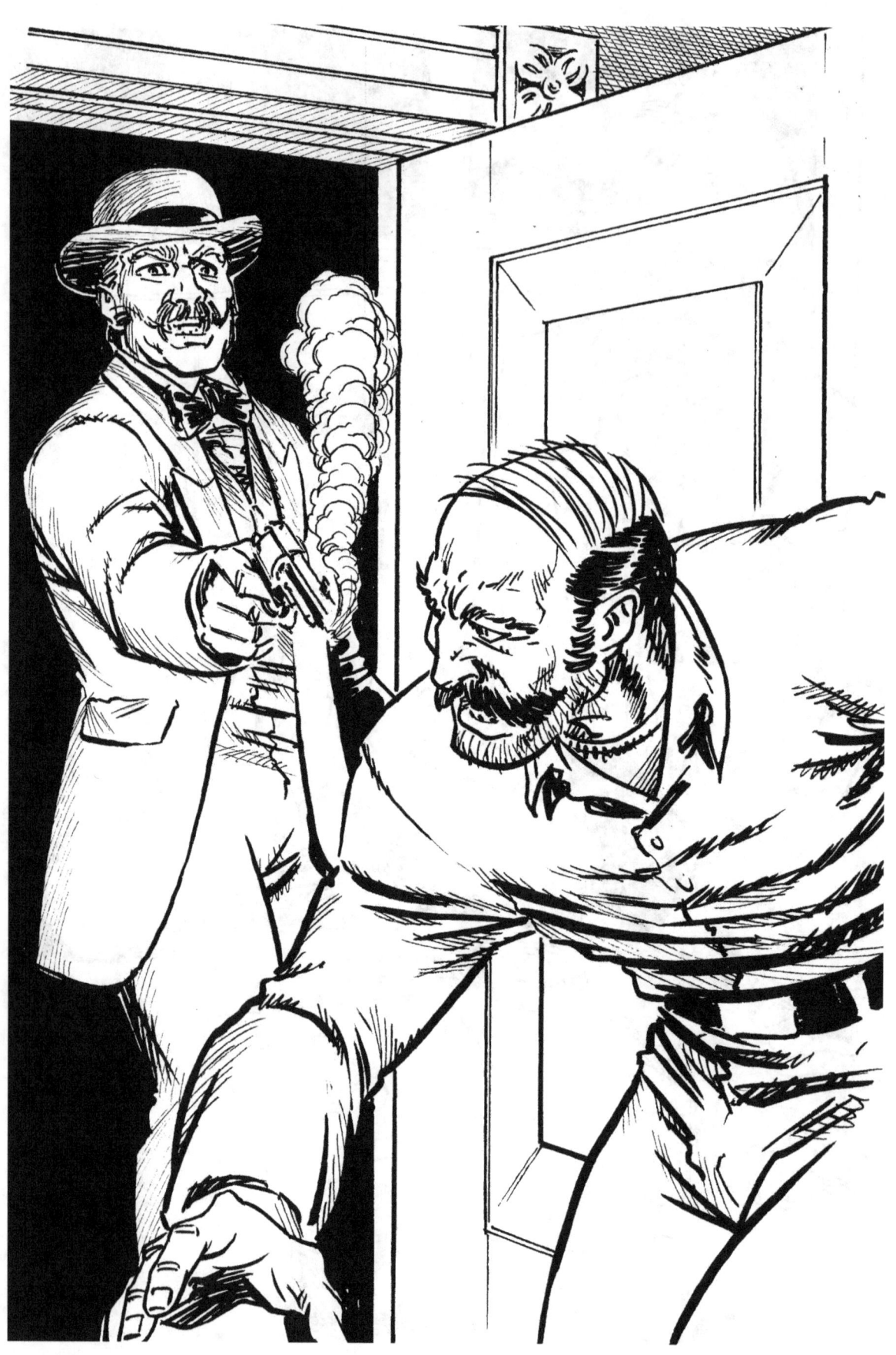

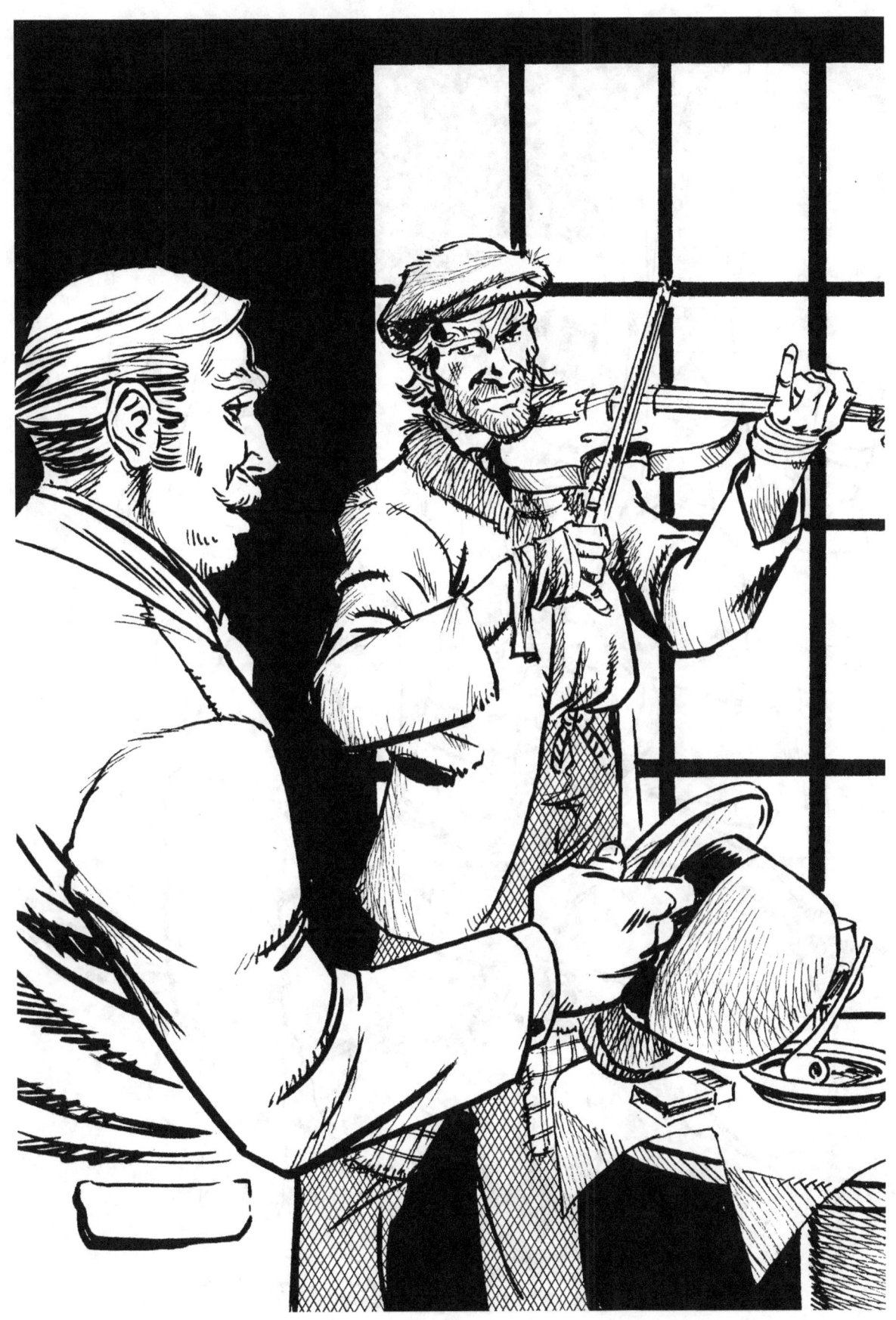

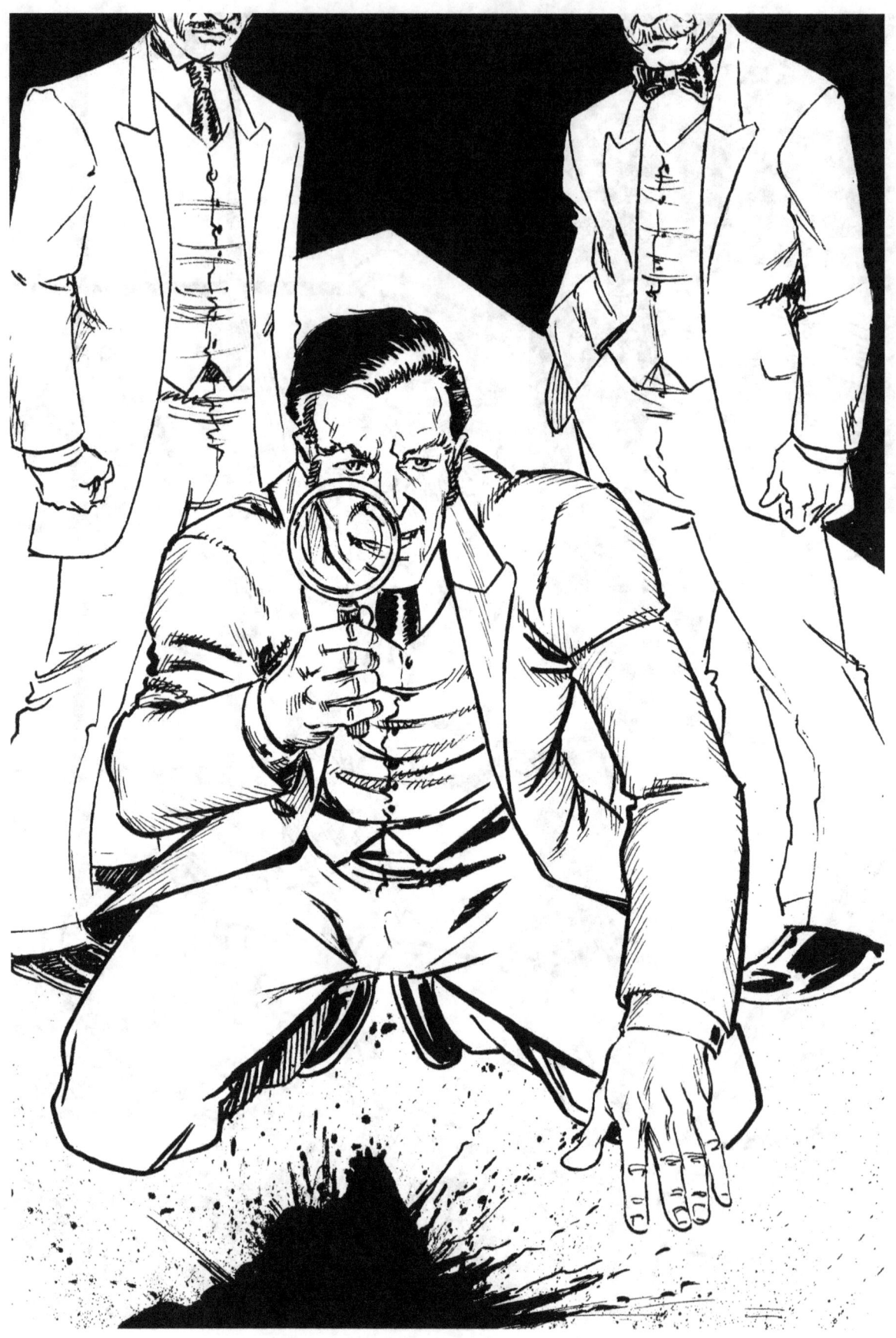

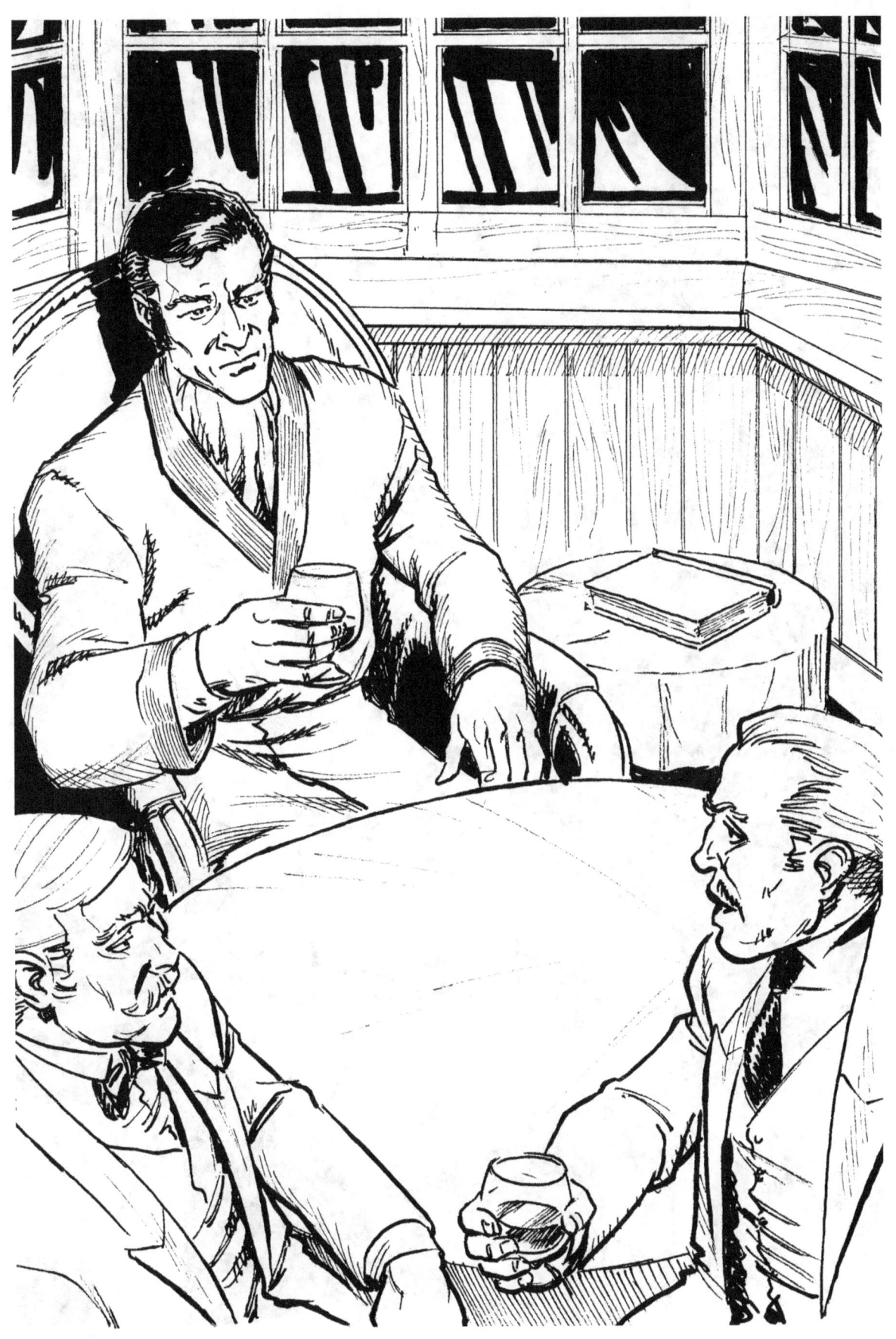

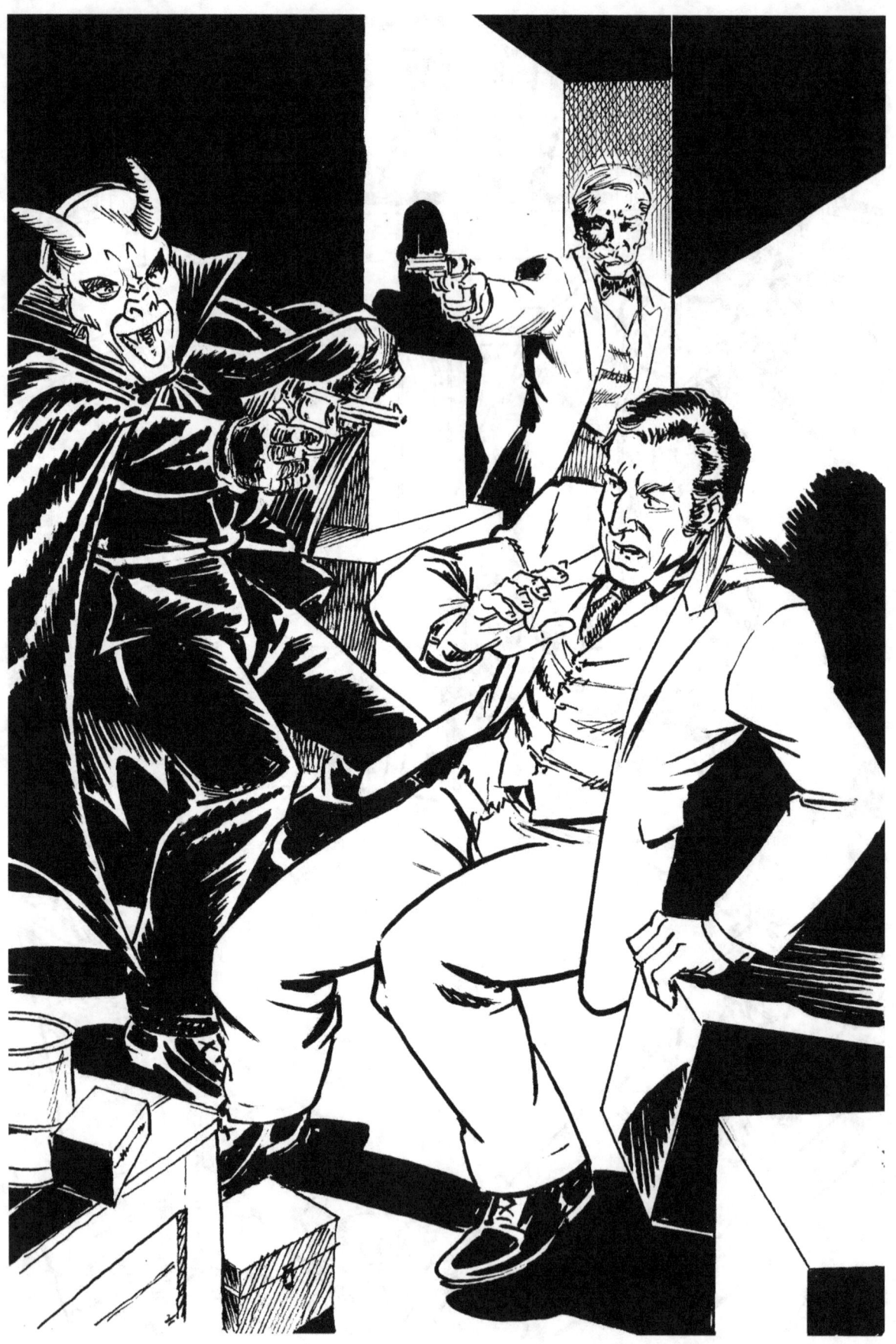

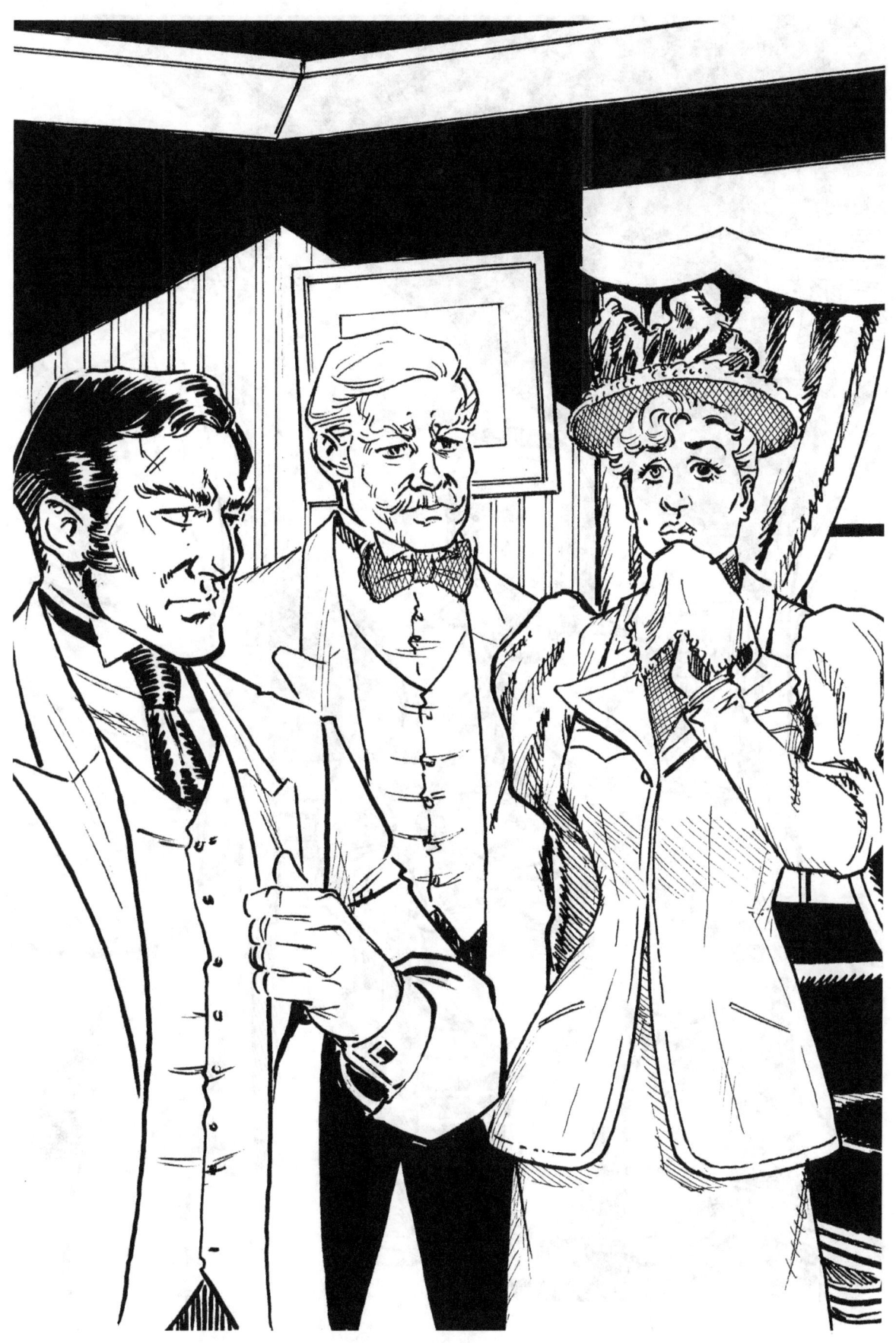

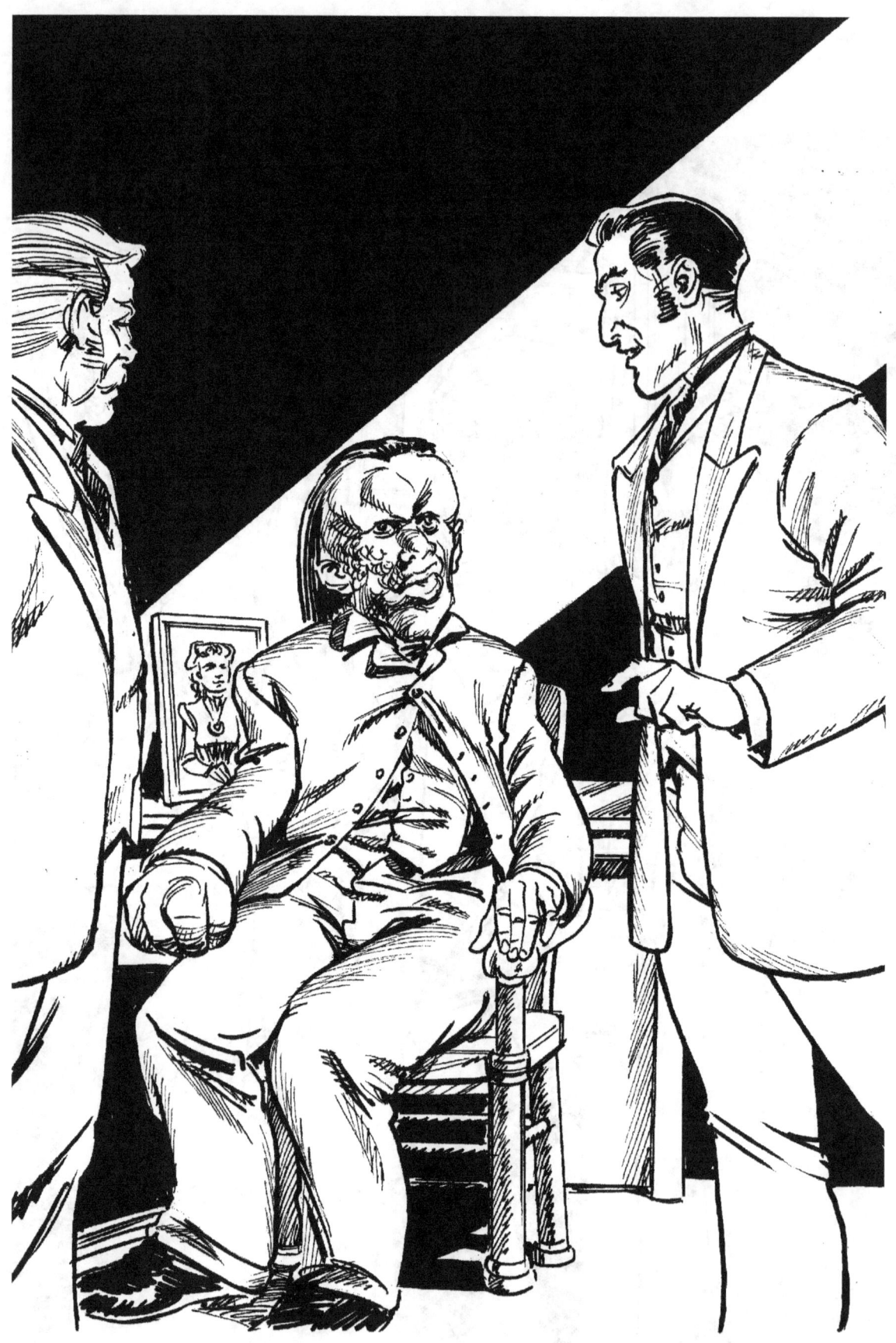

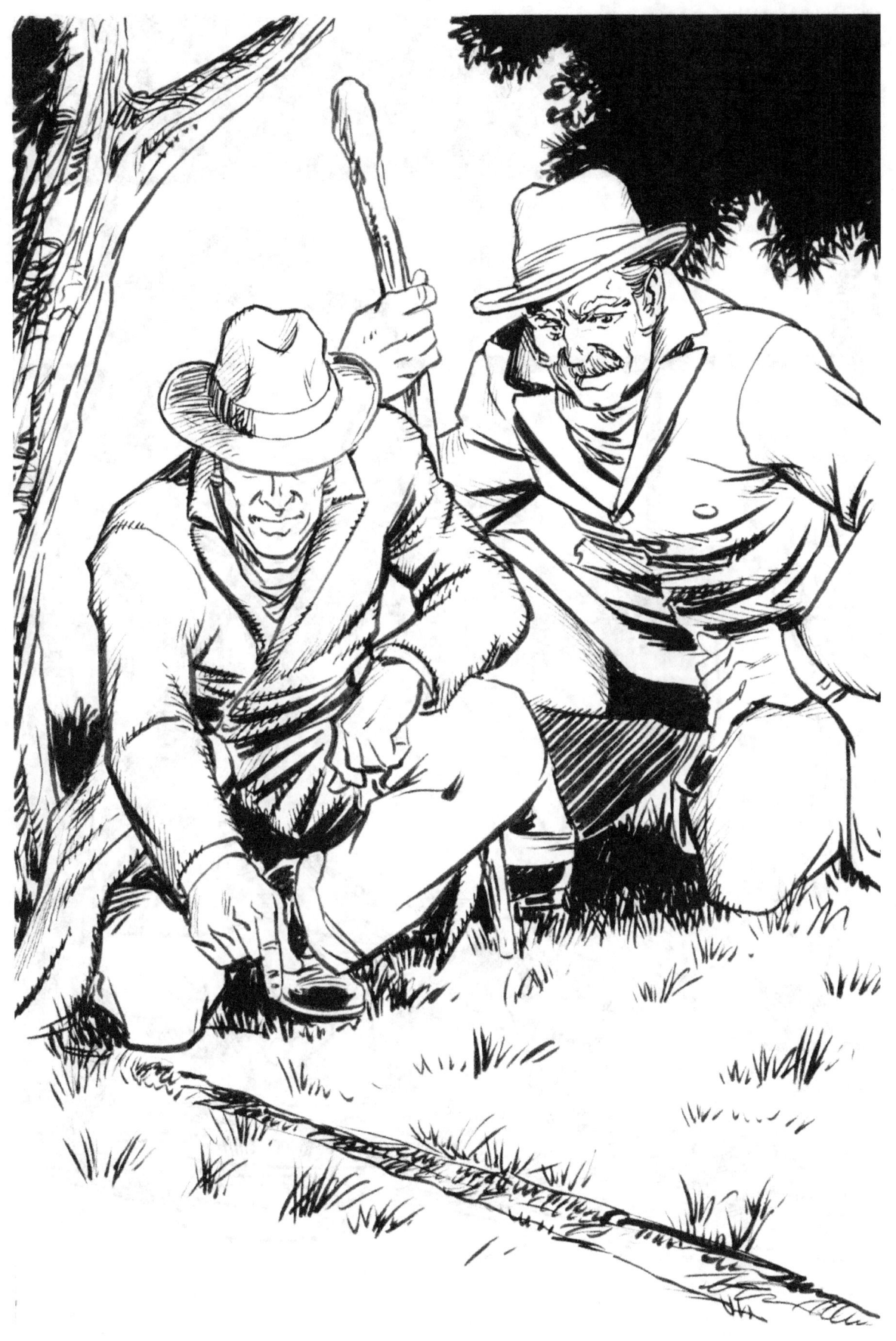

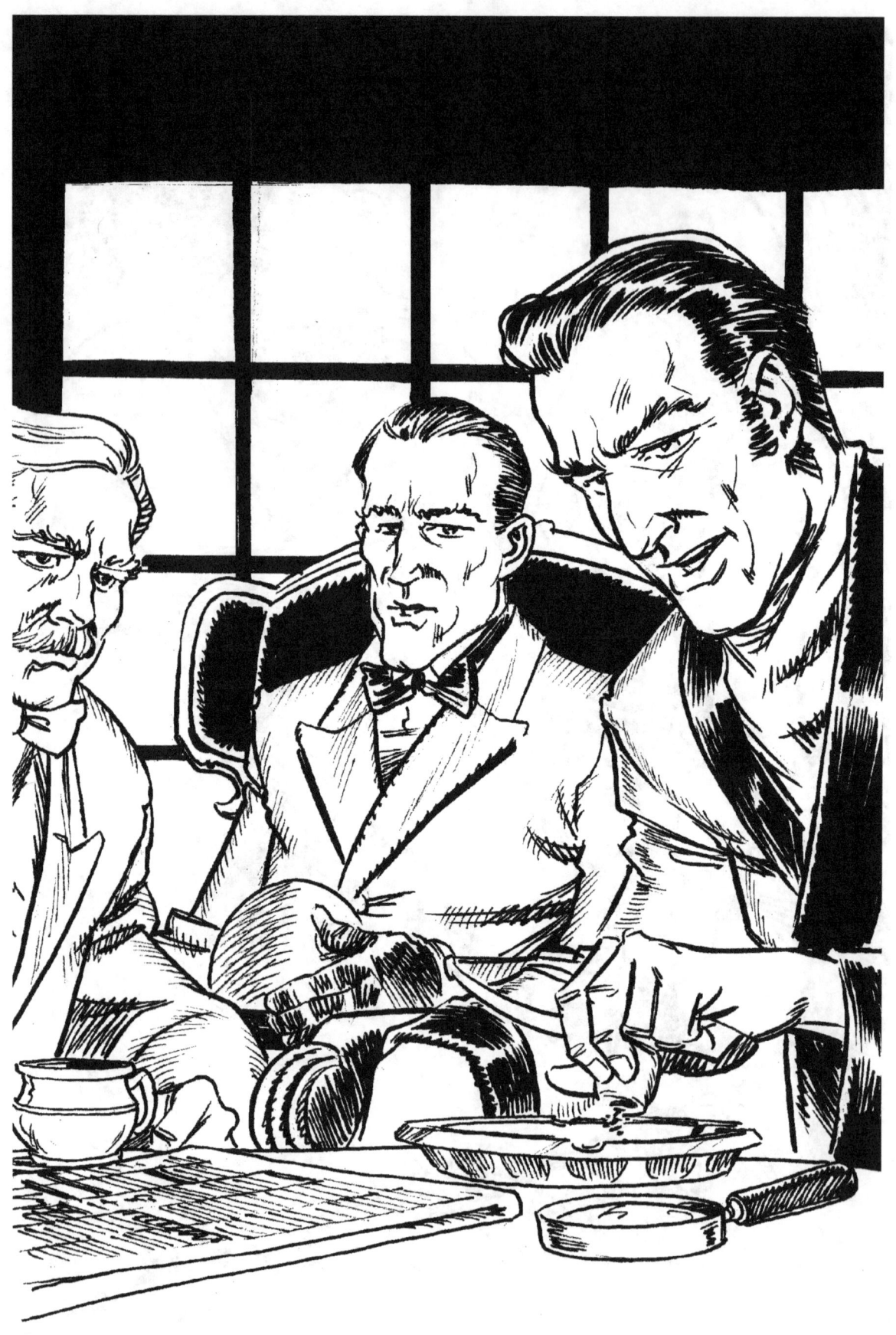

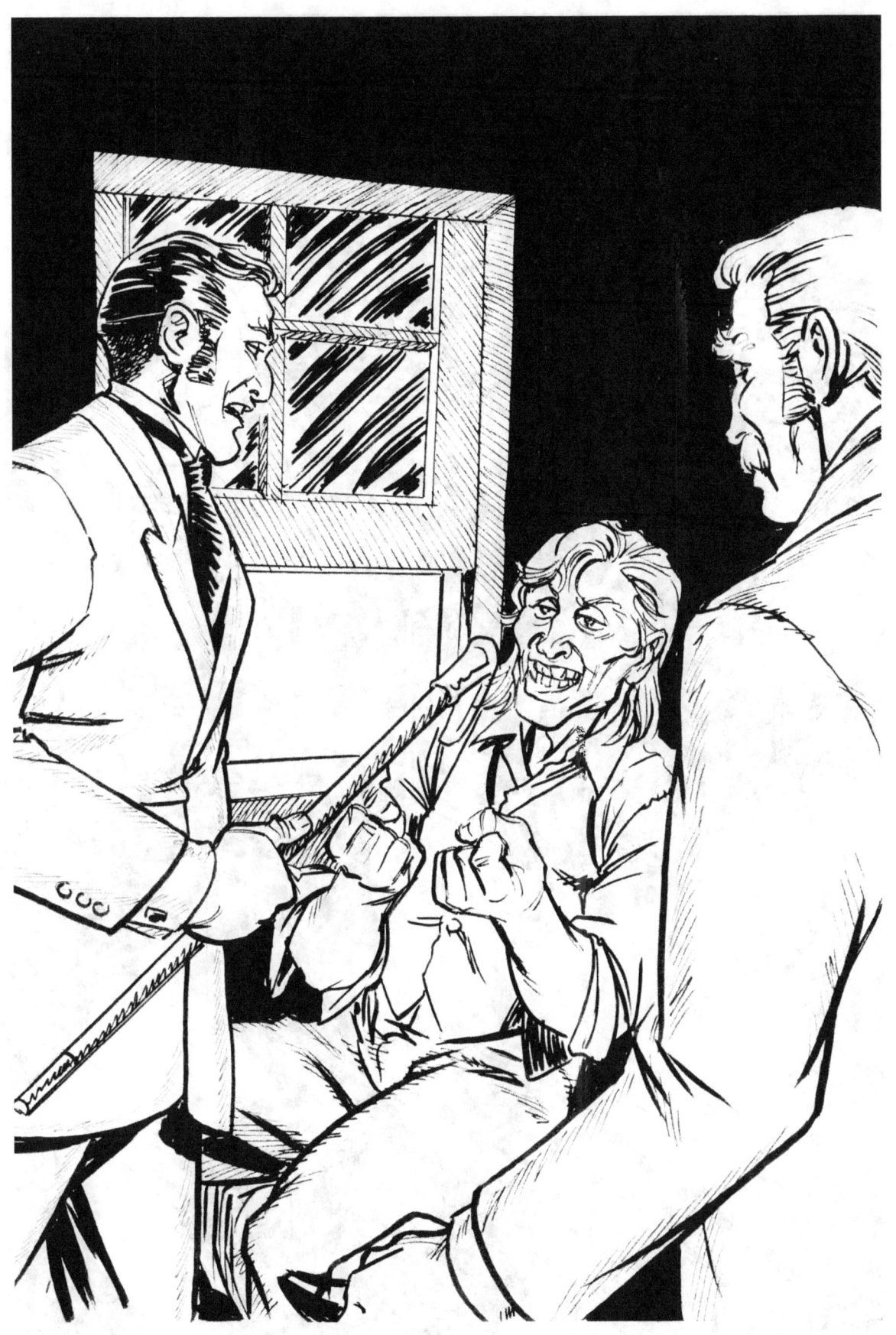

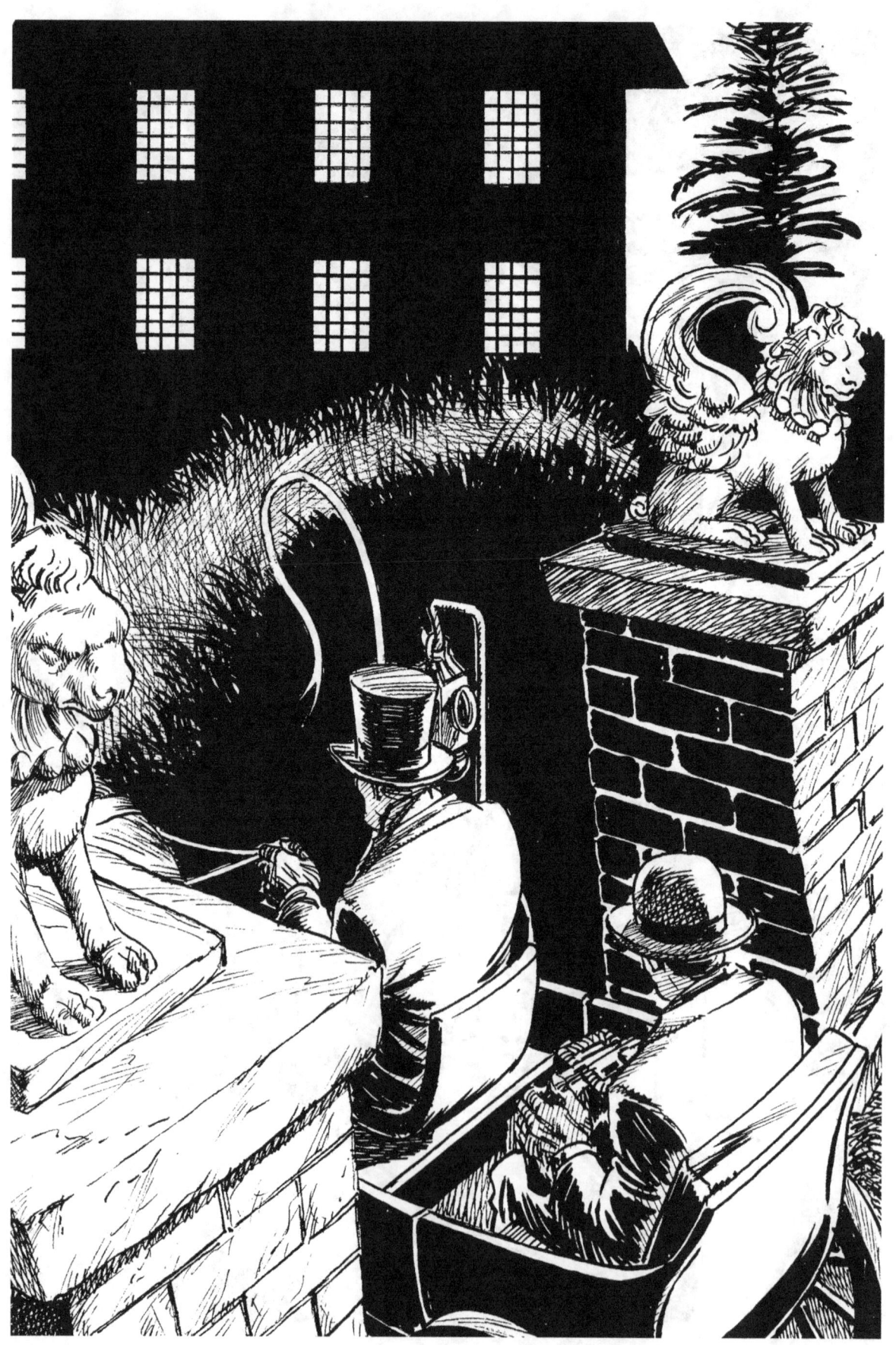

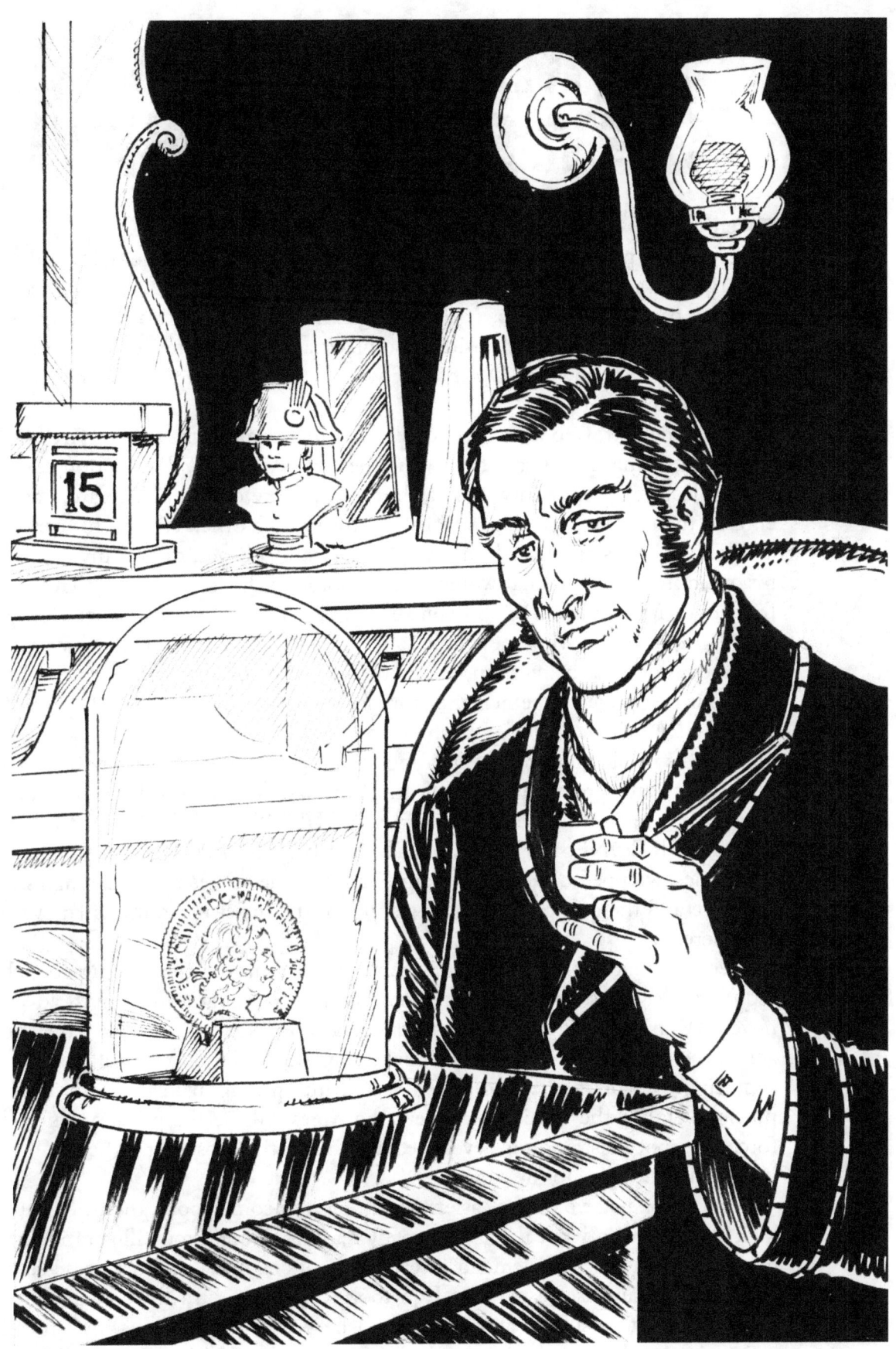

SOMETIMES WE GET SURPRISED

Ten years ago I approached my artist pal, Rob Davis, with the wacky idea of creating a publishing company that would publish new anthologies and novels featuring classic pulp characters from the 30s and 40s. And because I wanted these books to pay homage to those classic magazines, I wanted them to have gorgeous art, both on the covers and inside. The black and white interior pieces in classic pulps like the Shadow and Doc Savage were as much of a delight to the readers as were the stunning, painted covers.

To my delight, Rob actually said yes even to assuming the title of Art Director for this fledgling new dream that would become Airship 27 Productions. Now I'd known Rob for over twenty years as both of us were comicbook creators and had entered the professional arena within months of each other. I'd seen his early work in Malibu comics and it had impressed me greatly. I began to buy any comic with his art in it. Eventually that would include some of the best ever Star Trek comics from both Marvel and DC. So you see, I knew from the get-go that Rob was a gifted graphic artist who knew how to tell a visual story. And by the time Airship 27 Productions was being born, the two of us had realized a mutual goal of having done our first project together; the erotic horror graphic novel, DAUGHTER OF DRACULA, which we self-published.

But this whole pulp thing was going to be a totally different animal. I'd written two books that were ready for publication and handed them to Rob to handle the interior illustrations. The first was THE HOUNDS OF HELL and the second, BROTHER BONES: THE UNDEAD AVENGER. In both cases Rob dug into the stories, wrapped his creative energies around the scenes he was being asked to illustrate and then proceeded to draw some of the finest illustrations I'd ever seen anywhere.

Keep in mind, doing spot illos is about as far removed from doing comicbook sequential pages as writing a short poem is from penning a full length adventure novel. With a full blown comic, the artist has the luxury of multiple panels to get across the tale he or she wishes to show the world. Whereas a spot illo is all about capturing a single moment in the story and interpreting it in the best visual way possible. Unlike the comicbook where the pages will be the primary storytelling force, the spot illustration is never meant to usurp the prose but rather to enhance it, to add some spice to the stew.

And if you believe that is easier than doing the comicbooks, then I dare you to pick up a pencil and give it a go. For many reasons, doing a good illustration is a far greater challenge, which demands every ounce of creativity an artist possesses.

It was no surprise to me that Rob took to it like a bird to the air. What did surprise me was just how amazingly good he was at it. He didn't just spread his artist wings and fly, he soared to unimaginable heights. With each new illustration, I watched in awe as he found the core of every single scene he needed to draw whether it was a slam-bang action piece or merely two characters having a chat;

perhaps the most boring theme any artist ever has to deal with. And yet with each, Rob delivered drama proving the old adage about a single piece of art being worth a thousand words.

Within a few short years, Rob was yearly churning out dozens of quality illustrations and he became a master of the craft. So much so that by 2009, he won the first ever Pulp Factory Award for Best Interior Illustration for his work on the very first SHERLOCK HOLMES – CONSULTING DETECTIVE Vol One.

In fact he's become a recognized star in the field so that writers actually ask for him personally when submitting their new scripts to us. Everyone who has seen his work on Robin Hood, Sherlock Holmes, Captain Hazzard, Secret Agent X and all the other great pulp characters he's brought to life with his magic pencil, knows this is a true artist in every sense of the word. This is a creator who loves to tell stories, be it with lots of panels on just one amazing illustration.

Working with him side by side these past ten years has been one of my life's greatest pleasures. And it's poetically right that we recognize Rob's genius with this, the first ever volume dedicated to just a small sampling of his marvelous library of illustrations.

You see the truth about any real artist is this: they just keep getting better and better all the time.

Rob Davis surprised the hell out of me ten years ago and wouldn't you know, he still does it to this very day. God bless him.

Ron Fortier
6/1/2015
Fort Collins, CO

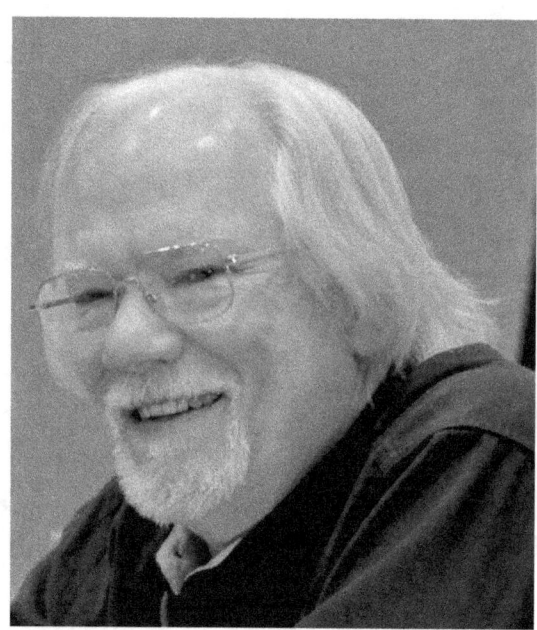

Rob Davis began his professional art career doing illustrations for role-playing games. Working with a number of independent publishers he began lettering and inking, then penciling comics—most notably for Malibu Comics on Scimidar with writer R.A. Jones. Rob began working on likeness-intensive comics like TV adaptations of *Quantum Leap* and Star Trek's many incarnations: primarily on the *Deep Space Nine* comics for Malibu but also on DC's Star Trek comics. Under his own publishing banner Rob has produced the graphic novels *Robyn of Sherwood* with writer Paul Storrie and *Daughter of Dracula* with writer Ron Fortier. Rob is Art Director, Designer and Illustrator for the New Pulp publisher Airship 27 Productions partnered with writer/editor Ron Fortier. Rob is the recipient of the Pulp Factory Award for "Best Interior Illustrations" in 2010 for his work on *Sherlock Holmes: Consulting Detective*. He works and lives in central Missouri with his wife and two children.

www.ingramcontent.com/pod-product-compliance
Lightning Source LLC
Chambersburg PA
CBHW080914170526
45158CB00008B/2103